KU-429-451

Bullying and Teasing
Social Power in Children's Groups

Bullying and Teasing
Social Power in Children's Groups

Gayle L. Macklem

Manchester Essex Regional School District
Manchester, Massachusetts

Kluwer Academic / Plenum Publishers
New York, Boston, Dordrecht, London, Moscow

Library of Congress Cataloging-in-Publication Data

Macklem, Gayle L., 1941–
  Bullying and teasing : social power in children's groups / Gayle L. Macklem.
    p. cm.
  Includes bibliographical references and index.
  ISBN 0-306-47974-5
  1. Bullying—Prevention. 2. School psychology. I. Title.

LB3013.3.M245 2004
371.5'8—dc22   2003061168

ISBN 0-306-47974-5

© 2003 Kluwer Academic/Plenum Publishers, New York
233 Spring Street, New York, New York 10013

http://www.wkap.nl

10 9 8 7 6 5 4 3 2 1

All rights reserved.

No part of this work may be reproduced, stored in a retrieval system, or transmitted in
any form or by any means, electronic, mechanical, photocopying, microfilming, recording,
or otherwise, without written permission from the Publisher, with the exception of any
material supplied specifically for the purpose of being entered and executed on a
computer system, for exclusive use by the purchaser of the work.

Permissions for books published in Europe: permissions@wkap.nl
Permissions for books published in the United States of America: permissions@wkap.com

Printed in the United States of America.

Preface

A keynote white paper presented at the Future of School Psychology Conference 2002 in Indianapolis, Indiana, addressed the critical issues that children must face in the 2000's. The issues of bullying and harassment were included among other pressing concerns such as alcohol and drug abuse, mental health issues and services, poverty and violence prevention. Bullying and harassment were included because these issues were described as generally ignored by schools. The authors pointed out that schools do not provide very much support for child victims of bullying (Crockett, 2003).

Pepler, Craig, and O'Connell (1999) have written about the bullying interaction and described it as a dynamic 'dance macabre'. This active and interactive dance takes place between the bully and the bullied. Goldstein (1994) described aggressive interactions as a 'person-environment duet', taking the social environment into consideration. He feels that the social environment determines whether or not aggression will escalate. Current research demonstrates that bullying affects all children in schools, not simply the several students who may be most visibly involved in an individual incident. In order to prevent escalation or to stop the action, something different must happen. The victim or the bully must change but this may not be easy. Importantly the classmates or the adults who witness the interaction have the power to change the interaction as well (Pepler, Craig, & O'Connell, 1999). Interventions using the bystanders and the school staff may be the best approach to decreasing the incidence of bullying in schools.

If school based mental health workers want to intervene to reduce or stop bullying they will have to address the entire system because the system includes not only the bully and victim, but also the bystanders, adults and the culture of the school. Context matters. Context affects the development of children. The bullying interaction must be viewed as an interactive social system. Practitioners will have to intervene on many levels in order the change the system. Victims need to be protected, external supervision and controls must be put in place to control the bully, and the bystanders must be trained to intervene. Beyond this, interventions must be extensive enough and be in place long enough to affect the power structure of children's groups and the power structure of the school as a whole.

Bullying is pervasive. It may be getting worse. The time to begin work to address bullying issues is past due. Olweus (1999b), the guru of bullying prevention, advocates that every child has the right to feel safe from bullies in school. We must act at many levels by creating interventions that are strong enough, in place long enough, and are deep enough to affect the power structure of schools.

Mental health workers including school psychologists, nurses, counselors, and social workers are becoming more and more interested in the social context of schools. Research in the field of school psychology, for example, is growing increasingly interested in the ecological context of learning. The field of school psychology is increasingly focused on prevention and systemic change.

Leaders in the field of school psychology are urging practitioners to study how educational processes and psychological/social processes interact (Kratochwill & Stoiber, 2000). They argue that it is critical to understand how a child's behavior relates to the system in which the student is functioning (Sheridan & Gutkin, 2000). Beyond this, school psychologists are beginning to understand that interventions must be made within the systems of families and schools. A student is part of the social system in which he or she functions. It is critical to pay attention to the context in which behavior occurs.

Feinberg and Barbarasch (2002) urge school psychologists to take leadership roles in developing and implementing programs that are school-wide. School psychologists are trained in program development. School psychologists have, additionally, accumulated expertise in improving school climate. It is for these reasons that school psychologists have recently begun to focus on bullying and destructive teasing in their schools. The planning, interventions, and preventative work that must be done in order to curb bullying fits well within the expanded roles of school psychologists.

This text is designed to arm school psychologists who want to take a leadership role in changing schools. The first several chapters provide school psychologists and other mental health workers with background information around definitions of bullying, the ways in which bullying is studied and incidence estimates. In addition, the relative contributions of the family, community and culture are explored along with the contributions of the school as a system to the problem of bullying.

The second several chapters provide in depth background information around the players who are involved in bullying in schools. The role of the bullies, the victims, the bully-victims, and the bystanders are examined. Bullying is a complex social or group phenomenon rather than a simple interaction between two children. The behaviors associated with bullying change as students get older and go through the school system from the early to the later grades. In addition, bullying is somewhat differently expressed according to gender variables.

In order to fully appreciate the phenomenon of bullying, it is important to look at what might be described as typical child developmental issues. A chapter addresses temperament and coping style variables that may contribute to the tendency of an individual child to assume one of the roles in the bullying interaction. The need that children have to belong to a group, to develop and maintain friendships, and to experience social power each contribute to the bullying phenomenon as well. A chapter is dedicated to friendship, social groups and peer power.

There is a clear need to develop school-based interventions to decrease bullying and to attempt to prevent the behaviors from occurring in the first place. The last few chapters address intervention in depth, from school-wide interventions to specific interventions for each of the players involved. School-wide interventions are covered first, including interventions at the classroom level and in the low structured areas of the school. Teasing needs to be examined carefully in that teasing behaviors are embedded in our culture. Some teasing behaviors may be tolerated and other teasing behaviors may be aggressive and even destructive. Interventions for bullies, bully-victims, victims and bystanders are examined separately in order to give school psychologists and others who work with children in schools some guidelines for developing interventions.

It is extremely important to acknowledge with deep gratitude the strong support and direct assistance that I received from Richard Macklem whose patience and tolerance is beyond comprehension. Sandra Ward's careful and critical reading of the manuscript along with her warm encouragement has been extraordinarily helpful. Janet Lemnah's talent in examining details in her review of the manuscript has been greatly appreciated as well.

The goal of this text is to provide school-based mental health workers with the background information that they will need to begin to address bullying within their own districts. It is hoped that this text will provide the impetus for individual school psychologists to take a leadership role in addressing the problem of bullying in their respective schools. It is hoped as well that this text will give practitioners enough assistance to begin to develop interventions in their respective schools so that children can learn to participate in groups that are more open and accepting, and can learn to treat each other with tolerance and respect.

Contents

CHAPTER 1

Definitions, Study Approaches, and Incidence

In order to understand the phenomenon of bullying, it is important to begin by defining bullying in the context of children's groups or in the context of school. Unfortunately, there is, to date, no universally accepted definition of bullying behavior. In addition, there have been changes in the way in which researchers have studied bullying in recent years.

DEFINING BULLYING

Ross (1996) reported that there was no clear consensus in regard to a definition of bullying as recently as the early 1990s. Achieving a consensus on a definition of bullying is important so that the results of one research study can be compared with another. Definitions of bullying range from quite broad to highly specific (Seward, n.d.). Definitions of bullying in the United States, for example, include a very wide range of behaviors from minor interactions between individuals to behaviors which are criminal in nature (Stein, 2001).

Since Dan Olweus' concepts of bullying are referred to most often internationally, it is important to look at his most current description of bullying behavior. In order to label a behavior bullying, Olweus feels that it must be intentional, repeated, and involve an imbalance of power. In addition, he feels that bullying often occurs without provocation and can be considered a form of peer abuse. Olweus would not label a behavior bullying if two children involved in an incident were of equal physical or mental power. Furthermore, he does not feel that an incident of bullying has to be physical or violent in order to be called bullying (Olweus, 1999b).

The concepts of power and peer abuse are associated with bullying behavior by many researchers (Haynie, Nansel, Eitel, Crump, Saylor, Yu, & Simons-Morton,

2001). Smith and Morita (1999) feel that bullies abuse *normal social power*. They feel that bullying is a subcategory of aggression. Bullying is the assertion of power through aggression according to Pepler, Connolly, and Craig (2000).

AREAS OF CONTENTION IN THE DEFINITION OF BULLYING

There are five areas of contention in regard to definitions of bullying. These are:

- whether indirect aggression should be included,
- whether the motivation of bully should be considered,
- whether bullying needs to occur repeatedly or can be an isolated incident,
- whether harassment as legally defined should be included, and
- whether teasing should be included.

First, the question of whether indirect aggression is included in the definition of bullying needs to be considered. Some researchers define only direct intimidation as bullying. Many other researchers include indirect and subtle behaviors as bullying. Swearer, Cary, Song, and Eagle (2000), for example, define bullying as anything from teasing or saying something mean, to physical aggression where one student or a group of students pick on someone over a long period of time. The inclusion of indirect aggression seems to be close to resolution given that researchers have increasingly included indirect bullying in their work.

Children's definitions of bullying behaviors are related to the issue of indirect aggression. Children's opinions about indirect bullying appear to differ from country to country. In one study, more Swedish students than English students consider leaving a child out bullying behavior, whereas, more English students consider name-calling a bullying behavior (Boulton, Bucci, & Hawker, 1999). Children may not realize that they are engaging in bullying behaviors if their definitions are different from adults, they may not report behaviors if they do not understand that they are being bullied, or they may not act in helpful ways if they are not identifying behavior as bullying. Although adults may feel that a power imbalance differentiates bullying, children do not seem to feel that an imbalance of power is necessary (Gropper & Froschl, 2000).

Younger children have broader definitions of bullying than older children, and include a wider range of behaviors when they think of bullying. Smith, Cowie, Olafsson, and Liefooghe (2002) talked to children about bullying in fourteen different countries. They determined that eight-year-old students used the term bullying to account for all sorts of negative behaviors. The understanding of bullying by younger children is less differentiated and more inclusive than that of older children, irrespective of cultural differences. Ross (1996) strongly states that if the child's perception is that he or she was being bullied, then this should define the behavior in spite of the possibilities that the victim exaggerates the behavior or underreports it.

The second area of debate in defining bullying behaviors has to do with the motivation of the bully, and whether or not it should be part of the definition. The motive for bullying is difficult to fit into a definition. When bullies are confronted, they tend to say that the child they targeted 'asked for it' or a bully will say that 'it was an accident'. Some definitions include *willfulness* on the part of the bully (Garrity, Jens, Porter, Sager, & Short-Camilli, 1994; Tattum & Tattum, 1992), or premeditation (Rigby, 2001). Understanding of bullying by some researchers includes the concept that the behavior is intentional and unprovoked (Gropper & Froschl, 2000; Ross, 1996).

The question for practitioners is whether or not hurtful or frightening behavior counts as bullying if it was not intended to hurt, intimidate, or frighten the victim. From a practitioner's point of view, motivation might be less of an issue in a definition, but more of an issue when consequences are considered. If a bully was clearly not aware that the victim was being affected by his or her actions, the consequence for the behavior might include education, as well as a consequence. The consequence, however, might be less major than if the bully appeared to enjoy the power he or she held over the victim. The question of motivation has not been resolved.

A third area of debate is whether bullying behavior needs to occur repeatedly as Olweus (1993) states in his definition, or whether a single incident might be called bullying. Many researchers insist that the behavior must be ongoing in order to be considered bullying (Rigby, 2001; Twemlow, Fonagy, & Sacco, 2001). The strong feeling of researchers that behaviors must be *repeated* in order to be considered bullying appear to be related to the issue of motivation, in that, if the behavior is repeated, it is more likely to be premeditated and deliberate.

In theory, an incident occurs the first time, and the bully is told that the behavior is unacceptable and that there will be consequences if it occurs again. The first incident might not be labeled bullying but the second incident *is* clearly designated as bullying behavior because the bully had been warned. From a practical point of view, it does not seem necessary to separate out the first incident as somehow different from a second incident. Consequences for the first and second incidents might differ however.

The fourth and fifth areas of contention have to do with whether to consider harassment and/or teasing as bullying behaviors or whether they are completely separate behaviors. If bullying is considered on a continuum, mean, but not destructive, teasing might fall at one end of the spectrum and harassment at the other end. Harassment is the easiest concept to separate from bullying since there are clear legal definitions of harassment. Harassment is defined as "a course of conduct directed at a specific person that causes substantial emotional distress in such a person and serves no legitimate purpose" (Under the United States Code Title 18 Subsection 1514(c)1).

Furniss (2000) argues that when a school is unable or is not willing to curb bullying it may be important for law enforcement to step in. Schwartz (1999) includes victimizing others on the basis of gender, race, ethnicity, religion, or sexual orientation as a specific type of bullying behavior. He describes these behaviors as a public display of power. Harassing students about their sexual orientation is now identified as a hate crime.

Teasing is much harder to deal with. Teasing is so much a part of our culture that individuals feel very strongly about it both positively and negatively. Some feel that teasing is part of normal family life, others feel that teasing is simply a mild form of bullying, and still others feel that teasing is typically mean or even destructive. Teasing has been considered a precursor of bullying, a subtype of bullying behavior, or an entirely different behavior. The consideration of teasing in definitions of bullying has not yet been resolved.

Although areas of disagreement continue, what may be most important, as far as intervention is concerned, is whether or not people in the same school agree on what is bullying. Although the definition of bullying may be important to researchers, in practice all of the people working with the same children need to be clear about acceptable and unacceptable behavior and the process of managing it (Kruger, 2002).

THE SCIENTIFIC STUDY OF BULLYING

A critical aspect in understanding the research around bullying behaviors is the way in which bullying behavior is studied. Most of children's behaviors associated with bullying take place where adults cannot see them directly. Another complication is that researchers have used several different approaches when they study of bullying behaviors. Typically, a survey is conducted and students are asked questions about their involvement in bullying and teasing. Researchers study bullying using measurement scales or surveys of children's perceptions, and/or parents' perceptions, and/or teachers' perceptions. When researchers collect peer ratings and teacher ratings of bullying, these measures tend to agree; but when students rate whether or not they themselves engage in bullying behaviors, or whether or not they are victims, their self-ratings do not agree closely with other measures. The most common approaches to collecting data on bullying include the following:

- surveys, questionnaires and interviews,
- peer nominations, and
- daily records direct observation.

These approaches are described below. Each measure has specific advantages and one method might be preferable depending on the research questions involved.

Surveys, Questionnaires, and Interviews

Surveys and interviews can tell us about a variety of aspects of the phenomenon of bullying. They can give us information about the *frequency* of bullying, about *attitudes* of children toward bullying, about the *bullies themselves*, and about the *incidents* that occur. They are not useful when researchers' questions involve the complexity of the bullying phenomenon.

It makes a difference whether questionnaires ask about direct versus indirect bullying. There is more agreement among all sources of information when the study involves direct aggression and bullying behaviors than when researchers include questions about indirect bullying (Pakaslahti & Keltikangas-Jarvinen, 2000). A questionnaire, survey, or interview about bullying may be designed to explore the child's point of view. Children's opinions are subjective, and they may not appreciate the complexity of bullying (Craig, Pepler, & Atlas, 2000). When a survey is used with children, researchers have found that it is important to clearly define bullying. Bullying is defined differently in various surveys. Some survey data is less representative of a particular country as a whole than others may be, which makes it difficult to compare data from study to study. It is important to make a distinction between small and larger representational studies and also between data collected in various ways.

Surveys or self-reports only identify children who are willing to say that they engage in victimizing others. Those who admit to bullying may also be willing to say that they feel positively about using aggression to get the power, objects, or outcomes that they want. On the other hand, there are, undoubtedly, bullies who are not willing to admit engaging in bully behaviors for a variety of personal reasons including worries about being identified (Gottheil & Dubow, 2001a, b). When surveys are involved, the risk is that students may not be reporting accurately (Craig & Pepler, 2000).

Ross (1996) adds that students may not understand that certain behaviors are actually bullying behaviors. Girls, in particular, may not understand that their negative social interactions are actually bullying. The number of girls who report that they themselves are bullies may be under estimated in survey data. Girls may be more challenging to study, because researchers find that girls are not as open when responding to self-report questionnaires, even when confidentiality is ensured (Seely, Krohn, Thomas, & Pomerantz, 2002).

When bullies identify themselves through surveys, there may be some bias introduced such as the bully's efforts to manage his image. Self-ratings of many behaviors often do not match other measures, but they do help us understand the thinking, feelings, and objectives of the individual's behaviors (Gottheil & Dubrow, 2001a).

Peer Nominations

Peer nominations are another approach that researchers may use to study bullying behaviors. Peer reputation, image, or status can be determined using peer nominations. Students list individuals whom they have observed being bullied or whom they know to have been victimized, in the peer nomination approach.

The image that the group has of the individual can be determined using peer nominations. Peer nominations and sociometric questionnaires are useful ways to study bullying behaviors. When studies are conducted to identify the bullies in a class or in a school, students in classes have been found to be good informants (Gottheil & Dubrow, 2001a).

If self-reports and peer nominations are compared, a higher level of victimization will be identified using self-reports. It is possible that self-reports are inaccurate and overestimate the degree of victimization to which a child may be exposed. Self-reports are *perceptions*, so it is difficult to determine how accurate they may be.

Daily Records

Still another approach to studying bullying is to ask students on a daily basis whether or not they have been harassed or bullied, or whether or not they have seen someone else receiving negative treatment from peers. This type of data collection lets researchers get at the repeated nature of bullying. It generates frequency data and overall levels of the negative behavior in a group, class, or school.

Direct Observation

In addition to studying bullying using surveys or by talking to children, observers go into schools to collect data by observing children directly. The advantage of this approach in studying bullying behavior is that when bullying is documented in context, external validity is increased. In addition, observers can record data not only about the bully, but also about all of *the other* children involved in an incident. Observers can study the group dynamic involved, and how context contributes to the cycle of behaviors. Observers may see incidents that children might not consider bullying and would, otherwise, be unreported. When cameras are used, film may pick up incidents that would not be seen by school staff (Craig & Pepler, 2000).

In the several studies that have used filming children, valuable data has been collected. The disadvantages of direct observation include the cost of data collection and analysis, the small number of students that can be involved in such a study, risks involved in invasion of privacy, and the possibility of ignoring students' rights (Craig & Pepler, 2000).

SUMMARY OF RESEARCH APPROACHES

If the goal is to understand the effects of bullying on individuals, self-reports are critical. If the goal is to look at the group phenomena or to explore the social status of students, peer ratings are critical. If the goal is frequency of bullying behaviors, daily recordings add to our understanding of the behavior. Direct observation allows for the collection of data that would have been lost and clarifies the complexity of bullying. Clearly, a variety of approaches is necessary in order to fully understand this complex behavior (Juvonen, Nishina, & Graham, 2001).

INCIDENCE OF BULLYING BEHAVIORS

In order to fully understand the need to address bullying behaviors, some appreciation of the incidence of bullying is necessary. Bullying is a problem in all schools and in countries around the world. Bullying has been described as the most common type of school violence (Swearer & Doll, 2001). To a large extent, our understanding of bullying behaviors has been learned from studies conducted in the Scandinavian countries, Great Britain, Ireland, Spain, Australia, the Netherlands, and Japan (Banks, 1997; Olweus, 1993).

It is important to look at an overview of the incidence of bullying in several different countries, because it demonstrates the universality of bullying behaviors. Rather than systematically looking at every country which has published data on the incidence of bullying, it is helpful to look at the incidence in a few countries, which have contributed to our understanding the phenomenon of bullying.

Incidence Studies in Norway

The Olweus Bullying Prevention Program is the best known and, perhaps, the best supported initiative to reduce bullying in elementary, middle, and junior high school students in the world. This program is a result of the systematic research, which began in the 1970s on bullying behaviors in the Scandinavian countries (Garrity & Baris, 1996). This definitive research in Norway was spearheaded by Dan Olweus and has been reported in a wide variety of sources.

The Scandinavian studies associated with Olweus' work involved 130,000 students. Olweus showed that fifteen percent of students were involved in bullying 'now and then' or more frequently. Nine percent of students said they were victims, seven percent admitted being bullies. Seventeen percent of the victims also bullied others. The percentage of students bullied in grades two through six was twice as high as in grades seven through nine. Bullying incidents dropped for boys in grade seven, because they became the youngest in junior highs or middle schools in Norway. Boys reported that they were more exposed to bullying than girls, especially in junior and senior high school, where four times as many boys as girls reported having been bullied. Nonphysical harassment was the most common form of bullying for both boys and girls. Thirty-five to forty percent of students who were victimized said that they were bullied by one student rather than a group of students. Most often a student reported being bullied by two or three other students.

Twenty percent of students said that they were frightened of being bullied during much of their school day (Garrity, Jens, et al., 1997).

Olweus (2001a) has recently determined that the incidence of serious bullying has changed in Norway. Rather than decreasing, Olweus reports that the incidence has actually increased by seventy percent since the 1980s. In spite of the impressive work by Olweus and his fellow researchers, researchers feel that teachers still are not well trained to deal with bullying. Data collected in 1997 showed that fifteen percent of students said they were bullied in class, and forty to seventy percent said that they were bullied outside of class.

Incidence Studies in Great Britain

In England and Wales there has been interest and concern about bullying since 1989. Data collected has indicated that one in every five children has been involved in a bullying incident. Studies of 6,700 students in Sheffield, England determined that twenty-seven percent of elementary-age students were victims 'sometimes' or more frequently. At the secondary level, ten percent of students reported that they were victims 'sometimes' or more frequently. Bullying around racial issues was a concern in some areas, and bullying of students with special needs was a concern as well (Smith, 1999). Another study of secondary schools determined that seventy-five percent of students were bullied during any given year. Severe and chronic bullying affected seven percent of students (Glover, Gough, Johnson, & Cartwright, 2000).

Canadian Studies

Craig and Pepler (2000) have conducted some of the most interesting research on bullying. They estimate that the rate of bullying behavior in Canada is almost four times that of Norway. Their original study indicated that twenty percent of students reported having been bullied, versus the nine percent identified by Olweus (1991). Harachi, Catalano, and Hawkins (1999a) estimate the prevalence of bullying up through middle school in Canada from twenty-one to twenty-eight percent.

Incidence Studies in New Zealand

Researchers in New Zealand are interested in the role of ethnicity and inter-cultural bullying. Maharaj, Rhyba, and Tie (2000a) suggest that the bullying label should be replaced with a broader concept such as "intimidatory practices" (p. 46). In a large study of secondary school students in New Zealand, researchers found that fifty-eight percent of all secondary school students said that they had been bullied and forty-four percent said that they acted as bullies and that 'it was fun' (Adair, Dixon, Moore, & Sutherland, 2000). Bullying seems to be more prevalent in New Zealand than in other Western countries, according to the Office of the Commissioner for Children in New Zealand (1999, reported in Maharaj, Tie, & Ryba, 2000b).

Incidence in the United States

Harachi, Catalano, and Hawkins (1999b) were asked to write about bullying in the United States in a volume that looked at bullying behaviors internationally. They found that the U.S. studies report prevalence estimates that vary a great deal due to different definitions of bullying in the U.S. studies, different methodologies used in studies, and the different ages of the subjects involved in the various studies. They did not find any national initiative to deal with bullying, or evaluation of programs as late as 1999 that involved prevention or intervention; nor did they feel that there has been adequate attention to developing programs in the United States.

In the past few years, however, there has been a flurry of interest in bullying in the United States. Incidence studies have been part of this interest. A 1993 survey in the United States found that approximately twenty percent of students reported having been bullied at one time or another (Whitney & Smith, 1993). The American Academy of Child & Adolescent Psychiatry (1997) reported that about fifty percent of all children are bullied while in school at one time or another. Of those who are bullied, ten percent were victimized on a regular basis. The Olweus model was implemented in South Carolina in 1998. A survey conducted as part of the program found that twenty-five percent of students reported being bullied, with ten percent of those students indicating that they were the subject of bullying 'once a week' or more (Lazar, 2002; Elliot, 2000).

Many incidence studies in the United States have focused on different age groups of students. A study of elementary, school-aged students conducted by Educational Equity Concepts and the Wellesley College Center for Research on Women found that teasing and bullying occurs frequently in grades kindergarten through three. Bullying and teasing is a part of what goes on typically every day in elementary schools (Froschl, Sprung, & Mullin-Rindler, 1998). A study by the Kaiser Family Foundation and Nickelodeon surveyed 1,249 parents and 823 children. They found that seventy-four percent of children eight to eleven years old said that teasing and bullying behaviors occur in schools at a higher rate than other risk behaviors. Among students aged twelve and older, eighty-six percent said that bullying and teasing occurs at a higher rate than other risk behaviors (Arce, 2001).

Studies have determined that middle school students do not feel safe in some schools, particularly those in urban areas. Up to eighty percent of middle school students in one study reported involvement in bullying behavior (Bosworth, Espelage, & Simon, 1999). Still another study study indicated that by fifth grade, almost fifty percent of students reported having been bullied (Jeffrey, Miller, & Linn, 2001).

The first nationwide research on bullying in the United States involved 15,686 students in grades six through ten. This survey, funded by the National Institute of Child Health and Development, indicated that more than sixteen percent of U.S. school children in grades six through ten said that others had bullied them during the current term. Almost thirty percent of students, who responded to the survey, reported that they had been involved as a bully, a victim, or both (Nansel, Overpeck, Pilla, Ruan, Simons-Morton, & Scheidt, 2001). Another way of looking at this data is to say that about 1.6 million students in these grade levels are bullied at least once per week (Ericson, 2001). Continued analysis of the data collected in this study indicates that bullying behaviors are a marker for involvement in violence-related behaviors later on. Engaging in bullying behavior places *the bully* most at risk for engaging in violent behaviors as time goes on (Nansel, Overpeck, Haynie, Ruan, & Scheidt, 2003).

Incidence Estimates from Observational Studies

Surveys are the least expensive way to collect incident data. However, incidence can be studied in ways other than self-reports. Innovative studies using observers have been conducted in Canada. A video camera was used to observe on a playground in Toronto. Over four hundred incidents of physical bullying were observed on the playground during a fifty-two hour period. This is, most likely, to be an underestimate, because the camera could not count verbal bullying, which is even more prevalent than physical bullying (Hazler, 1996).

When observers watched children in Toronto, they found that a child was bullied on the playground *once every seven minutes.* Surprisingly, observers also reported that bullying occurred in the classroom *once every twenty-five minutes.* Children said that more boys were engaged in bullying others, but the observers reported that both girls and boys bullied at about the same rate (Pepler, Connolly, et al., 2000). Girls' behaviors were not always interpreted as bullying.

A more recent study (Craig, Pepler, & Atlas, 2000) showed that four and one half incidents per hour of bullying took place on the playground, and almost two and one half incidents per hour occurred in classrooms. The interactions were quite short. The average duration of a bullying incident outside on the playground was 33.6 seconds, and the mean of incidents occurring in the classroom was 26 seconds in length.

Craig and Pepler (2000) reported another study in which six and one half bullying incidents took place per hour, lasting an average of thirty-eight seconds each. Half of the time the aggression was verbal, and in twenty-nine percent of the situations, it was physical. In twenty-one percent of incidents, both physical and verbal interactions took place. Direct bullying took place in eighty percent of the incidents observed, and indirect bullying took place in two percent of the situations observed. Racial bullying was involved in four percent of situations. Only one bully was involved in ninety percent of the incidents observed. Boys were involved in

5.2 incidents per hour and girls in 2.7 incidents every hour. Boys tended to target boys more than girls targeted girls. In sixty-seven percent of incidents, students went after other children in the same age group. Observers felt that many of the incidents were serious; in fact, they were described as 'tormenting' in seventy-nine percent of the cases.

CURRENT FOCUS IN THE UNITED STATES

Many researchers feel that bullying and retaliation occur more frequently in the United States than in Europe, possibly because violence is a normative aspect of behavior in the United States. Violence is more accepted in the United States than Europe (Garrity, Jens, et al., 1997; Walker, Colvin & Ramsey, 1995). An alternate explanation is that bullying and teasing are increasing. There is evidence to suggest that aggressive behavior has been increasing in both amount and severity. Aggression is seen at earlier ages than in the past in the United States (Schwartz, 2000).

Bullying affects up to five million students yearly in elementary and middle schools across the United States (Liberman, 2001). It is widely considered to be an antecedent to violence in schools in the higher grades (Saufler, 1998). A number of states have initiatives for teasing and bullying prevention including Massachusetts, Pennsylvania, New York, Florida, New Hampshire, California, and Maine (Mullin-Rindler, 2001). Legislation has been passed in Georgia, New Hampshire, and Colorado to force schools to act against bullies. Legislation is being considered in Michigan, Illinois, Washington, and Oregon (Matson, Ju, Knierim, Hansen, & Knierim-Fatras, 2002). In addition, groups such as the National Education Association are conducting national bullying awareness campaigns (National Education Association, n.d.).

A report by the American Medical Association's Council on Scientific Affairs concluded that seven to fifteen percent of children engage in bullying behavior and ten percent are victims. From two to ten percent of children are involved as both bullies and victims. These conclusions were made from a review of research conducted from 1985 to 2002. This group recommended that doctors become vigilant for signs of bullying in children (American Medical Association, 2002).

Also in the United States, the Department of Education at the federal level contracted with the National Association of School Psychologists through the Center for Effective Collaboration and Practice. The Department engaged the National Association of School Psychologists to write *Early Warning, Timely Response: A Guide to Safe Schools* and a follow up document *Safeguarding Our Children: An Action Guide to Implementing Early Warning, Timely Response* in 2000 (Fagan, Gorin & Tharinger, 2000). In the spring of 2002, post 9-11 ideas were generated during the National Association of School Psychologists Convention in Chicago. One of the chief violence prevention activities recommended was to develop policies and programs to reduce bullying. The point was made that "school safety is an inside job" (Poland, 2002).

School violence has contributed to intensified interest in bullying behaviors. The final report of the *Safe School Initiative* of the U.S. Secret Service and the U.S. Department of Education determined that in the thirty-seven incidents of violence examined, many attackers felt that they had been bullied by others. The authors felt that bullying behaviors should be addressed in schools because they are so common.

The American Medical Association adopted a policy in 2002 to help doctors identify bullying (Tanner, 2002). The American Medical Association announced in July of 2001 that it would address bullying as part of its anti-violence program. The National Education Association established a National Bullying Awareness Campaign early in 2002. The federal *No Child Left Behind Act* encourages programs to protect students and teachers and encourage responsibility. It anticipates violence and, therefore, requires states to report school safety statistics on an individual school basis. Districts must use federal school safety funding to develop and implement a plan for keeping schools safe and drug free (Ashby, 2002). Several states have developed policies against bullying including Colorado, New Hampshire, and West Virginia. Massachusetts is in the process of spending one million dollars to implement school-wide interventions in a number of schools (Lumsden, 2002).

A National Bullying Prevention Campaign has been mounted in the United States and is set to kick off in September of 2003. This campaign is the largest effort that has ever been mounted. The goal is to address the needs of nine to thirteen year olds to help prevent bullying. It will be led by the Health Resources and Services Administration's Maternal and Child Health Bureau of the U.S. Department of Health and Human Services and is funded by the Centers for Disease Control and Prevention National Youth Media Campaign.

SUMMARY

Bullying is a common experience of children who attend schools in all countries around the world. School is where children gather in large numbers and learn to function in group situations. It is where children learn about their peer world. Mental health workers and school administrators have become more aware of the incidence of bullying behaviors and are beginning to realize how context influences children's social and emotional development.

Research around the bullying phenomenon has been conducted in a number of countries around the world. The study of bullying is challenging because of the difficulty of establishing a universally-accepted definition of bullying and because there have been a variety of approaches in gathering data. The broader the approach to studying bullying, the more complete picture of bullying that can be obtained.

The incidence of bullying from around the world is startling. It appears to be increasing. School violence has served as an impetus to large-scale efforts to address the problem. Yet, even in countries where work has been ongoing for the greatest length of time, researchers are finding that bullying is increasing. Changing school culture appears to be an enormous task. It is time to begin to tackle the problem of bullying in schools everywhere.

CHAPTER 2

Family and Societal Influences on Bullying

In order to develop more effective interventions to decrease bullying, it is important to look at some of the important correlates of bullying and of victimization, as they are currently understood. Of the various correlates of bullying behaviors including family factors, parenting style, sibling relationships, and more general cultural influences such as television viewing, video games, and the Internet, each may contribute to bullying behaviors.

FAMILY CORRELATES

Families in the United States, and in many other countries, are diverse. The structure and stability of families and the number of hours parents work differ, as do the resources available to families. Children, growing up in all kinds of families, learn how to deal with family relationships early on (McGurk & Soriano, 1998).

Although parents influence the behavior of their children, the relationship between parenting and the behavior of their children is no longer considered a one-way street. The relationship is bi-directional, with each influencing the other. Just as parents influence their children, children influence the behavior of their parents. Parents also socialize the expression of emotions in their children. This is an interactive process as well (Zhou, Eisenberg, Losoya, Fabes, Reiser, Guthrie, Murphy, Cumberland, & Shepard, 2002).

There are well known family correlates related to the development of aggressive behavior in children and to the development of victimization in children. For example, aggressive behavior is elevated in children who witness violence in their homes (Sudermann, Jaffe, & Schieck, 1996). The behavior of aggressive girls appears to be more strongly influenced by parents who exhibit depressive or aggressive behaviors than boys are affected (Delligatti, Akin-Little, & Little, 2003). In more extreme cases, children who are maltreated by parents have been found to exhibit more aggressive behaviors including bullying behavior with peers. Students abused by parents are disruptive in school and have difficulty controlling their emotions. Abused children are victimized by peers, as well as by their parents. They are also more likely to be bullies or victims of bullies although not all abused children become bullies or victims. They are disruptive and dysregulated. It is the emotional and behavioral dysregulation that the children demonstrate, which increases the likelihood that they will be involved in the bullying system (Shields & Cicchette, 2001).

Parent's Role in Bullying

Children first learn to function socially at home with parents and siblings. Parents scaffold the skills and strategies needed in order to interact with others. Parent teaching is direct. Parents are emotionally involved with their children, making them powerful models (Bigelow, Tesson, & Lewko, 1996). Parents may teach negative and even aggressive behaviors. There are parents who want their children to learn to defend themselves and to compete. These parents do not seem to think that bullying is a big problem (LeBlanc, 2001). Parents may also contribute to bullying by ignoring it. In adolescence, the influence of the family does not protect adolescents from engaging in negative behaviors such as bullying, in the same way that school factors may be protective (Crosnoe, Erickson, & Dornbusch, 2002).

Power Relationships at Home

There is some evidence to suggest that bullies have authoritarian parents, and they typically disagree with their parents (Baldry & Farrington, 2000). Harsh management strategies and low warmth of parents have been demonstrated to relate to bullying behavior in the children of these parents (LeBlanc, 2001). Peers reject some children who engage in bullying behaviors. Parents of children who are neglected or rejected by peers behave differently than parents of typical children. They use more direct commands, make more negative statements, and are less consistent in their use of commands with their children (Franz & Gross, 2001). Rejection is related to both bullying behaviors and to victimization.

Parenting Style

Parents may have also indirect influences on bullying and victimization. Parenting style is associated with a student's social competence, school functioning, and poor choices. All of these are related to bullying and victimization (Haynie et al., 2001).

Eron, Huesmann, and Zelli (1991) determined that aggression is learned before age six, so that by this age, children have already established negative patterns of behavior. In studying several aspects of parental style, they found that when children are rejected *and* are harshly punished *and* they do not identify closely with their parents, they are more likely to behave aggressively later on. In effect, research suggests that aggression *must* be learned before age six in order to identify direct ties between child-rearing practices and later aggression.

Families and Aggressive Behaviors

Perry, Hodges, and Egan (2001) propose that a variety of parent-child interactions could facilitate the development of aggressive behavior in their children. There are several combinations of parent-child interactions that might influence the development of specific child behaviors. One style of interaction would involve psychologically controlling parents and defiant children. Another would involve coercive parenting and an avoidant child. Still others would involve a laid-back parent who doesn't follow through with a defiant child or a laid-back parent with an avoidant child. These combinations of parent-child relationships, combined with child-specific variables, would be more likely to produce aggressive children. Researchers have also found a relationship between a rejecting and unresponsive parenting style and a child's tendency to use inappropriate, aggressive behavior (Rosen, 1998).

The data that supports family antecedents of aggression explains the behavior of children who engage in high rates of aggression (Smith & Sharp, 1994). Children learn oppositional behaviors from coercive relationships with parents who get into powerful confrontations with their children, in which they allow their children to be aggressive toward them. For boys, a coercive relationship with their mothers and low levels of affection together result in increasing aggressive behavior over the first few years of elementary school. Unresponsive mothers, who used social coaching, were able to ameliorate their sons' tendencies to be aggressive. Both boys and girls who have negative relationships with their fathers tend to be aggressive with peers. These children also have been shown to have more negative interactions with peers. Children who feel that their parents reject them are more likely to think peers are against them (Ladd, 1999).

Olweus (1991) suggests four factors that are related to the development of an aggressive, behavioral pattern from studies of aggressive boys:

- negative, emotional attitudes of parents when their children are young,
- failure to provide limits when the child is aggressive toward them or others,
- use of aggressive management of the child such as yelling at or hitting the child when rules are broken or commands are not followed, and
- temperament.

Children who might be described as having a hotheaded temperament may be more prone to be aggressive in their interactions with others.

When parents do not follow through after giving a directive, the child learns not to comply. Their discipline practices predict aggression in their children (Craig,

Peters, et al., 1998). Over time, the children master the skill of resistance and become very controlling in their relationships with family members. They continue the behavior because it works, it is powerful and rewarding. They do as they please rather than doing what their parents ask. Their motivation in interacting with others becomes an issue of control. Power, domination, and control of others is the primary motivation for these children when they interact with others outside of the family. Unfortunately, the behavior does not change once children enter school. When they enter school, and teachers or other school staff become angry with them, the children are not impressed and they continue to do as they wish and challenge the authority of adults (Goldstein, 1995).

Developmental Progression for Bullying Behaviors

A developmental progression for bullies begins at home, where there is poor discipline and monitoring. Authoritarian and/or coercive parents, who lack warmth, permit aggression, and handle limit setting inadequately set their children up for the development of bullying behaviors (Goodman, 1999; Mullin-Rindler, 2001). The parent may ignore positive behaviors (Patterson, DeBaryshe, & Ramsey, 2000). Once the bullying behaviors develop, they lead to high status among other children early on, with no initial negative, social, or academic impact (Mullin-Rindler, 2001; Strawn & Paradiso, 2001).

Studies in England determined that bullies understood or thought of their families in terms of power relationships (Smith, 1999). Bullying behavior is associated with power displays and externalizing behaviors. The effect of the family on the association between bullying and externalizing behaviors is indirect. For girls, there were no age differences in the association between bullying and externalizing behaviors; but in the case of boys, the association between bullying and externalizing behaviors was stronger when boys were younger and decreased for ten and eleven year olds (Craig, Peters, & Konarski, 1998).

Studies investigating how family environments predict bullying behavior have primarily involved boys. There isn't as much research on the development of bullying in girls as it relates to the family. There is, however, some data to indicate that when girls are harshly punished, it is likely to teach them to behave aggressively toward people they live with later on. When children are disciplined physically at home they learn that hitting back is acceptable (Schwartz, 1999). This may relate to physical bullying.

Victimization and Family Influence

Students who are victims of bullies come from families in which there are not many positive interactions. Punishment is inconsistent as well. This type of family environment appears to be very similar to the family environments of students who engage in bullying behaviors. However, the children in families with few positive interactions and inconsistent punishment react differently to this type of parenting, in that some may become bullies, and some become victims of bullies (Craig, Peters, et al., 1998).

Ross (1996) feels that various social risk conditions facilitate being the victim of bullying. It appears likely that particular experiences in a child's family may increase the likelihood that a child experiences victimization at the hands of classmates. Three parent behaviors appear to be associated with the likelihood that a child will become a victim of peers. Insecure attachment, overprotective parents, and the combination of controlling and coercive parenting are related to victimization (Perry et al., 2001).

Attachment issues may be related to victimization. Children, who have an anxious resistant attachment to their mothers, have difficulty separating in new environments and are distressed when they have to face situations alone (Ross, 1996). Olweus (1978) feels that the child, who is a victim, communicates vulnerability. Others suggest that the victim is different in some way, so that bullies are attracted to him or her. However, there isn't much evidence to support specific differences in victims other than reduced physical strength in the case of boys (Ross, 1996).

Children may develop internal beliefs about themselves as victims. Children who are fearful and compliant blame themselves and do not feel that they can stand up to threats. They tend to be preoccupied and cling to parents when stressed. They also have difficulty separating from their mothers and have difficulty with age-expected behaviors. These children can be described as exhibiting 'debilitated coping'. Boys who exhibit 'debilitated coping' behaviors and who believe that they are overprotected by their mothers tend to behave as if they are victims. This style of coping is also a risk factor for anxiety or depression (Perry et al., 2001).

The parenting styles that relate to victimization differ in boys and girls. Boys are more likely to become victims, if parents are too close and over solicitous. Girls are more likely to respond as victims when parents are harsh, coercive, or use love withdrawal (Perry et al., 2001). Family correlates of victimization include maternal overprotection of boys and hostility on the part of mothers of girls (Ross, 1996).

The relationship between family functioning and affective issues in children is indirect, but is stronger for girls than for boys. Victimization is associated with both internalizing behaviors and externalizing behaviors. For girls, the relationship between family functioning and internalizing behavior increases at ages ten and eleven, but there are no age differences in boys. There are no age differences in the association between family functioning and externalizing issues for girls, but the association decreases for boys at ages ten and eleven (Craig, Peters, et al., 1998).

Siblings' Role in Bullying

Sibling relationships are different from parent-child and peer relationships. Contrary to what most people may think, siblings are less involved with a given child than a child is involved with other relationships outside of the family. There are exceptions, however, and some siblings may be supportive in the same way that peers are supportive. For most children, peer relationships are more relevant. Siblings provide opportunities for practicing social skills and competencies, just as peers provide opportunities for children to practice social interaction skills. Children can try out skills and friendship making and maintaining strategies with siblings that might have negative consequences if they were tried out with friends. Friends, obviously, can leave the relationship, but siblings are trapped in their relationships during childhood (Bigelow et al., 1996).

There are situations in which siblings play a strong role. One situation involves a younger sibling with an older, more aggressive sibling. Younger children must learn to get along with or get around their more aggressive, older brothers and sisters. Patterson (1986) describes siblings as individuals who provide *training* for bullying. He also describes conflict among siblings as the most common form of aggression in families. There is some data to support his views. Bullies who come from homes where mother is the only parent see their siblings as quite powerful (LeBlanc, 2001). Of particular influence is the pairing of an older aggressive brother with a younger sister. This produces an aggressive girl who may engage in bullying behaviors with peers. In adolescence, a highly aggressive, older brother may model aggression for a young brother and draw him into more serious aggressive behaviors. When an older brother exhibits negative behaviors, and a younger teenage brother identifies with his older sibling, he may be influenced in the same direction (Ardelt & Day, 2002). If a child has siblings who are delinquent, there is an increased risk of later violence, because antisocial siblings increase the risk for a younger adolescent to follow the footsteps of an older sibling. Interestingly, this influence is stronger for girls (Hawkins, Herrenkohl, Farrington, Brewer, Catalano, Harachi, & Cothern, 2000).

A study in Great Britain determined that students who bully others think of their brothers and sisters in terms of power relationships, just as they think of their parents in terms of power relationships (Smith & Sharp, 1994). Bullies, in general, tend to have a negative relationship with their brothers and/or sisters (Rosen, 1998).

Parents' Role in Teaching Children to become Bystanders

It is important to explore the role of parents in influencing bystander behaviors, which are important contributers to bullying in children's groups. Children who witness bullying behaviors are bystanders. They may behave passively or actively. They may feel sympathetic or rejecting toward the victim. If the bystander observes that the victim feels upset, and the bystander feels upset himself or herself, the student is experiencing empathy. Empathy is the emotion or affective response. People who can feel the distress of another person are more likely to respond actively in some way. In this way, empathy is related to whether or not a bystander might intervene when bullying is observed. When parents interact warmly with their children and tend to express positive emotions when they interact, their children are more likely to feel empathetic in stressful situations. In addition, they are more likely to feel guilty when they observe victimization, which may prevent them from joining in (Zhou et al., 2002).

NEIGHBORHOOD AND COMMUNITY INFLUENCES

Meta-analysis of the relationships between later violent behavior and community and neighborhood factors suggest that poverty, community disorganization, availability of drugs and guns, and knowing adult criminals when the student is fourteen to sixteen years old are related to youth violence (Hawkins et al., 2000). There is little data to demonstrate direct relationships to bullying.

Some communities are viewed as high-risk communities, and some of these communities are engulfed with violence. In these communities, violence is the norm and is not considered deviant. The families in these neighborhoods who try to shield their children are faced with overwhelming odds of keeping their children away from damaging role models and protecting them from the rewards and dangers of violence. Parents may not be able to accomplish this alone. Schools located in these areas need to think about finding ways to help families who are trying to protect their children connect with one another (Coie & Jacobs, 2000).

CULTURAL INFLUENCES

The influence of culture is pervasive. Behavior is culture-specific. Child rearing practices, values, and expectations that parents have for their children vary from culture to culture. Children must learn how to interact socially in the culture in which they grow up. They learn about the status system of the culture, and the way in which people play and communicate (Jahoda, 1998).

The United States has a heterogeneous school population, and a more violent culture, in general, than many other countries. The American culture tolerates, and at times condones, aggression. In the best of all worlds, prevention would take place on a national scale, because isolated programs are unlikely to make permanent change when cultural influences are so great (Coie & Jacobs, 2000). Some psychologists feel that there is a general atmosphere of meanness in American culture, where teasing and taunting have become the norm among most students (Bowman, 2001). This may be one of the several cultural influences, which appear to contribute to a high rate of bullying. It is extremely difficult to change cultural influences. In the United States, where there is no centralized educational system or centralized curricula and it is impossible to standardize well-researched

ST. MARY'S UNIVERSITY COLLEGE
A COLLEGE OF THE QUEEN'S UNIVERSITY OF BELFAST

interventions for the prevention of bullying in schools across the nation (Stein, 2001).

Influence of Television

The media has been implicated in exacerbating the aggressive culture in the United States. Violence is glorified in the media where it reinforces aggressive ideas and values. Many students tease because they see teasing, put-downs, sarcasm, and lack of respect on television, in the movies, and in the video games that have become part of American childhood. These influences model, and may even teach, negative behaviors (Freedman, 1999).

Television viewing has been demonstrated to cause multiple learning and behavior problems in some children (Hyman, Dahbany, Blum, Weiler, Brooks-Klein, & Pokalo, 1997). The American Psychological Association Commission on Violence and Youth gathered data on the effects of television on violent behavior. Television shows often depict negative behavior, including teasing and bullying behaviors and defiance of rules. Children in the United States watch an average of twenty-eight hours of television each week. Children's programs have more violence than adult programs (Muscari, 2003).

Although some students are influenced more than others, students who watch a good deal of television violence may develop positive feelings about using aggressive behaviors to solve problems. Just as serious, very frequent television watchers apparently become more tolerant of aggressive behavior. Heavy television watchers may determine that the world is not safe. A child's worldview may be affected in a frightening way (Hyman et al., 1997; Murray, 1997).

The largest study of media was the National Television Violence Study of 1994. Researchers found that heavy television watchers believe that the world is frightening and dangerous. *Attractive* television characters engaged in thirty-nine percent of violent incidents. Their attractiveness made them powerful models. Perpetrators were not punished in seventy-three percent of cases, nor did they feel badly about their behavior. Fifty-five percent of incidents did not show the victim suffering (Aidman, 1997). The message for children is clear. Aggressive power feels good and does not have emotional or actual repercussions for the perpetrator or the victim.

The effect of watching television violence is not related to other risk factors, but has a strong enough effect on aggression to be significant. It is important to keep in mind that although the portal of aggression through television programming has a significant effect on aggressive behaviors in children, it is *not* as strong as other environmental variables. Students may imitate the specific behaviors that they see in the media, but the environment must reinforce these behaviors if there are to be long-term increases in aggression for a given child. It should also be noted that not all children are equally affected by media violence; some are more likely to be affected than others (Coie & Jacobs, 2000; Huesmann & Miller, 1994).

Influence of Video Games

Other forms of entertainment media may also influence children. For many years, parents and educators have felt that video games include excessive aggression and aggressive models. Griffiths (1999) reviewed the research in this area and found that the studies are uniformly weak and consider only short-term outcomes. However, young students were observed to become more aggressive after they watched or played with a video game that had violent content. Younger children are more likely than older children to imitate the behavior of characters in the video games (Brody, 2000).

Internet Influences

According to the web site project for the Foundations of Information Technologies at the University of British Columbia (2002), bullies are using the Internet to create web sites that target victims. There have been several cases of this type of bullying in Canada. It is referred to as 'cyberbullying' or 'twenty-first century bullying'.

Bullying via the Internet is a new area for researchers to explore. Children's charity NCH commissioned a survey in the United Kingdom. The data showed that 25% of children reported having been threatened when using their computers or cell phones. The BBC news reported that the sixteen percent of students surveyed between the ages of eleven and nineteen had been subject to bullying or threats via computer or cell phone. An additional seven-percent reported having been harassed in Internet chat rooms. Some experts feel that Internet bullying is particularly intrusive because it occurs in a child's home (British Broadcasting Company News Online, 2002).

Electronic bulletin boards and usenets make the Internet interactive. Bullies may feel safe using the Internet, because they can access it in their own homes and send messages using false identification. If a bully puts up a website targeting a victim, the audience is, potentially, very large compared to a hidden area of the playground, according to speakers at the European Conference on Initiatives to Combat School Bullying (1998).

SUMMARY

Parents of students who exhibit aggressive behavior contribute to their children's aggression in several ways. They do not teach their children to comply with authority, nor do they model positive problem solving. They reward aggressive behavior. These parents either ignore or over punish behavior while they are modeling aggressive behavior.

Some parents may literally train their child to be aggressive when they interact with others. In these families, the child learns to behave aggressively, in order to cope with a parent's coercive behaviors. Over time, the intensity of negative interactions in the family increase as each member tries to control the other. There is little teaching of prosocial behaviors while this is occurring. Siblings also contribute to the development of aggressive behaviors including bullying.

The general degree of violence in a culture may be related indirectly to bullying behaviors. Attitudes toward aggression and about aggression are taught through cultural influences in the media. Aggression on television influences some children negatively, although it is not as strong as other environmental influences and must be reinforced in the 'real world' in order to have long-term affects on a child. Video games and the Internet may also be related to bullying.

Finally, the community or neighborhood in which a child grows up can influence the degree to which a child exhibits aggressive behavior. Violence in the community can also influence feelings of fear in children.

CHAPTER 3

The School as a Factor in Bullying

The school violence literature points to the fact that school staff can create conditions that foster and support negative behaviors (Dill, 1998). Baker (1998) feels that the violence which occurs in some schools is associated with a weak sense of community. The more aggressive students do not form the relationships with others or with staff that might deter their behavior. These students arrive at school with a history of poor attachment which makes them less trusting, more anxious, and likely to expect that others will reject them. They are less connected to the school than their peers. This can be identified as early as the third to fifth grades.

BULLYING OCCURS IN CONTEXTS

Studies indicate that bullying is taking place in schools much more frequently than it occurs going to or from school (Ross, 1996). Importantly, not all schools deal with bullying behaviors to the same degree even when external differences would not account for differences in behaviors. The risk of being victimized in some schools is four or five times higher than it is in other schools (Olweus, 1999).

Bullying can be thought of as the interaction between the student and the contexts or systems of which the student is a part (Song & Swearer, 2002). A student's behavior does not occur in isolation, and seldom is the child the only variable in the occurrence of behavior. The school environment itself plays a role in both fostering and perpetuating bullying behaviors. In fact, there are a number of different, school-related factors that play a role in bullying and destructive teasing behaviors in schools. School culture and school climate influence the bullying and destructive teasing behaviors of students and staff in their interactions with one another. Teachers' attitudes and behaviors are crucial variables in exacerbating or deterring bullying behaviors.

Of the many negative school climate factors that are related to school violence those that would seem to be more related to bullying behaviors include discipline practices and the failure of schools to address bullying behaviors (Dill, 1998). The discipline practices that contribute to bullying include use of suspensions to address bullying, humiliating students as punishment, and discipline that is rigidly administered without careful thought. Schools that overuse punishment exacerbate misbehavior. These schools have high rates of violence (Hyman et al., 1997). Most researchers feel that bullying and teasing are not managed well by schools (Ross, 1996).

SCHOOL CULTURE AND SCHOOL CLIMATE

Some experts feel that whether or not bullying occurs has much more to do with the school climate than it does with the behavior of the victim (Brady, 2001). The culture of a school refers to unwritten expectations that develop over time. It also involves the opinions that members of the culture develop and the way that problems are solved. It includes all of the rules that tell members of the system how to behave and interact with one another. School culture includes the events that individuals celebrate together and the stories that are shared which communicate the values of the school (Peterson, 2002). School culture and the social system within the school determine the quality of the school environment. School culture includes both staff climate and the student climate.

School climate includes all aspects of the school environment: the discipline policies and implementation of the policies, the physical building and grounds, available resources (physical, financial, and people resources), communication channels, support services, and morale. In each of these areas, there are issues that affect bullying behaviors in schools. For example, the number of and training of non-teaching staff to supervise low structure areas in the building affects the extent of bullying in the school (Hyman et al., 1997). The low structure areas in schools are the locations where there is a low level of adult supervision and activities are not formalized. They include corridors, the lunchroom, bathrooms, and the playground.

Experts consider the school climate an aspect of the school culture that has potential for prevention of problems within the school. Studies show that when bullying behavior is prevalent in a school, it affects the climate of the school negatively. Those specific school climate factors that are most associated with bullying behaviors include:

- modeling of bullying behaviors by staff and dominant students,
- ignoring and/or reinforcing bullying, and
- accepting bullying behavior as normal and expected behavior.

In addition, when school disciplinary policies are either too tough or too easy-going, bullying may increase or, at least, be supported (Song & Swearer, 2002).

Although school climate is viewed as having a strong potential for decreasing school violence, it does not seem that all children are affected equally. A study of junior high students in Israel (Benbenishty, Astor, Zeira, & Vinokur, 2002) has provided some evidence to indicate that girls are more affected than boys when the school climate is positive. Even if school workers focus on changing school climate, it may not reduce all students' worries associated with victimization unless a great deal more is done.

An interesting study which explored the relationship of school and family factors as they affect behaviors of teenagers identified several *school factors* were critically important in this age group. School factors, such as achievement and attitudes toward school, were protective for adolescents, in that, these factors prevented association with deviant peers (Crosnoe et al., 2002). It may be that whether or not a school is coeducational may make a difference in the amount of bullying in a school. Ross (1996) reported a study conducted in 1991 in which individuals felt that there was less bullying in coeducational schools, when students of the opposite sex did not approve of the behavior by children.

SCHOOL SIZE

School size did not tend to make a difference in bullying behaviors in the early major studies of bullying behaviors in schools (Olweus, 1991). One reason may be that Swedish, Finnish, and Norwegian schools tend to be smaller than schools in the United States. Neither class size nor school size were related to bullying in the several major studies conducted in these countries (Ross, 1996).

In the United States there is some data to indicate that secondary schools that are smaller than five hundred pupils have a better chance of reducing alienation of marginal students and bullies by encouraging participation. There is more social control by the adults in smaller schools, better monitoring of behavior, and the possibility of interfering with the power of cliques is improved in smaller high schools (Garbarino, 2001).

TEACHERS' ROLES IN BULLYING BEHAVIOR

The way in which teachers interact with different children, the degree to which they concentrate on negative behaviors, and the modeling they do in the classroom each may affect bullying in a school. Issues such as tolerance of bullying, poor supervision in low structure areas, ignoring bullying behaviors, crowding in hallways and on playgrounds with very little play equipment, and lack of systematic approaches to bullying are major variables acting to perpetuate bullying in schools (Ross, 1996).

Studies of classroom behavior and the influence of teachers on the classroom behavior of students indicate that inadequate or inappropriate instructional practices may explain more than fifty percent of student discipline problems (Hyman et al., 1997). Researchers feel that when teachers concentrate on negative behaviors, fail to reward positive behaviors, and engage in coercive behaviors toward students themselves they maintain, or even increase, aggressive behavior in some students (Reinke & Herman, 2002).

Teachers are not always aware of the differences in their own behavior when they interact with various students. Students who behave in ways that stress teachers believe that their teachers don't like them and do not have their best interests at heart. These students gravitate toward others like themselves, in spite of teachers attempts to discourage this association. When stern discipline is used toward these students, they withdraw from the adult staff and act out their feelings in class. Teachers clearly play a role in perpetuating acting out behaviors (Baker, 1998).

Benbenishty et al. (2002) found that teachers could affect the behavior of students with whom they have good relationships. They have less effect on other students in the school environment. Teachers will have difficulty controlling the behaviors of students who feel that they are not valued in the classroom. Teachers have a great deal of power with younger children. The way they interact with a child who may be only a little different can affect how the rest of the class sees that child. Children can be seen as very different or can be accepted by the group depending on how the teacher interacts with that child. Differences either increase or become meaningless in this way (Ross, 1996).

Teacher Identification of Bullying Behaviors

Craig and Pepler et al. (2000) suggest that teachers have difficulty identifying bullying behaviors. Teachers and other adults in schools may become so used to seeing bullying behavior that they no longer react to it. They may not take it seriously, because some bullying behavior fits the male stereotype (Barone, 1997; Paulk, Swearer, Song, & Carey 1999; Wiler, 1993). Teachers, typically, feel that the pushing and shoving in corridors is accidental. Students at the middle school level disagree. Middle school students report that the school hallways are one of the key areas where bullying takes place (Barone, 1997).

Middle school teachers are even less accurate in identifying bullies and victims than are elementary school teachers. Middle school teachers have less contact with individual students. The teasing and bullying behaviors at the middle school level are more hidden and covert. Teachers identify only fifty percent of the bullies and victims that students can identify. In addition, adults tend to rate student behavior according to the relationship that they have with that particular student. Students judge peers in the same way. Bullies are powerful individuals and may be quite likeable, so teachers may have positive relationships with them. Their personal relationships with bullies may make it harder to consider these students in a negative light (Leff, Kupersmidt, Patterson, & Power, 1999: Paulk, Swearer, et al., 1999).

Teachers' Beliefs about Bullying Behaviors

The attitude of teachers toward bullying plays an extremely important role in the amount and frequency of bullying in a school. Teachers, in general, are more likely to identify physical than verbal aggression as bullying (Craig, Henderson, & Murphy, 2000). Research on the attitudes of teachers, counselors, and prospective teachers has demonstrated that adults correctly label physical aggression and threats of physical aggression as bullying behaviors. Professionals viewed these aggressive behaviors as serious and felt that they required a reaction or consequence. However, verbal and social bullying were not felt to be as serious or as requiring a strong response (Craig, Henderson, et al., 2000; Hazler, Miller, Carney, & Green, 2001).

A survey in Irish schools showed that teachers in twenty-seven percent of elementary schools and fifty-three percent of what is considered 'second-level' schools in Ireland, did not feel that bullying was a problem in their schools (O'Moore, 1997). Even if teachers become aware of bullying, they may not feel that it is in their job responsibility to stop the behaviors. There are several reasons for this. One reason is that teachers may not feel responsible for bullying behavior that occurs outside of their own classroom. Teachers are more likely to deal with behaviors that occur in class as compared to behaviors that occur on the playground or in other low structure areas. Teachers at the elementary level are more likely to deal with negative behavior on the playground than are teachers at the middle school level (Astor, Benbenishty, Marachi, Haj-Yahia, Zeira, Perkins-Hart, & Pitner, 2002).

School staff may feel that the milder forms of bullying are normative and, do not intervene for this reason. Because school personnel tend to stop the *physical* aggression that they observe, they may believe that they are adequately controlling bullying on the playground. Teacher intervention is inconsistent, partly because the incidents are so short and hard to detect. When incidents are ignored, this serves to exacerbate bullying behavior rather than to decrease it (Craig & Pepler, 2000).

There are still other reasons why teachers may not intervene when they see bullying incidents. The poor social interaction skills demonstrated by victims may not draw adults to help them. When teachers do intervene, they tend to deal with the bullies rather than the victims (Batsche, 1997). This may increase the perceived power of the bully. Unfortunately, some forms of bullying behavior amuse teachers and other adults, especially if sexual teasing is involved. Adults who are amused trivialize sexual teasing (Gropper & Froschl, 2000).

Some school personnel tend to 'look the other way' when bullying behavior is occurring. This is upsetting to students (Ross, 1996). Studies of teachers and children conducted in kindergarten through grade three in New York, and in

Massachusetts, showed that adults were uninvolved or ignored seventy-one percent of the incidents that they observed. Some teachers appeared unaware of what was going on, but others, when they were asked, offered a variety of explanations for not stopping the bullying behaviors. They said that they felt they wanted children to learn to work things out themselves, wanted to discourage tattling, or they believed that the behaviors were natural (Froschl & Gropper, 1999). In addition, teachers may not take bullying behaviors seriously when they are indirect (Batsche, 1997).

Many teachers and other adults feel that students should learn to deal with their own problems. This way of looking at bullying is unfair, because there is an inequity of power involved in bullying; it would be very challenging for a victim to deal with the behaviors alone (Garrity, Jens, et al., 1994).

Teacher Interventions

Gropper and Froschl (2000) found that adults failed to get involved in seventy-one percent of the incidents observed. In one study teachers stopped *only one in 25* bullying incidents (Pepler, Connolly, et al., 2000). Researchers directly observing children on the playground recorded staff intervening in only four percent of bullying episodes (Craig & Pepler, 2000).

Teachers may have low awareness of bullying behaviors. A study of children's opinions in an elementary school in Greece determined that just about half of the students said that they did not know whether or not the teaching staff even knew that bullying was taking place. These students also reported that teachers did not discuss bullying and victims to the same extent as parents discussed it at home (Houndoumandi & Pateraki, 2001). More important, students do not believe that teachers will stop bullying (Banks, 1997). In one study, forty percent of students in elementary school and sixty percent of students in junior high said that teachers don't try to stop bullying very often (Wiler, 1993). Researchers agree that teachers in elementary school are more likely to intervene than are middle school teachers (Behre, Astor, & Meyer, 2001).

When students were interviewed following bullying incidents, both boys and girls wanted their teachers to become involved rather than ignoring the incidents. Eighty-one percent of boys felt that the teacher was looking when the incident occurred, but only sixty-two percent of the girls reported that they thought the teachers were looking. Students might feel that adults condone bullying, especially because students felt that the teachers saw the incidents occur and did not act to stop them (Gropper & Froschl, 2000).

Teacher Bullies

As painful as it may be for school staff to admit the fact, teachers can engage in and model bullying. A recent study found evidence to suggest that some teachers may provide two percent of the bullying themselves. Alternatively, teachers may model excellent problem-solving strategies and skills of conflict resolution (Ross, 1996).

There is very little data on the extent to which students may be ridiculed, humiliated, or be the recipient of verbal aggression from teachers. However, emotional maltreatment by teachers may be strongly related to the alienated and acting out behavior of some children in school according to researchers (Hyman et al., 1997). In one study, students said that they were picked on most often in classrooms (Willenz, 2001). There are estimates that at least one teacher-bully models bullying in most schools (Ross, 1996). Goldstein (1999) feels that the number may be higher, he estimates that 10% of teachers are involved in bullying.

SOCIAL DYNAMICS OF THE PEER GROUP

Student Climate

Student climate has to do with the psychosocial environment of the school. The student climate includes whether or not students feel accepted by various groups within the school and the expectations that students have for themselves as determined by the group. It includes the decision making that the group *may allow* an individual student to make. Student climate relates to the extent to which students control their behavior (McWhirter, McWhirter, McWhirter, & McWhirter, 1998). The social environment may stimulate and support aggressive behaviors (Wright, Lindgren, & Zakriski, 2001).

Social Context

The social context of an individual school can effect the extent of bullying that occurs in the school (Astor, Benbenishty, et al., 2002). The social dynamics of the peer group are important. If they are positive, bullying may be lower in a given school. When the group is not supportive, the likelihood of bullying behaviors is higher.

CLASSROOM VERSUS LOW STRUCTURE AREAS IN SCHOOLS

Classroom Bullying

In class, more boys are bullied than girls. More indirect or covert bullying has been observed in the classroom. Direct bullying in class is more likely to be stopped by a classroom teacher, because the classroom space is smaller and supervision is closer. In the classroom, bullying can interfere with the lesson which would make it more likely that a teacher would stop it so that order is maintained and curricula goals are accomplished (Craig, Pepler, & Atlas, 2000).

Playground and Other Low Structure Areas

Bullying occurs more often during recess, at lunch, in the corridors as children move from class to class, and in boys and girls bathrooms. In elementary schools, the playground is a key area with particularly low structure. Olweus (1993) reported that teacher density was a key factor in bullying behaviors. The more visible the teacher supervision in the school, the fewer reports of bullying reported by students. Teacher supervision is critical for controlling bullying in schools. A low degree of supervision and poor supervisory practices on the playground and in other low structure areas are maintaining factors in bullying behavior. Students learn that aggression *works* when they see it occur and see it rewarded. The chance of observing bullying, seeing it rewarded, and being bullied are more likely to occur on the playground than in the classroom (Craig, Pepler, & Atlas, 2000). Children as well as researchers say that bullying occurs more on the playground than in other places (Olweus, 1991).

Craig and Pepler (1995, 1997, and 2000) conducted impressive observational studies at lunchtime and on school playgrounds using videotape in Canada. It appears to be quite difficult for staff to distinguish between general rough play and teasing. It may also be quite challenging for school staff to identify indirect forms of bullying, where a child manipulates classmates to bully or when a child uses the social structure to bully others. In these Canadian studies, researchers were interested in the behavior of staff who actually observed the bullying episodes. These adults, who directly observed bullying, intervened in only four percent of the situations and appeared to be unaware of what was going on.

On the playground, there are many more students interacting at a significantly higher activity level than in the classroom. The high activity level and the percentage of the behaviors that involve close contact may make it difficult for supervising staff to identify what they were observing as bullying behavior. Play spaces are large, and there is a great deal going on. Because almost twice as much verbal as physical bullying is taking place on the playground over a large or extended space, it is very hard for supervisory adults to catch children who are engaging in bullying behaviors. In general, the consequences for bullying on the playground occur infrequently. This lack of consequences rewards bullying behavior (Craig, Pepler, & Atlas, 2000).

Monitoring student behavior is challenging on the playground. Teachers were observed to stop only one in six bullying incidents on the playground as compared to one in five incidents in class. This indicates a low level of intervention in both environments. Bullies could easily interpret the lack of intervention as a low risk of being caught in bullying behavior (Craig, Pepler, & Atlas, 2000).

Bullying on the playground occurs once every 2.4 minutes, whereas it occurs every thirty-seven minutes in class (Craig, Pepler, & Atlas, 2000, p. 24). Craig, Pepler, and Atlas (2000) did not find any difference in the rate of *students* stopping bullying in class as compared to the playground. Peer attention reinforced bullying in both environments equally, but children were more likely to be victimized on the playground. The reasons that there may be more incidents on the playground include the fact that there are more children on the playground as compared to supervising adults. In addition to the high frequency of active play on the playground, the play space is large, and there are many different types of unstructured play occurring at the same time on a typical playground. Finally, because twice as many incidents of bullying involve verbal as compared to physical aggression, it may be difficult to hear all of these comments with large numbers of children all making a good deal of noise. Direct bullying is found more frequently on the playground than the classroom partly because there are fewer clear rules and fewer consistent rules. Rules on the playground in some schools vary from adult to adult, who may be on duty.

Supervision of Low Structure Areas

Addressing bullying concerns on the playground or during recess periods in schools is challenging. Adding to the researchers observations already outlined, activities are typically loosely organized or are organized by dominant children who control both who participates and the rules of the game. The children who have little power in the peer group perceive this as unfair. Games form and reform quickly. Children join in and leave games frequently. The rules are often unstated, unclear, and change depending on which adults are present. Adults who are present may or may not actively monitor students. They many or may not enforce whatever rules are common. They may create their own rules on the spot. They may or may not intervene when they observe an incident but in addition, may or may not intervene when a child reports an incident they did not observe themselves. Adults 'on duty' may or may not even know the unwritten rules, know the students who get into frequent difficulty or know the students who tend to be isolated during recess. The weather may alter the rules restricitng the play area, limiting play areas to children who have proper clothing for the day, or change the rules for safety issues. These changes in rules along with the fuzzy nature of the rules is extremely difficulty for many children (author's observations).

On playgrounds where the supervision is decreased and more casual, students can easily be drawn into negative, social exchanges with one another. Verbal exchanges can escalate into physical situations. Aggressive students have difficulties in several areas when they are on the playground. Aggressive children have difficulty joining in smoothly without upsetting the action, when games have already started. They over-react to mild teasing and to verbal challenges, and they have a good deal of difficulty responding to adult limit setting (Walker et al., 1995).

Although children are engaged in positive, play activities most of the time when at recess, interview, survey, and observational approaches have demonstrated that a large number of children experience bullying and aggression now and then on the playground. In one study (reported in Boulton, 1994) it was not unusual to find eight-year-old students spending time fighting and bullying. Girls engaged in bullying 2.6 times per hour and boys engaged in bullying 3.7 times per hour. This was less than for eleven-year-olds but negative behaviors still occurred to girls 1.1 times per hour and boys 1.4 times per hour in the eleven-year-old group. Craig and Pepler (1997) found that ninety-two percent of the bullying incidents in the low structure areas involved only one child who was being victimized. This is a very frightening situation for the targeted child. Most of the time, children were about the same age in the bullying incidents that were observed.

The inconsistency with which bullying is stopped, the difficulty of distinguishing it from rough and tumble play, and the shortness of each incident each contribute to the high rate of bullying on school playgrounds (Craig & Pepler, 1997). The low structure areas present formidable challenge to adults who attempt to reduce or stop bullying behaviors.

SUMMARY

A weak sense of community can influence the occurrence and perpetuation of bullying in schools as can school discipline policies that are rigid and punishing. School climate is an important variable. When bullying is modeled, tolerated, or ignored in a school, school climate is negatively affected. The professional staff affect bullying when they interact differently with different children, including bullies, and when they concentrate on negative behaviors to the exclusion of prosocial behaviors. Teachers may model bullying behaviors, appear to tolerate bullying, and may not take bullying seriously or feel responsible for stopping it. Students tend to believe that staff will not intervene to help them or to stop bullying behaviors.

Although bullying occurs in all school environments, bullying occurs at an alarmingly high rate in the low structure areas of schools such as playgrounds. Teacher density is a critical factor. More direct than indirect bullying occurs on the playground with even non-aggressive children involved. Bullying also occurs in classrooms, although it is less frequent, more indirect, and covert.

CHAPTER 4

The Bullies

The bullying interaction involves bullies, victims, and bystanders. We probably know most about the bullies of the various roles involved in a bullying incident, because children who are aggressive have been of particular interest to researchers for some time.

ACTIVE OR AGGRESSIVE BULLIES

Aggressive bullies are the most common type of bully (Newman, Horne, & Bartolomucci, 2000a). Bullies are not only aggressive; they are also hostile and domineering. The typical bully feels positively about violence, is dominating, has little empathy for others, and may also be impulsive (Olweus, 1991; Smith & Sharp, 1994). Bullies tend to be stronger or bigger than peers and they may have more status in the group than that of the victim (Olweus, 1991). Most bullies pick on more than one child. Bullying occurs when it pays off, when the community supports it, and when the bully gets what he or she wants.

Aggressive bullies need to be in control. When they are caught, they do not take full responsibility for their behavior and may say they were provoked into bullying others. They are comfortable in blaming their victims (Banks, 1997; Haynie et al., 2001; Schwartz, 1999). Bullies need power and they feel powerful when they dominate others. They have positive attitudes toward aggression. They experience satisfaction when others are upset or hurt. They also need prestige. The culture teaches 'power over' and winning. Bullies want others to think that they are tough, and they do not want to risk any possibility that they might be victims (Smith & Sharp, 1994).

Bullying may start with teasing and progress to verbal and/or physical abuse. Bullying develops from less serious incidents to more serious incidents over time (Alsaker & Vakanover, 2001). Victimization of peers is a behavior that is consistent across contexts (Craig, Peters, et al., 1998).

Some aggressive bullies act alone. Other bullies act in pairs or small groups when they victimize another child. Bullying behavior is extremely frightening for the victim when groups of students engage in bullying behavior. Aggressive students attract each other, which helps them feel that their behavior is really okay and is accepted by their own group. When aggressive boys group together, the groups are formed of bullies along with boys who are secondary helpers and on-lookers. The onlookers give the group positive feedback for the negative behaviors and support the behavior of the smaller, aggressive pair or small group (Rodkin, Farmer, Pearl, & Van Acker, 2000).

Bullies tend to pick on students who exhibit victim behavior because they are weaker and they don't fight back. Victims are unpopular and bystanders won't help them, so bullies may feel that it is *socially acceptable* to pick on students who behave like victims (Bernstein & Watson, 1997). Olweus (1993) described bullies as showing *aggressive reaction patterns*. By the time that bullies are preadolescents, they act to dominate others without feeling badly about their behavior. When bullies are called on their behavior they avoid blame or they may say that the victim had a part in his or her victimization. They may say that the targeted child 'asked' for trouble (Ross, 1996).

Gottheil and Dubrow (2001a) used self-report measures, peer group nominations, and a measure in which children were asked to take the point of view of peers in rating themselves, to study bullying behaviors. Boys who bullied in grades five and six were somewhat aware of what their classmates thought of them, but they did not seem to pay much attention to this information. They discounted the feedback they received from their peers or were not motivated to change. Girls who bullied tended to think their classmates' views of them were probably correct, but this didn't stop their behavior.

Bullying begins with a lower level of hassling, roughhousing, or teasing. The bully uses these behaviors to determine whether or not the child who they have targeted is a good candidate to be bullied. Once a victim is selected, the bullying can escalate to a serious degree (Ross, 1996).

Elementary children beyond grade three who bully others most frequently are the least anxious children (O'Moore & Kirkham, 2001). Telling children that bullies have low self-esteem will be difficult for a targeted child to accept, when a confident looking and powerful peer is threatening the child. It is, clearly, inaccurate information to give a child and could even be dangerous if the child decided to fight back with put-downs or other behaviors. When a less powerful child fights back physically or verbally, bullying may intensify. Boys who are bullies have high self-concepts by the fifth grade (Kaukiainen, Salmivalli, Lagerspetz, Tamminen, Vauras, & Poskiparta, 2002).

Students who bully but are not victimized use a wide variety of bullying techniques and engage in more negative behavior as compared to students who bully but are also victims (Cary, Swearer, Song, & Eagle, 2001). Olweus (1991) describes these active bullies as exhibiting an *aggressive personality pattern*. The aggressive student who bullies others typically has more physical strength than his peers.

Bullying behavior is a relatively stable behavior. Gottheil and Dubrow (2001a) cite several studies to indicate that bullying will persist over the school year, even when the child moves on to another building, changes teachers or peer groups, and even when there have been interventions to stop the behaviors.

Aggression is a strategy the bully uses to dominate other students. Active and aggressive bullies may have some social weaknesses, but they don't typically have trouble controlling emotions. They are *effectual* aggressors according to Schwartz (2000). Bullies are easily drawn to situations involving aggression (Craig, Peters, et al., 1998).

PASSIVE BULLIES

Passive bullies are a mixed group according to Olweus (1991). Eighteen percent of bullies are described as *passive bullies*. These students are intensely loyal to aggressive bullies. They are anxious, explosive when angry, have low self-esteem, and are likely to be rejected by peers. The passive bully gets in trouble at school and at home (Strawn & Paradiso, 2001). These are students who will not initiate bullying themselves, but who will join or follow a bully in harassing or victimizing other children in school (Sudermann et al., 1996).

The passive bully is dependent, insecure, and lacks social status. The passive bully readily joins in when a bullying incident begins but seldom starts a bullying episode. Passive bullies have also been described as anxious or neurotic. They are eager to be friends with active bullies. They are less well liked and less popular than active or aggressive bullies (Ross, 1996). There are also secondary players in bullying incidents. These are the students who encourage, manipulate, or dare others to become involved in the bullying interaction (Lazarus, 2001). These subtypes of bullying have not been studied in any depth at this time. It appears, however, that bullying is rewarded by participation at any level (Newman, Horne, & Bartolomucci, 2000a).

VARIOUS ASPECTS OF BULLYING BEHAVIOR

Types of Bullying Behaviors

Bullying can be viewed as a behavior which takes three forms according to Ericson (2001): physical, verbal and psychological. Physical bullying can include threatening physical violence and destroying property. Pushing, scratching, butting shoulders, tripping, or destroying the victims personal property are examples of physical bullying. Verbal aggression includes teasing, intimidating, milder threats, name calling, negative comments, and making intimidating phone calls. E-mail messages and slam books may fall under this category, although some practitioners would call this written aggression and include graffiti and note passing as well. Psychological bullying includes behaviors including exclusion, spreading gossip, spreading rumors, and making racial slurs. Ericson's characterization of psychological bullying which involves both verbal and/or nonverbal behaviors generalting a feeling of fear and powerlessness in another child includes behaviors that are more commonly described as social bullying and threatening behaviors. Social bullying involves behaviors such as spreading rumors; threatening behaviors would include behaviors such as intimidation or extortion.

Gray (2001) describes a number of different types of bullying. She suggests that both verbal bullying and using written messages to bully others occur most, followed by physical bullying and social or what Gray describes as relational bullying. Gray also includes backhanded bullying, in which bullies use kindness to mislead the victim, and the making of absurd requests along with an offer of friendship which is designed to embarrass or make fun of the victim. Bullying can also involve active shunning of a target child (Lumsden, 2002).

Bullying can be direct and open when repeated and hurtful acts and words are used, or when a victim is harassed physically or verbally. Bullying can also be indirect, such as when children isolate a target child and intentionally exclude the child from the group. Indirect bullying may involve social isolation, exclusion, or non-selection (Goodman, 1999). Whether direct or indirect, bullying is a game of one-upmanship (Lingren, 1996).

As children age, indirect bullying may become more complex. Teenage girls engage in indirect aggression to include excluding others and spreading false stories. When interviewed by researchers, some girls report that their motivation is to create excitement or to engage in behaviors that they believe will make them part of the group (Owens, Shute, & Slee, 2000). Among adolescent females, one of the most common types of bullying is 'talking about' a victim. Additional behaviors that teenage girls use include starting and facilitating the rumor mill, telling confidential information, and having a quiet conversation that is just at a level so that it can be heard by the victim. Bullies may leave mean messages for the victim to find, make fictitious phone calls, huddle together looking and laughing at the victim, or simply glare at the victim with an angry and cold stare. In addition, peers may use code names for a victim, so that witnesses cannot testify the group was engaging in bullying (Owens, Slee, & Shute, 2001).

Motivation for Bullying

Ross (1996) describes two motivations for bullying behavior, a *payoff* and *power*. If the bully's goal happens to be some sort of payoff, the bully would select out a child who will easily give in. If the bully's goal is power, the bully might select out a child who is disliked by peers and who will make a fuss but would still be easy to dominate. Olweus (1999) noted that bullies seemed to get satisfaction from causing distress and injuries. They also appeared to gain prestige from their peers when they engaged in bullying behavior.

In a study of fifth graders, girls described bullies as 'crowd pleasers'. Some of the girls interviewed felt that nothing could be done to stop bullies but none of the boys felt this way. Some boys who are identified as bullies are described as having poor emotional control by others, but these boys are not the 'active' or aggressive bullies (Khosropour & Walsh, 2001).

Bullying and Aggression

In deepening our understanding of bullying behavior, it is important to distinguish between bullying behaviors and the broader category of aggressive behaviors. There are distinctions between aggression and bullying. Boys who are primarily aggressive may be aggressive in all circumstances and with everyone. Bullies are *selective* in who they attempt to dominate. Early on, bullies tend to be involved in positive activities with the groups. Bullies are popular when they are young in the early grades (Ross, 1996).

Espelage and Asidao (2001) feel that bullying differs from aggression, because bullies choose the children they target and manipulate situations so that they can control the situation as well as the children involved in the situation. Bullies tend to go after the same kids over and over. They engage in more than one type of bullying.

Rejection and Bullying

Although aggressive children may be popular when they are young and may continue to find friends as they go through school, over time peers dislike aggressive children more and more (Warman & Cohen, 2000). Peers reject children who are more extreme in their use of social aggression, just as they reject those who are extreme in their use of physical aggression (Henington, Hughes, Cavell, & Thompson, 1998). Aggressive children do not constitute a single group of students. Aggressive behavior and being rejected by peers are related, but do not predict future outcomes in the same way. Rejection tends to affect later adjustment; whereas, aggression predicts delinquency (Yoon, Hughes, Cavell, & Thompson, 2000).

A study in the Netherlands determined that peer rejection is not stable. When kindergarten children were followed for five years, children rejected early on were later accepted over time. Only the children who remained rejected engaged in high levels of bulling behaviors (Haselager, Cillessen, Van Lieshout, Riksen-Walraven, & Hartup, 2002). Other studies show that children who remain rejected over time tend to be disruptive and off-task in class, and exhibit high levels of verbal and physical aggression. Students identify one-third of rejected students as highly aggressive (Mounts, 1997).

Fear of being rejected by classmates is most acute in middle childhood. Boys in particular want to be accepted by the group. Girls want to be accepted by their closest friend or friends. When peers do not accept aggression, some students are able to appreciate that they are engaging in aggressive behaviors. Students who are accepted by their classmates will underestimate the degree to which they engage in aggressive behaviors (Keltikangas-Jarvinen, 2002).

Social Status of Bullies

Self-views, beliefs, or cognitions of bullies have to do with how a student views himself or herself, and what the student believes or thinks about whether or not a particular behavior is acceptable. In addition, beliefs about whether he or she is competent to do whatever it is he or she wants to do, and whether the student believes the behavior will get him or her what he or she wants are important in bullying (Gottheil & Dubow, 2001b).

Bullies tend to have *average or above average* self esteem, contrary to popular opinion (Sudermann et al., 1996). A very interesting study of fourth to sixth grade boys showed that aggressive boys could be very *popular* and *accepted* by the other children in the school. These boys were good at sports and were considered 'cool', tough, and skilled in exploiting others. They were not considered good students, however. Bullying was a major part of their social status (Rodkin et al., 2000). Bullies enjoyed the rewards of bullying, lacked empathy, and liked to control and dominate peers (Olweus, 1991; Pepler, Connolly, & Craig, 2000; Miller & Rubin, 1998).

Although many parents tell their children that bullies tease and are mean because they don't feel good about themselves, or are jealous of the child who is being teased, research does not support this point of view. Bullies have *positive* feelings about aggressive behavior. Bullies don't feel bad about themselves, and they are not anxious (Banks, 1997). Self-esteem is not one of the issues with which bullies have to contend, and programs which tried to improve the self-esteem of bullies have backfired. They have produced better bullies (Mullin-Rindler, 2001b; Strawn & Paradiso, 2001).

Bullies feel just as attractive physically as peers, and feel just as popular. Older bullies have been found to be the least anxious of all those who participate in the bullying sequence actively or as bystanders (O'Moore & Kirkham, 2001). The fact that bullies experience less, or at least no more, anxiety or insecurity than others has been known for some time (Olweus, 1991).

Aggressive children, in general, are very positive about their own competence and social relatedness (Hughes, Cavell, & Prasad-Gaur, 2001). Although positive views of self are helpful, when self-views are positive in the extreme and are also incorrect, the result may be adjustment difficulties and problems in social functioning. A current question for researchers who are interested in bullying behavior is whether unrealistically positive self-views might result in aggression; or, whether peers are afraid of giving negative feedback to aggressive children and for this reason aggressive students are not likely to become aware of the feelings of others. Some studies indicate that students with strongly positive self-perceptions behave more aggressively. A group of rejected, aggressive students older than eight years of age overestimated both their acceptance and their competence. It may be that they were able to see themselves positively by discounting others' views (David & Kistner, 2000).

Information-Processing Bias

Emotion is a variable that influences thinking. Students process social information differently depending on the degree of emotion that they feel when they are problem solving. Aggressive children may process social situations differently than nonaggressive children, and this may be related to the emotion tied to a given situation (Ledingham, 1991).

Aggressive students in general tend to believe that others have a hostile intent when the social situation isn't clear. At least some bullies behave as if they are biased in regard to their understanding of the behavior of others. When aggressive students are presented with hypothetical social situations that required problem solving, they tend to suggest aggressive solutions. By the time that aggressive students are teenagers they deny their participation in aggressive acts. When they do admit a role in an aggressive act, they distort the circumstances. Students who are willing to own up to their aggressive behavior feel positively about themselves. They belong to groups and know how others view them. Aggressive students are rejected by some peers but are supported by others (Cairns & Cairns, 1991). It could be that aggressive children project their goal of *control over others* (Yoon, 2000).

Aggressive students may tend to interpret the behavior of peers as hostile toward them because they have difficulty processing the *intentions and motives* of others. They believe that aggressive action is usually successful in getting them what they want. They do not think of aggression as inappropriate and are confident in their ability to behave aggressively and be successful in doing so (Teglasi & Rothman, 2001). Their style of problem solving along with their impulsive and aggressive temperaments puts them at risk for problems beyond bullying and teasing (Bernstein & Watson, 1997).

Problem solving in social areas has to do with the effort to reach the social goals that are important to the individual. The Waterloo Longitudinal Project, which followed students in grades one and two, indicated that peers who were considered aggressive were less likely to think of cooperative strategies when they wanted something. The aggressive children were more likely to react with negative behavior when they thought that something had been done to them on purpose. The aggressive children also attributed negative intentions to others. Their peers easily drew the aggressive children into exchanges that become riddled with conflict (Rubin, Bream, & Rose-Krasnor, 1991).

Some of the aggressive children behaved in ways that would draw the attention of the peer group to themselves, such as calling out and making challenging statements. They were more intrusive and disruptive in their use of methods that they suggested when they were presented with hypothetical social situations. Not only did these children suggest aggression as a strategy to use in the hypothetical social situations, they typically used aggression in their real-world play to get what they wanted. They tended to use bargaining or offer something positive, so that they could manipulate the other child into doing what they wanted. Importantly, these behaviors *frequently worked* in the real world. They were successful and effective. The children were reinforced for the aggression they used by the peer group (Rubin et al., 1991).

Some aggressive children appear to appreciate negative feedback when it is directed toward other children, but not when it is directed toward them. Aggressive children are hypersensitive to negative feedback. It has been hypothesized that aggressive children who are rejected are actually more sensitive to rejection than their peers. This is seen in their tendency to believe that others are hostile, while they continue to believe that they are liked by others in the peer group, and that they are personally very competent. An information-processing bias appears to be in effect (Hughes, Cavell, et al., 2001).

When studies have been conducted to determine whether there may be a relationship between attributional bias and aggression, researchers have found evidence to support the idea that a child's behavior is related to differences in processing social information. The connection is stronger for aggression in reaction to perceived threat. Students who act in anger because they feel threatened, learn that accidents can happen that are not intended *later* than other children. Children who are both aggressive and rejected by peers are most likely to think others intend to threaten them (Orobio deCastro, Veerman, Koops, Bosch, & Monshouwer, 2002).

OUTCOMES FOR BULLIES

The bullies don't do well later on. Bullying behavior may be an early indicator of an antisocial behavior pattern. There is a strong correlation between chronic bullying and negative outcomes for the bullies, in part because bullying behaviors are stable. Early aggression is the best predictor of later aggression (Banks, 1997; Pepler, Connolly, & Craig, 2000; Teglasi & Rothman, 2001). Students identified as bullies in elementary and middle schools are more likely to be involved in sexual harassment and assault than their peers when they reach high school (Khosropour & Walsh, 2001).

Bullying behavior is among the warning signs of later highly aggressive behavior. School bullies are more likely than others to break the law when they reach adolescence (Osofsky & Osfsky, 2001). Girls who bully learn to be aggressive in interpersonal interactions. Researchers think that this could affect their parenting style in the future (Garrity, Jens, et al., 1995). Serbin, Moskowitz, Schwartzman, and Ledingham (1991) followed a small group of aggressive girls and found that they did have difficulty as parents. They also performed less well in school and had more medical problems.

Bullies tend to either feel quite depressed or do not feel depressed at all. The two types of bullies are extreme in this regard. Norwegian studies of eighth grade students indicated that bullies experienced symptoms of depression, with higher rates of depressive symptoms among girls who bully others (Roland, 2002). There is also some data available to indicate that bullies may experience suicidal ideation. In an attempt to explain the association between bullying and depression, researchers suggest that there may be a subtype of bully that is aggressive with comorbid depression (Swearer, Song, Cary, Eagle, & Mickelson, 2001).

Studies of students in grades five through eight in Canada show that bullies say that they started dating at younger ages and are more aggressive in those dating relationships than their peers. Bullies report that their opposite-sex relationships are not very supportive and power is not equal in their dating relationships. They seem to be dating before they have adequate maturity to manage a dating relationship. Adolescents who bully are more likely to do things that others would not do in order to hold on to relationships. Both boys and girls who are bullies may carry this behavior over to dating relationships, possibly, because they have already learned from participating in bullying that aggression is power. Bullying in childhood may be one of the precursors of violence in dating (Connolly, Pepler, Craig, & Taradash, 2000).

In addition to adjustment difficulties, bullies tend to have general problems with school rules and difficulty obeying school norms. They do not follow school rules as well as others, and are late for school or are absent frequently. They also experience problems with school achievement. Aggressive bullies have lower school achievement than either the victims or children who are victims but who also bully others. They are not as invested in academic performance as their peers (Song, Swearer, Eagle, & Tam Cary, 2000). With time, there is an impact on school success for bullies, along with problems in early adulthood (Mullin-Rindler, 2001; Strawn & Paradiso, 2001). Chronic bullying has a cost for society as well as for the individual and, of course, the victim. Bullies are more likely to require special education services, social services, mental health services, and juvenile justice services (Craig, Peters, et al., 1998). Prevention programs to address bullying might have the affect of decreasing general violence among adolescents in the community later on (Andershed, Kerr, & Stattin, 2001).

Longitudinal Outcome Studies

Bullies are more likely than their peers to participate in other anti-social behaviors in addition to bullying (Center for the Study and Prevention of Violence, 2001). Bullying behavior may be an early warning sign of long term difficulties for aggressive children. About sixty percent of boys who were bullies in middle school had at least one conviction by age twenty-three years. From thirty-five to forty percent of boys who had engaged in bullying behaviors had three or more convictions (reported in Limber, 1996).

Olweus (1993) conducted a longitudinal study involving boys in Sweden. He found that sixty percent of the students who had been called bullies in grades six through nine had committed a crime by age twenty-four. Of that group, thirty-five to forty percent had three or more convictions. By the time they were adults, these boys who were aggressive bullies demonstrated a four-fold increase over their peers in committing criminal acts (Olweus, 1994, 1999).

An important longitudinal study of boys from the Pittsburgh Youth Study has documented several different pathways to more serious misbehavior for students showing early aggression. One pathway starts with annoying peers and bullying. This pattern is followed by fighting and interpersonal violence. Bullying was clearly a precursor to later violent behavior for this group, although, of course, not all bullies would persist along this pathway toward violence (Kelley, Loeber, Keenan, & DeLamatre, 1997).

FROM BULLYING TO SEXUAL HARASSMENT

As children who bully others get older, they may become involved in more serious behaviors. These behaviors fall in the category of harassment. Harassment is extremely important to distinguish from bullying, because it is a violation of civil rights under the law. The Department of Education in the United States at the federal level defines harassment to include crude name-calling, threats, and physical or sexual assaults (US Dept. of Education, 1998b). The relationship between bullying and sexual harassment is currently being explored by researchers in Canada who feel that the way that bullies have learned to use aggressive power in elementary school will be seen in the same way in dating situations later on (Connolly et al., 2000).

Unfortunately, harassment can be ignored just as bullying behavior can be ignored, until a student is seriously hurt. Just as some bullying behavior is passed off as inconsequential, some types of harassment behaviors are not considered significant by school staff. However, harassment is *not typical* and is clearly inappropriate behavior. Sexual harassment in particular may appear to be insignificant because it occurs at the time that students are maturing physically. Sexual harassment appears to be related to expressions of sexual interest in the opposite sex (McMaster, Connolly, Pepler, & Craig, 2000).

As students progress through elementary and middle school and enter high school, bullying decreases. Sexual harassment, on the other hand, increases (Connolly et al., 2000). Sexual harassment includes behaviors such as grabbing, pulling, brushing up against, leering, making inappropriate comments that are suggestive, spreading sexual rumors, making sexual jokes, referring to sexual orientation, graffiti, and other behaviors (Hyman et al., 1997).

Same sex harassment often includes homophobic references, spreading rumors, and can extend to hazing behaviors (McMaster et al., 2000). Researchers have reported both student-to-student and adult-to-student, sexual harassment. Studies of harassment in schools suggests that school administrators have not responded consistently to sexual harassment (Hyman et al., 1997).

Students of both sexes harass others sexually in early adolescence. At this developmental period, boys and girls are harassed equally. Boys engage in more same-sex harassment than opposite-sex harassment at this age, but the boys who engage in same-sex harassment are not the same students who harass girls. Homophobic put-downs appear to be a common way for boys to aggress toward other boys (McMaster et al., 2000).

The American Association of University Women Educational Foundation (2001) conducted the first nationwide survey of sexual harassment in the United States. They collected data on 2,064 children in grades eight through eleven. They found that four out of five school-aged children said that they had experienced sexual harassment in their schools. According to this study, eighty-five percent of girls were victims, whereas seventy-six percent of boys reported harassment. Middle- and secondary-level boys increasingly are reporting harassment in school contrary to the studies of slightly younger students in Canada. All students find sexual harassment upsetting, but girls say that they are more affected than boys say they are affected. One in every four girls reported cutting a class or staying home because they were afraid. Just as bullying occurs in the classroom, sixty-one percent of physical harassment and fifty-six percent of non-physical harassment occurs in classrooms, where teachers are present most of the time.

Adolescents are attracted to aggressive behaviors, and girls in particular are drawn to it. It appears that boys competing for access to girls, and girls competing with their same-sex peers to get attention from the most dominant males, accounts for the increase in harassment behaviors (Pellegrini & Long, 2002). Bullying behaviors become sexual harassment later in adolescence among a subgroup of students (Pellegrini, 2001b).

In the American Association of University Women (AAUW) survey in 1993, about half of the time students who engage in harassment are trying to demonstrate their power or to get something they want. This behavior occurs at a high rate. Eighteen percent of students feel frightened some or most of the time in school (AAUW, 2001). Like bullying, incidents of harassment are occurring in the presence of teachers in school hallways. A surprising seven percent of students reported being harassed by the teachers.

Some harassment behavior is part of aggressive behaviors, including bullying, that appear to be fairly stable over time. McMaster et al. (2001) feel that bullying changes over time in its appearance and becomes more broad based. Pepler and her research team feel that sexual harassment is a form of bullying evolving in the middle school years. Correlational studies show that students who are bullies are more likely to say that they abuse alcohol significantly more and use drugs significantly more than their peers. Bullying and sexually harassing classmates appears to teach certain individuals about interpersonal power and increases the risks of drug and alcohol use and abuse in high school (Pepler, Craig, Connolly, et al., 2001).

Schools are responsible to act in cases of harassment, and a school district can be held responsible when it responds indifferently to charges of harassment among students (Office of Civil Rights, 2001, January). Brady (2001) pointed out that some of the behaviors that we excuse between children would instigate a lawsuit if adults engaged in the same verbal or physical behaviors.

SUMMARY

Bullies are powerful children. They engage in bullying when it gets them what they want in the form of power over others with little to no cost to themselves. Bullies do not seem to care much about negative feedback from the peer group at large, and are not motivated to change their behavior. They believe that their own associates and friends support their behavior. Aggressive bullies have low anxiety, high self-regard, and little empathy for their victims. Bullies engage in physical, verbal, and social bullying. They may exhibit direct and indirect bullying. Their motivation involves power, dominance, and prestige. Their behavior is stable over time. Passive bullies are followers who do not instigate bullying but who join in readily. Other bullies may be motivated by a desire to be accepted by a powerful bully or by the popular crowd.

Bullies do not do well later on. A portion of the group who engage in bullying may have adjustment difficulties as they go through school and may become involved with violence in dating relationships and even criminal behavior eventually. Some bullies are rejected because of their aggressive behaviors. These bullies are at risk for becoming involved in anti-social groups. Bullies, as distinguished from the broader group of aggressive children, are selective in the children they target to dominate. They go after the same target over and over, and use a variety of bullying behaviors. Bullies have average to above average self-esteem, and many have unrealistically positive self-views. Some bullies attribute hostile intent to others, while at the same time they believe that they are liked and are competent. Some of the characteristics of bullies appear to be due to the fact that in the real world, bullying works rather well.

As bullying decreases in late middle school and in secondary school, sexual harassment increases. Sexual harassment may increase as students learn ways of interacting with individuals of the opposite sex. Although both boys and girls are sexually harassed, boys increasingly report incidents although girls are still harassed more than boys. One in every four students is often a victim of these behaviors in the United States.

CHAPTER 5

Age and Gender Variables in Bullying

It is important to explore age and gender variables associated with bullying, because there are distinct differences in how bullying takes place and is experienced by children according to these variables. It is important to keep in mind, however, that grade differences are less important than school context variables (Astor, Benbenishty, et al., 2002).

AGE VARIABLES

As age variables are explored, it is important to keep in mind that age and grade effects depend on the way in which schools are organized. In the United States, for example, there is a wide variety of school organizations. Elementary school may be organized by grade kindergarten through grades 5 or 6, or by kindergarten through grade 8. Middle schools or junior high schools may be organized around grade levels 5 through 9 or 6 through 8. There may be other grade level organizations in various towns and communities. In reviewing research, it appears that school transitions are associated with increases in bullying behaviors, so that the rate of bullying varies around school transitions. There are several key transition periods to consider; in particular, the transition from preschool to kindergarten and the transition from elementary to middle school.

Also, when age variables are considered the role of peers in bullying behavior is relevant. Although we know that aggressive children have particular characteristics such as difficulty delaying gratification and that their parents tend to be inconsistent in management, the peer group also plays a role in the maintenance of aggression. Peers play a role in allowing aggressive children to get their way by rewarding the behavior, and allowing the aggressive behavior to continue. Peers also do not let their aggressive classmates know that they do not like the bullying behaviors, possibly because they are worried about escalating the behavior or because they prefer to simply stay away from aggressive classmates (Coie & Jacobs, 2000). In general, the percentage of students who are targeted by bullies seems to decrease with age (Olweus, 1993).

Teasing and Bullying among Young Children

Some researchers feel that it is the youngest children who are at greatest risk of being bullied (Basche, 1997). Olweus (1993) found that the percentage of children targeted by bullies decreased as students went through elementary school. He found that the number of children who are victimized by bullies is twice as high in elementary schools as compared to secondary school. At the same time, the number of students engaging in bullying behavior stays the same. Olweus further found that the highest percentage of students reporting being bullied by others was in second grade, where about one third of students said that they were victimized. However, this was the youngest age group that he studied. Kindergarten and first grade students were not assessed in the Swedish studies. When attempts were made to assess children at the kindergarten and first grade level, researchers found that very young children were not reliable reporters (Astor, Benbenishty, et al., 2002; Ross, 1996).

Bullying in the Elementary Grades

Although younger children were not represented in the early studies, it is well known that teasing begins as early as kindergarten in schools. The transition from preschool or nursery school to kindergarten appears to be a period in which children are more likely to be victimized than at other times. Kindergarten children are more likely to say that they are bullied than children reporting at other ages. Kochenderfer and Ladd (1996) looked at different ways in which kindergarten children are bullied. Verbal aggression was more common than physical aggression in this age group. The most common types of bullying at this age involved being 'picked on' or when peers made 'mean' statements about a child. Almost half of the kindergarten children complained that they were picked on or that kids said 'bad things' about them. Each of the different types of bullying affected victims who reacted by feeling lonely and who want to stay away from school. Boys and girls were equally likely to be victimized in kindergarten (Kochenderfer & Ladd, 1996). About twenty percent of kindergarten children, as compared to ten percent of children in third to sixth grade, were identified as victims of teasing and bullying in schools in one study (Leff, Kupersmidt, Patterson, & Power, 1999).

Younger children are bullied most, with first through fourth graders bullied more than any other age groups (Lazar, 2002). Ross (1996) suggests several reasons why younger children may report being bullied. Young children may use bullying behaviors because they are less verbally and socially competent than their peers. It may also be that younger students exaggerate the bullying interactions. Children who have been bullied once may hold on to this memory, confusing the time frames used in interviews and surveys. Each of these confounding issues could inflate the reports of younger students.

Young children's definition of bullying may be quite broad and inclusive, as compared to older students, so they report higher rates (Ross, 1996). At the same time, Harachi, Catalano, and Hawkins (1999b) suggest that young boys may use bullying as a way to approach others in new groups, because they have fewer proactive skills than older children. In addition, they may be more rewarded for their behaviors because younger boys feel positively toward a percentage of the boys who engage in bullying behaviors. As students progress through school, the children who are victimized may decrease, as students become more selective in the specific students they target (Pelligrini & Long, 2002).

Bullying behavior is also common between grades four and six, or seven. Astor, Benbenishty, et al. (2002) found that children in grades four through six were concerned about being threatened and being bullied. However, children reported a lower level of being victimized than children in kindergarten through grade three.

Transition from Elementary to Middle School or Junior High

School transitions appear to be particularly common but critical times during which children are teased or bullied. Researchers think that as children's groups form and reform students try out aggressive behaviors, randomly, on everybody. Once students figure out who will react and who won't, bullies tend to narrow the focus of the teasing to specific children. After the transition period, the group has figured out which children react most. The bullying, then, tends to concentrate on a smaller group of students (Kochenderfer & Ladd, 1996).

As students move from elementary school to middle school in the United States, they report an increase in teasing and bullying. Students know that bullying intensifies at this time, and they become nervous about the transition to middle school. Once the newly formed groups stabilize in the new school, teasing and bullying tends to decrease a little (Asidao, Vion, & Espelage, 1999; Kochenderfer & Ladd, 1996; Pellegrini & Bartini, 1999). Research in the United States shows that direct bullying increases in middle childhood, peaks, and then declines (Banks, 1997). Studies in Great Britain have also found that bullying and other aggressive behaviors increase when students first enter middle school. Boys use bullying behavior to demonstrate power over others. This display of dominance is used as students move into new social groups. In the United States, middle schools and junior high schools have been criticized because they change and disrupt the social supports that are available for children, who may be vulnerable and need the supports in order to successfully fit in. The competition that is so strong among students at the middle school level may be an additional factor that increases bullying (Pelligrini & Long, 2002).

The group structure changes when students change schools. Friendships are restructuring, and groups break up with the sudden disruption. Old classmates and new classmates, all of whom are struggling to find a place in the peer group that will maintain their self-esteem, surround students. This change in group structure has to do not only with the change in schools, but it also occurs due to the fact that children are maturing quickly. A study of African American students between ten and twelve years old provided evidence that students who experienced harsh and inconsistent discipline at home and who acted out, were more vulnerable to bullying if they *also* were early maturing (Ge, Brody, Conger, Simons, & Murry, 2002). Once the students enter the new school, they are faced with the need to make new relationships and figure out their status in the group hierarchy. They may no longer fit in the same place, because of their internal rate of physical development and the presence of new peers who may replace them in their old group (Pellegrini, 2001b).

Pellegrini and Long (2002) describe bullying as deliberate aggression to achieve high or powerful status in the peer group. Another impetus for the increase in bullying behavior is that girls in early adolescence are attracted to males who are more aggressive. Attention from girls may be the goal for which boys who bully others are competing. In like manner, girls hurt other girls to prevent them from gaining access to socially powerful males. In a study using multiple methods of measurement, Pellegrini and Long found that boys not only increasingly used both direct and indirect aggression but also felt more positive about it from grades five to seven. The evidence that the increase in bullying is associated with changing schools is supported by the fact that it occurs primarily in countries where students attend middle schools which are separated from the elementary schools. Boys attempt to dominate other males and girls attempt to dominate other girls as new groups come together. In middle schools that start with grade six, students have more stable status in their new groups by seventh grade.

The picture is clear. As students enter elementary school, an independent or different middle school, or a different high school, groups need to reform to include new members out of an increased group of contestants for positions in the group. Researchers feel that aggressive behavior is used to establish dominance in students' new social groups. Bullying appears to increase during school transitions. Once the hierarchy of the peer groups is re-established, bullying decreases and aggressive behavior, in general, decreases.

Bullying in Middle School

Bullying is a behavior that is common in middle schools in the United States. The Safe Schools/Healthy Students Initiative in the United States is a project of three federal agencies: the Department of Health and Human Services, the

Department of Education and the Department of Justice. National data collected through this initiative in regard to school violence and policy referrals, show referrals and mandatory suspensions greatly increasing in middle school (Massey, Armstrong, Boroughs, Santoro, & Perry, 2002). If behavioral controls in general are seen more frequently in students in middle school, it would not be a surprise if bullying were seen at high levels in middle school.

There is a strong connection between bullying and popularity in sixth grade when the sixth grade is the beginning of middle school. Sixth to eighth grade bullies are as popular and have as many friends as those who treat their peers better. Boys use mild bullying behaviors, including teasing, as a way of interacting in grade six, and they use bullying in determining their social status in middle school. Boys bully more than girls at this age, even when aggression is described verbal as well as physical, and they act aggressively more toward other boys than they do toward girls (Espelage & Holt, 2001; Pellegrini, 2001b). Pelligrini and Long (2002) also reported that boys were victimized by boys more than boys victimized girls in middle school. In like manner, girls tended to victimize girls more than boys would victimize girls in middle school. Direct bullying is more common among boys, and indirect bullying is more common among girls (Astor, Benbenishty, et al., 2002). Girls in middle school use social exclusion, ostracism, manipulation of the attitudes and opinions of others, and character defamation in bullying interactions (Cairns & Cairns, 1991). Bullies, generally, do not change their tactics for establishing dominance in a group that they have mastered when they were younger. Students who are identified as bullies in second grade are still engaged in bullying behavior when they are in sixth grade (Garrity & Baris, 1997).

It may be that as boys begin to want relationships with girls, they show that interest initially by teasing. The teasing may be playful and include minor physical contact. Boys protect themselves from being rejected by girls, because should a girl not like the attention or embarrass the boys, the boys can say that the behavior was accidental. They pretend that they are not actually interested in girls. Boys engage in more positive behaviors with girls at this age as well. The more dominant boys are considered to be more desirable by girls (Pellegrini, 2001b).

In one study, eighty percent of middle school students said that they had behaved as bullies in the previous month. Teasing, name-calling, threatening, social ridiculing, and physical aggression were common, yet, the students did *not* describe it as serious. In another study, twenty percent of boys, as compared to seven percent of girls, admitted bullying at a high rate in grade eight (Espelage & Holt, 2001). On average, eighty-to-ninety percent of middle school students reported that they were victims, and that they also bullied others (Asidao et al., 1999).

In a second study of American middle school students it was also found that both students and teachers identified more students whom they described as bully-victims than they identified students whom they described as solely bullies or solely victims (Paulk et al., 1999). Some students reported that they joined in the bullying, but some of those who participated did not feel very good about it. Unfortunately, *they did it anyway* (Asidao et al., 1999).

Using a survey developed by psychologists at the University of Nebraska-Lincoln, researchers determined that sixth grade students in a middle school had different perceptions of bullying, depending on the role they played in the bullying episode. The bullies said that they meant no harm to victims. Victims did not agree that the bullies meant 'no harm' (Carey, Swearer, Song, & Eagle, 2001).

Bullying in Secondary Schools

Aggression is overt as students move into secondary school, and a significant proportion of the aggression that students exhibit involves bullying. Students at the secondary level do not consider aggression as negatively as they did in elementary school. Some researchers feel that this is because the bully represents a challenge to adult views and authority which many students admire in this age group (Pellegrini & Long, 2001). Aggressive behaviors continue to be used to establish the hierarchy of the group. 'Successful' bullying appears to be used strategically as the new groups are formed at the secondary level.

As the new groups stabilize in secondary school, bullying behavior tends to decrease but sexual harassment increases. Pellegrini (2001b) found that the bullying behavior which boys engaged in as they entered middle school turns into harassment within a year or so. Bullies want to have relationships with individuals of the opposite sex, even though they may feel negatively about other students in general. Bullies date at younger ages than their peers (Connolly, Pepler, Craig, & Taradash, 2000). Unfortunately, because they have already learned to express power in relationships through bullying, bullies may use bullying in their dating relationships.

GENDER VARIABLES IN BULLYING

Higher rates of bullying and of aggression, in general, have been reported in boys worldwide (Ross, 1996). Gender differences depend on the definition that researchers use when studying bullying, and more specifically, whether or not indirect bullying is included in the bullying definitions. Some researchers feel that boys are much more likely to engage in *direct* bullying behaviors than girls (Mullin-Rindler, 2001a). In early elementary school, boys initiate three to four times as many incidents involving bullying behavior as girls, and are victims twice as often (Froschl & Gropper, 1999; Newman et al., 2000a).

Researchers hypothesize that the more girls play with boys, the higher the level of bullying on the playground because boys tend to engage in more bullying behavior in general (Astor, Benbenishty, et al., 2002). Ross (1996) suggests that girls who bully others tend to be of the same age as their victims. Boys, who bully others, tend to be older than their victim. Olweus (1993) found that the number of girls who victimize others decreases with age.

An *observational* study of children aged five through eight years in four schools explored gender differences in bullying. In this study, there was typically only one bully, but when there was more than one child who started the bullying sequence, the students were both of the same gender. Boys were three times more likely to tease and bully than girls in this study, although boys and girls were both bullied. Physical behavior was more prevalent than verbal behavior, and when boys were bullied physically, they responded physically. Girls responded verbally (Grooper & Frischl, 2000).

More boys than girls say they are victimized from the fifth to the seventh grades. Girls disapproved of bullying in grade five, but accept it more and more as they get older (Pellegrini & Long, 2002). Girls at this age say that bullies attack others by pointing out weaknesses in academic performance or athletics. These girls also report that engaging in mean games and making negative comments about race or disabilities are the bullying behaviors that they see. Boys in middle school report laughing when others are upset, or when others cry or fall, more than girls report this type of bullying (Khosropour & Walsh, 2001).

Incidence studies typically use self-reporting data collection methods. Ross (1996) argues that girls may not appreciate that their behaviors are bullying, and, therefore, do not report it even though they may know that their behavior is 'mean'. Girls' self-reports underestimate the degree to which they are engaging in bullying. Boys say that they engage in direct, physical bullying more than girls. Girls talk more about engaging in and being the recipients of indirect bullying than boys. There does not appear to be much difference in direct *verbal* aggression between boys and girls (Ross, 1996).

Researchers who include both direct and indirect bullying in their definition of bullying behavior indicate that boys and girls bully in almost equal numbers. Bullying behaviors are manifested differently in boys and girls. As described earlier, boys who bully threaten to hit or take things from peers, and boys who bully tend to be stronger than their peers and need to control others. Girls use nasty, dismissive glances and gestures, start and spread rumors, gossip, send intimidating notes, threaten others with social ostracism, play mean games, manipulate friendships, and/or leave a classmate out of the group. Strength is not as important for girls who bully; in fact, girls who bully tend to be physically weaker than their peers (Banks, 1997; Pepler, Connolly, et al., 1997; Khosropour & Walsh, 2001; McCoy, 1997; Mullin-Rindler, 2001a). When adults are asked about girls bullying behavior, they say that girls who bully others are often trying to get attention from peers. Being included often means leaving out particular students. Teachers hypothesize that girls bully because they are bored and want to create excitement, or that they are acting out television soap operas (Owens, Slee, et al., 2001).

Young boys who are bullies report that they engage in both physical and verbal aggression. Older boys who bully say that they use mostly verbal aggression. As boys get older, they use more varied bullying, so the percentage of bullying that is physical decreases and verbal bullying increases. Bullies are significantly less anxious and less depressed than others who may be involved in bullying as victims or involved in bystanders roles (Craig, 1998).

By middle school age, boys are doing most of the bullying (Garrity & Baris, 1997). Olweus (1991) in his Scandinavian studies concluded that boys more frequently acted as bullies and more frequently reported bullying others. In his studies, the percentage of students experiencing indirect bullying was about the same for boys and girls, but more boys were directly bullied. Studies indicated that more than eighty percent of boys were bullied by boys, whereas about sixty percent of girls in grades five to seven were the victims of boys.

Social or Relational Aggression in Girls versus Boys

There has been more research conducted on bullying among boys than in girls. This may be related to the ways that aggression has been viewed by researchers in the past (Henington et al., 1998). Interest in aggressive behavior among girls is increasing dramatically. As stated earlier, girls prefer indirect bullying and verbal harassment, while boys are more comfortable with physical bullying, although verbal harassment is also often used by boys (Alsaker & Vakanover, 2001). More specifically, girls enagage more in social or relational bullying than boys. Bullying that is indirect or relational enables the bully to have power over others by controlling relationships or friendships.

Although research suggests that more boys than girls bully, when data is collected by survey approaches, when researchers on the playground observe children, or when social bullying is included in the definition of aggression, the discrepancy is not as great. Using the broader definition, girls are rated as bullying as often as boys (Henington et al., 1998). Henington and colleagues (1998) estimate that if bullying is measured without including relational bullying in the definition, sixty percent of aggressive girls would be missed, but only seven percent of aggressive boys would be missed.

Relational bullying has to do with the manipulation of a targeted child's social relationships or damaging a student's reputation or status in the peer group (Crick, 1993). Although both boys and girls bully others physically, girls stop bullying physically before boys stop physical bullying (Craig, Pepler, Connolly, et al., 2001). Girls tend to use relational aggression when they bully others. In relational aggression, students hurt others by causing problems with their friendships, or they may use exclusion to isolate another child (Garrity & Baris, 1997). Relational aggression is easily observed as early as preschool (Crick, Nelson, Morales, Cullerton-Sen, Casas, & Hickman, 2001). Children are capable of using indirect bullying by the time they are five years old, and at least in the five to seven year old age group it is used equally by boys and girls (Alsaker & Vakanover, 2001).

Between eight and eleven years of age, girls continue to use more and more relational aggression. They appear to be choosing the form of aggression that is most hurtful to others, and the type of aggression that is most *tolerate*d by the peer group. Girls who use more extreme relational aggression are likely to be rejected by others, but boys who use relational aggression are less likely to be rejected, unless they are also physically aggressive (Henington et al., 1998). Because relational aggression is used more as children grow older, it is considered *more advanced* behaviorally (Lagerspetz & Bjorkqvist, 1994). Verbal aggression increases with language development.

International studies suggest that girls between the ages of eight and fifteen years of age use indirect aggression, but whether they use more or less indirect aggression than boys varies from country to country (French, Jansen & Pidada, 2002). Studies suggest that girls in the United States, Finland, Italy, Poland, and Israel use more relational bullying than boys; whereas, in Russia and China this is not the case, at least with young children (Crick & Grotpeter, 1995; French et al., 2002).

When a number of studies are reviewed, it appears that in the first several grades, boys use both relational and direct bullying. As students progress through the grades, boys, as compared to girls, do not show different degrees of indirect bullying. Although some studies indicate that fourth and fifth grade boys are still showing more direct and relational bullying than girls (David & Kistner, 2000), other studies suggest that somewhere between eight and eleven years of age, boys decrease use of indirect bullying. Even when relational bullying is part of the definition of aggression, among this age group, thirty percent of boys are considered aggressive and only twelve percent of girls (Henington et al., 1998). Studies vary in wording of items on scales used to measure the several types of aggression and in sample characteristics (David & Kistner, 2000).

Relational Bullying and Rejection

Classmates reject children who use extremely mean relational aggression (Henington et al., 1998). Students who only use relational aggression have a lower rate of behavioral issues, but are rated by the broader peer group as exhibiting a low level of positive social interaction (Wolke, Woods, Bloomfield, & Karstadt, 2000). However, among students older than age eight, classmates will put up with boys who use direct aggression, as long as they do not exhibit indirect bullying. Yet, there is some evidence to indicate that boys seem to be more willing to put up with indirect bullying than girls are willing to do so (Salmivalli, Kaukiainen, & Lagerspetz, 2000). Peers reject girls who use extreme direct aggression, and they feel that girls who use primarily relational bullying are withdrawn and depressed (Henington et al., 1998). Students who use both direct and indirect bullying tend to exhibit the most behavior issues. A child who uses relational aggression is a powerful manipulator and is in total control (Wolke, Woods, Bloomfield, et al., 2000).

Students who use relational aggression are not the same group of students who use physical aggression, in that some of the students who use relational aggression also report close, exclusive relationships with their friends. This may give relationally aggressive students a good deal of power over their friends, both because of the intimate knowledge they may have and because the friendships of the peers who are not aggressive are restricted by the relationally aggressive child. Students who exhibit relational aggression tend to use their aggression against their friend(s), whereas, students who are physically aggressive exhibit their aggression toward children outside of their small group (Mounts, 1997).

Hypotheses Around Relational Aggressions

Researchers feel that girls may use more indirect aggression because they mature earlier than boys. Higher social intelligence is required for indirect aggression than for verbal aggression, and is least needed when students are physically aggressive (Pepler & Sedighdeilami, 1998). Indirect aggression is the most sophisticated of indirect, verbal, and physical aggression (Bjorkqvist, Osterman & Kaukiainen, 2000). Relational aggression in a mild form could, theoretically, be considered social strategies that require skill (Archer, 2001).

Relational Bullying in Middle Childhood

Middle childhood is a time when relational aggression can be particularly pronounced. Ross (1996) suggests that girls value friendship, and depriving another girl of friendship by excluding her, or arranging for her to be excluded, is particularly frustrating for girls. The extraordinary number of ways that girls in middle school participate in social or relational bullying include the following (Boulton & Hawker, 1997; Crick, Nelson, et al., 2001; French, Jansen & Pidada, 2002; Henington et al., 1998; Lagerspetz & Bjorkqvest, 1994; Pepler & Sedighdeilami, 1998; Ross, 1996; Smith, 2002):

- telling lies about a targeted child,
- starting and/or supporting mean rumors,
- excluding a student from parties or sleepovers,
- activing as if the targeted child doesn't exist or otherwise ignoring the student,
- writing nasty meassges and passing them around the classroom,
- talking about the victim or pretending to talk about the victim,
- scapegoating,
- persuading or mobilizing classmates to dislike or reject a targeted child,
- refusing friendship,

- becoming friends with someone they don't care about to get revenge on a victim or to make the targeted child jealous,
- telling secrets,
- laughing at someone's misfortune,
- damaging a child's reputation with the peer groups,
- withdrawing friendship if the more powerful girl does not get her way,
- distributing photocopies of personal information,
- whispering as someone walks by,
- shunning a victim in various ways (moving awary from the lunch table one by one until the targeted child is left alone),
- sending harassing e-mail messages or thinly disguised e-mail messages, and
- leaving negative comments or messages so that the victim finds them.

It is important to keep in mind that boys can enagage in these behaviors as well although it may not be their primary mode of bullying. These behaviors are intended to damage the victim's feelings about herself or her relationships with peers.

Effects of Social Bullying on Girls and Boys

Although both direct and indirect aggression can have harmful influences on children, relational aggression is particularly painful for girls. Interpersonal bullying has a powerful effect on girls when it affects their friendships (Crick, Grotpeter, & Bigbee, 2002). Girls who make significant use of relational bullying tend to be rejected and lonely. They are at-risk for problems later on as well (Crick & Grotpeter, 1995).

When children are rejected or excluded they may react in one or more ways. Younger students who are the victims of relational aggression may react by being relationally aggressive in return, whereas if they are physically bullied they may not react with physical aggression. School staff may support a child who is the victim of physical aggression but may not support a victim of relational aggression (Crick, Nelson, et al., 2001).

When provoked by manipulating relationships, students who use indirect aggression are more likely to experience sad feelings (Crick, Grotpeter, & Bigbee, 2002). Students who are socially aggressive tend to internalize stress, according to teachers. More recent studies indicate that they are also likely to be impulsive, defiant, and blame others; and so they exhibit both internalizing and externalizing behaviors. Girls who are physically aggressive, and boys who are relationally aggressive, tend to be less well adjusted, perhaps because their respective behaviors will be reacted to more negatively because they are less normative. Researchers suggest that relationally, aggressive students tend to hide their behavioral difficulties and do not admit to them on self-reports (Crick, 2000).

SUMMARY

Bullying behaviors begin early and can be observed in preschool. Students transition from preschool into kindergarten and bullying behaviors increase. Young children report far more bullying behavior than older children report. Some of the high incidence may have to do with age effects; for instance, younger children may have a broader definition of bullying behaviors or bullying incidents may have greater significance. At the same time there may actually be more bullying behaviors in early childhood, because of the rough play of young boys or the fact that children have not yet learned proactive ways to get what they want.

As children go through elementary school, bullying appears to decrease, just to increase again as students transition to middle school. Bullying appears to be a strategy that students use to establish status in new groups. Once new groups are established in middle school, bullying decreases again. Although bullying does not appear to increase in secondary school, sexual harassment does increase.

There are differences in the incidence of bullying behaviors reported by girls and boys. More boys report that they bully others and more report being victims. The most current data collected from children includes types of bullying that are indirect or social. When bullying is reported with this broader definition of behaviors, the by-sex prevalence of bullying is less extreme. Girls engage in more social or relational bullying and indirect bullying than boys.

Girls use relational bullying earlier than boys, which may be due to the more sophisticated nature of relational aggression. Relational aggression requires more verbal ability and maturity than verbal or physical bullying. As children mature, they appear to use the types of aggression that hurt their victims most. Since relational bullying hurts girls more, and girls bully other girls more than they bully boys, it makes sense that girls would use relational bullying against their victims.

CHAPTER 6

The Victims of Bullying

Schools usually do not keep records of children who are victimized by bullies, and so victimization in schools may be more widespread than was previously thought. In fact, an estimated 160,000 children do not come to school each day because they are afraid of being victimized by bullies (Walker et al., 1995). The abuse of children by their peers is underestimated (Corsaro, 1997). Most commonly, peers abuse students verbally but both boys and girls may be assaulted physically and sexually as well. Girls may be victimized by children they hardly know or by boyfriends who they thought they trusted.

VICTIMS CANNOT ESCAPE

Students who are bullied in schools have no escape from bullying other than feigning illness and staying home which is a very temporary reprieve. If they could stop the bully, they would have already done so. Children do not have choices about which children they are placed with in small groups or in classrooms. The other students with whom they can work and play are quite restricted by the structure and decision-making policies of schools. Placement decisions in schools are often determined by efforts to balance classes according to gender and abilities, and teachers may be motivated to break up friendships that children have established either to reduce discipline issues or to encourage independence. Ross (1996) suggests that bullying is common, because children are 'trapped' in their school environments. They cannot easily move to another class or school (Corsaro, 1997). The child who is victimized by bullies in schools cannot easily get to a safe place (Alsaker & Vakanover, 2001).

THE STUDY OF VICTIMIZATION OF CHILDREN IN SCHOOLS

There are several major approaches to studying victimization. In one approach, students subjectively rate their own degree of victimization. In a second research approach, peers rate the social reputation of their classmates, in regard to whether or not they are victimized by others. The two approaches are only moderately correlated, sharing only about sixteen percent of the variance (Juvonen et al., 2001). The frequency and amount of bullying may be underestimated, because children are afraid to report that they have been victimized or have witnessed another child being bullied (Grills & Ollendick, 2002).

Schuster (1999) feels that peers are the best informants of the one or two victims that are found in each classroom. Teacher reports correlate with peer identification approaches. When children are asked about victimization, their responses will depend on how bullying is defined. Bullies may not report that they engage in indirect aggression; they may not even realize that these behaviors fall into the bullying category (Craig, 1998).

INCIDENCE OF VICTIMIZATION IN SCHOOLS

Experts estimate that there are approximately two students in every classroom that may be victims of bullies (Garrity & Baris, 1996). Seven to ten percent of students are repeatedly victimized (Bernstein & Watson, 1997). Although earlier studies suggested that more boys are bullied than girls, Canadian studies of students aged four through eleven years indicated that one in fourteen girls and one in twenty boys are victimized. More girls ages seven to nine say that they have been bulled, but among younger and older students, boys and girls report being bullied equally (Craig, Peters, et al., 1998).

Looking at all grade levels, about one in ten children will experience victimization during school (Miller & Rubin, 1998). When middle school-aged children were surveyed, one study found about seventy-seven percent of students had been bullied (Ladd & Ladd, 2001). Bullying in middle school most often involves same-sex aggression.

Once a child is victimized in school, it is likely that this child will be at risk for quite a while (Olweus, 1993). Victimization often results in rejection. Once a child becomes a scapegoat of the peer group, the teasing and bullying increases. The child behaves in an avoidant and fearful manner, and the children around the victim begin to feel uncomfortable and less safe.

Retrospective studies indicate that people who were bullied during childhood report that victimization was best recalled from age eleven to thirteen years of age. It could be that middle childhood is the time that bullying behavior may be the worst (Eslea & Rees, 2001). Victimization in general decreases with age as the peer group focuses on specific scapegoats (Astor, Benbenishty, et al., 2002).

FAMILY PATTERNS

There may be some family patterns related to whether or not a child learns to be a victim. Victims tend to be close to their parents, especially their mothers, and are often carefully protected by parents (Banks, 1997; Bernstein & Watson, 1997; Strawn & Paridiso, 2001). Mothers of boys who were victimized treated their children who were bullied as if they were younger than their age. Fathers of victims tend to have been victims themselves (Bernstein & Watson, 1997). Olweus (1991) reported that boys who are victimized are not assertive when they interact with others, and may be overprotected especially by mothers. Olweus describes the overprotection that victims of bullying are given as both a cause of bullying, and as a parental reaction to the bullying of their child. It should also be noted that parents of victims are involved in schools (Nansel, Overpeck, Pilla, et al., 2001).

Victims tend to exhibit an insecure/resistant attachment to parents. Parents of victims do not encourage autonomy and often respond with overprotection. The children easily become anxious when threatened and give up their toys when challenged or get visibly upset. The developmental progression is from insecure attachment and overprotection at home, to being targeted in school (Ross, 1996). This group of students approaches others tentatively, and they try very hard to please others. They want to be included, but once rejected by peers, poor academic performance follows. A reputational bias then follows these children through school (Bernstein & Watson, 1997; Strawn & Paradiso, 2001).

THE BEGINNINGS OF VICTIMIZATION

Ross (1996) reports that the bullying of specific children starts in preschool. Bullying is not unusual in day-care and preschool environments. Assertive students take over in these environments. The way that boys in particular react during preschool is related to continued victimization. Fighting back at this age makes things worse.

Although preschoolers who are victimized are more anxious than their peers, physical appearance differences do not seem to make much difference at all in regard to which students are targeted, according to some researchers. In other studies, victims tend to be somewhat physically different from their peers; smaller, weaker, or disabled. However, *most often*, victims do not differ from their peers or stand out significantly (Asidao et al., 1999; Miller & Rubin, 1998; Pepler, Connolly, & Craig, 2000). Among older children, victims are not significantly different than other children, with the exception of smaller size among boys who are victimized.

Victims are not all alike; in fact, there are several different groups of children who are victimized (Miller & Rubin, 1994). Twice as many boys of short stature reported they were victimized when those differences become salient in late middle school and secondary school (Voss, 2000). Students who are overweight, have a visual, hearing, or speech handicap, are physically unattractive, or who do not do well in school report being teased and bullied at rates higher than peers (Sweeting & West, 2001).

PASSIVE VICTIMS

One group of students who are victims tends to be anxious, sensitive, insecure, and cautious. These children are *passive victims*. They don't attempt to retaliate when they are mistreated. They tend to be isolated or socially withdrawn. Many victimized students have somatic complaints, which might be better described as anxiety symptoms.

Passive or submissive victims tend to have difficulty standing up for themselves when engaged in peer groups. They relate better to adults than to other children (Center for the Study and Prevention of Violence, 2001). Passive victims are the most frequently targeted group of students. They usually don't have a single, solid friendship among their classmates (Garrity and Baris, 1996; Newman et al., 2000a). Students who are victims remain that way throughout their school career, even when classes change and they have the opportunity to make new friends among a new group of children. They believe that being teased and bullied is inevitable (Bernstein & Watson, 1997).

Olweus (1993) described victims as demonstrating an anxious or *submissive reaction pattern*. He interpreted his observations to indicate that the behavior and attitudes of children who are victimized appear to signal insecurity to others, along with the message that they will not retaliate. When this occurred, combined with physical weakness in boys, victimization was most likely. Olweus (2001b) does not 'blame the victims' even though he describes them as signaling weakness to peers who bully. Olweus feels that passive victims are actually dealing with an uncontrolled and aggressive environment developed by their classmates. In Olweus' work, the boys who were passive victims did not provoke the aggression to which they were they were subjected. In addition, they had adequate interpersonal skills, so that it was not lack of ability to interact appropriately with others that resulted in their victimization.

Behavior of Passive Victims

Once the group has singled out a child as a victim, the child's behavior appears to fit the characteristics of a victim. Victims tend to look to adults when there is conflict. They react negatively to losing when playing at recess (Newman, Horne, & Bartolomucci, 2000a). Victims score higher on internalizing behavior, are lonelier than their peers, and tend to be fearful of new situations. They have fewer good friends than their classmates. Girls who are victimized worry about being evaluated negatively by others or worry about being left out (Haynie et al., 2001).

Victims tend to be quiet and shy. They are variously described as lacking in physical strength, and exhibiting a low propensity for violence (Olweus, 1993). Passive victims act in a withdrawn and submissive manner. They do not exhibit assertive behavior very often (Schwartz, 2000).

Some students who are victimized use inappropriate entry behaviors when trying to get into peer groups; for example they may enter groups in ways that disrupt the ongoing activity. They tend to have difficulty controlling their feelings and score higher on internalizing and psychosomatic behavior scales. They have fewer friends and less peer protection than other children (Bernstein & Watson, 1997; Goodman, 1999). Boivin, Hymel, and Hodges (2001) found that when a child exhibits withdrawal from the peer group *or* aggressive social interactions *and* this is combined with low status in the group, these variables interact to increase a child's risk for being harassed by peers. Aggression in response to bullying is explored in the next chapter.

Culture of Silence

In many children's groups, telling is not accepted and tattling is taboo. Telling goes against the group norm in a culture which values conformity. Children who are bullied often don't tell school staff. Some children who are bullied do not tell because they don't believe that school staff will manage the situation carefully. Some feel embarrassed because they are unable to make the bully stop, and because they know that that they can't emotionally handle the situation. Others feel that they don't deserve to receive relief because they are so incompetent and cannot meet the expectations to cope that they perceive from other children and from adults (Ross, 1996). Many victims don't tell because they think that the teasing will only get worse. To some extent, this may be a realistic appraisal of the situation given that the bully has already determined the child's vulnerabilities. Although children find it easier to talk with parents than teachers, one third of victims who don't tell parents tell researchers that they did not want to upset their parents, and therefore, did not share being bullied with them (Banks, 1997; Bernstein & Watson, 1997; Limber, 1996).

Victims continue to remain silent even after efforts have been made to put programs in place to teach them to tell. Thirty percent of students still admit that they have not told anyone about their plight, even after they participated in programs designed to teach reporting bullying behavior (Smith & Shu, 2000).

Both girls and boys will say that they are bullied when students are asked to complete questionnaires. A higher percentage of younger children report experiencing victimization more frequently and more directly than older children report. The youngest children in schools tend to say that older children bully them. Older children are more likely to say students of the same age or classmates bully them (Pepler, Connolly, et al., 2000).

There is a decrease in victimization across grade levels (Pepler, Connolly, et al., 2000). Boys who are withdrawn and rejected are more likely to be bullied than girls who are withdrawn and rejected (Boivin et al., 2001). When all types of bullying are considered, boys are more likely to be victimized in elementary school and girls in high school. (Mullin-Rindler, 2001b). Girls report experiencing more indirect and social bullying, except in the youngest groups (Grills & Ollendick, 2002; Owens, Slee, & Shute, 2001). Although boys and girls are equally likely to be victimized, boys get hit and pushed more; whereas, girls receive more verbal aggression (Barone, 1997; Kochenderfer, & Ladd, 1996; Pepler, Connolly, et al., 2000).

VICTIMIZATION OVER TIME

Once labeled a victim, a student's status in the group drops (Juvonen et al., 2001). Studies that follow children over time have found that a small percentage of children continue to be bullied as they go through school. Ladd and Ladd (2001) followed children from kindergarten to the end of third grade. They found that four percent of students were bullied for the entire period to different degrees. However, Craig, Pepler, Connolly, et al. (2001) in their Canadian studies did not find that there is a decrease in physical bullying or an increase in verbal aggression with age but they did find an increase in sexual harassment with age. As children grow older, most research indicates that physical bullying decreases while indirect aggression and verbal aggression increases.

As students go through early adolescence, they spend more time with students of the opposite sex. Students of both sexes report that they have experienced more same-sex than opposite sex harassment, although they experienced both types of harassment. Boys tend to be harassed with comments implying homosexuality; girls tend to be harassed by attempts to damage their reputations or by negative mean comments about their appearance (Craig, Pepler, Connolly, et al., 2001).

Early and Late Maturation and Victimization

Some students are at increased risk for victimization during this period, especially early maturing girls and late maturing boys. Early maturing girls are at risk, not only from boys but also from other girls. The harassment that children experience at this stage of development often has sexual content. Boys bully girls more until high school, when girls are more likely to be bullied by girls. Sexual harassment increases during high school toward girls. It may be that girls who mature early are sexually harassed, because boys are noticing their advanced development and this represents interest that some researchers feel is not entirely intended to be inappropriate. Sexual harassment appears to be related to puberty, sexual identity, and romantic interactions (Craig, Pepler, Connolly, et al., 2001; Mullin-Rindler, 2001a).

Interviews with white high school girls indicated that about twenty percent were bullied once a week or more often (Lampert, 1998). Adolescent girls report more significant emotional reactions to indirect bullying than boys report (Owens, Slee, et al., 2001). They may engage in talking to themselves or ruminating about negative events and feelings, which makes the situation worse. Other girls at this age may retaliate, and still others may be able to use effective coping strategies. If a student is new to the school, does not have friends, or is not able to respond assertively this student is at greater risk of experiencing continued social bullying than their more skilled peers (Owens, Slee, et al., 2000).

RELATIONAL VICTIMIZATION

Some researchers feel that if relational bullying is not included in studies of bullying that seventy percent of the girls who are bullied by classmates will not be identified. An additional fifteen percent of boys would be overlooked. Relational aggression begins around age three years, where observant preschool staff and families can easily identify it. Even in young children, relational aggression has negative affects (Crick, Nelson, et al., 2001).

Crick, Nelson et al. (2001) described relational bullying as normative, especially among boys, when it is used occasionally. When it is used frequently by students or when it is used in powerful ways, it can no longer be considered normative. A child may be strongly affected by a single instance of relational aggression when it is intense. Boys who are relationally bullied at this age are more likely to start to avoid social interactions with peers. Girls at this age who are the subject of relational aggression exhibit decreased self-control. Adolescent boys and girls both consider relational bullying as 'okay' in romantic relationships. Girls may be most active in this type of bullying.

When you ask students, boys report that physical aggression is more hurtful than social aggression, but girls rate social and physical aggression equally harmful. As girls get older, they rate social aggression as increasingly hurtful. Girls say it gets worse as they get older. Boys say social aggression decreases (Galen & Underwood, 1997).

Observers in school lunchrooms report that children who are rejected are more often the target of relational aggression than other groups of children. Teachers say that rejected students are bullied by students who manipulate their relationships with peers. It does not appear that rejected children who have friends, have friends who are skilled enough or willing to help and support them (Crick, Nelson, et al., 2001).

EFFECTS OF VICTIMIZATION BY BULLIES

Bullying occurs in a social context, and it affects all participants: the bully, the victim and the bystander (Teglasi & Rothman, 2001). A single bullying incident may be devastating for some children. Other children may show significant symptoms of stress only when bullying takes place more than once. For many children, the result of having been victimized can be far reaching (Corsaro, 1997). Bullying can leave lasting emotional and psychological effects, which can follow victims into adulthood (Barone, 1997; Ericson, 2001).

Victims react to teasing and bullying with anxiety, tension, fears, low self-esteem, low risk taking, anxiety, and even depression (Banks, 1997; Leff, Kupersmidt, et al., 1999; Pepler, Connolly, & Craig, 2000; US Department of Education, 1998b). Researchers have found that by sixth grade, being bullied is associated with higher levels of depression than is found in other students (Swearer, Cary, Song, & Eagle, 2001). Almost all students who are victims of bullying are rejected (Schuster, 1999). Being the victim of bullying is related to sliding grades, absenteeism, poor academic adjustment, being lonely, exhibiting withdrawal behaviors, difficulty acting assertively, or being aggressive (Banks, 1997; Schwartz, Farver, Chang, & Lee-Shin, 2002). Children who have been bullied will say that they have more problems with their general health than peers report (Craig, 1998). A three-year study of secondary students showed that those who had been bullied during their first two years of high school, experienced delayed physical symptoms during the last two years of secondary school (Rigby & Slee, 1999).

Olweus (1991) found that children who are bullied are anxious and less secure than peers. He has described them as cautious and sensitive. They react by crying or withdrawing, and they feel badly about themselves and what they have to deal with in school. They feel shame and believe they have failed. In school, the children who are bullied feel that they are alone. Olweus believes that some boys signal their weakness to the bully through their anxiety and physical weakness.

Loneliness and Isolation

All of the different types of bullying affect their victims by causing children to feel lonely and isolated. Kochenderfer and Ladd (1996) found that verbal bullying caused victims to dislike school. Young children, who were intimidated *verbally* when the school year began, did not participate in class to the same degree as others later in the year. Children who were bullied in kindergarten *physically* were described by teachers as more active, less socially skilled, and more aggressive than others.

One effect of bullying is isolation. Withdrawal because a child is rejected by peers places the child at greater risk than is the case for children who prefer to play alone or who are socially anxious (Goosens, Bokhorst, Bruinsma, & vanBoxel, 2002). Victims reported adjustment issues, difficulty starting new friendships, and loneliness (Nansel, Overpeck, Pilla, et al., 2001).

Olweus (1994) conducted a follow-up study of individuals who had either bullied other students or who were victims of bullies, for at least three years between the grades of six and nine, when they were twenty-three years old. Although the victims experienced higher rates of depressive symptoms and lower self-esteem, they were not victimized as young adults. By the time they were adults, they were not stressed and did not lack social skills. This suggests that the individuals were not bullied as children because they were incompetent. It also suggests that the anxiety or depression that children feel when they are bullied is a result of the bullying rather than playing a causal role in victimization.

Emotional Functioning of Victims

Self-esteem drops once a child becomes a victim. Self-views are unlikely to change for the better, unless the child who has been victimized becomes more accepted in the group (Juvonen et al., 2001). The more often that a student experiences bullying, the lower his or her global scores on self-esteem measures (Grills & Ollendick, 2002; O'Moore & Kirkham, 2001). If the child is being teased about something specific, the child might lose self-esteem in that domain. When a child is bullied verbally, the child may believe what is said about him or her, even if the statements are fictitious or exaggerated. Each type of bullying may affect a child differently, and if a child is subject to more than one type of bullying, the affects appear to be additive and intensified (Ladd & Ladd, 2001). Children who are bullied are often isolated from their peers; isolation further contributes to low self-esteem. Being bullied is associated with lower global scores of self-worth in students older than eight years of age (Grills & Ollendick, 2002; Salmivalli, Kaukiainen, Kaistaniemi, & Lagerspetz, 1991).

Studies show that victims of bullying who are passive when they are being victimized are able to think of good solutions to social problems when they are given hypothetical social problems to solve. The problem is not related to lack of knowledge. The interfering variable is that they don't *believe* that they are competent socially. They blame themselves for being victimized, and either give in quickly or respond in a disorganized manner when they are teased or bullied (Perry et al., 2001). Submissive children may believe that if they used assertive behavior or aggression, it would not work. When boys feel this way they typically don't use aggressive responses. The passive reaction to being bullied is associated with being bullied by peers (Schwartz, 1999). An additional serious effect of teasing and bullying is that children may begin to believe what is said about them (Kochenderfer & Ladd, 1996).

Victims are aware of what others think of them. They rate themselves in the same way that others rate them, which indicates that their self-perceptions are accurate. The knowledge of how they are viewed by others does not motivate them to act differently, possibly because they feel helpless (Gottheil & Dubow, 2001a). Being victimized by a bully or bullies has been found to relate to both internalizing and externalizing behaviors. Victims become upset quicker than their peers, and their elevated anxiety may put them at risk for continued victimization (Craig, Peters, et al., 1998).

Victims of bullying report anxiety, tension, and fears, in addition to low self-esteem (Pepler, Connolly, & Craig, 2000). Girls report higher anxiety than boys report as a result of victimization, and they also report feeling badly about themselves. If a boy has stronger feelings of self-worth, he may be better able to handling bullying (Grills & Ollendick, 2002). Depressive symptoms are more likely to be present when bullying is chronic. Hawker and Boulton (2000) determined that having been bullied by peers increased the chances of depression. Craig (1998) feels that depression may be part of the child's functioning rather than specifically tied to victimization, whereas anxious vulnerability may be characteristic of children at risk for being bullied.

Although victims typically do not act on their feelings, they may also feel angry, think of revenge, and feel sorry for themselves after specific incidents (Skiba & Fontaini, 2000). Self-reports of low acceptance by peers is related to being victimized by peers. Girls who reported being victimized also reported acting out (Khatri, Kupersmidt, & Patterson, 2000).

Although we often think that social support and opportunities to talk about one's feelings would ameliorate the damage from being bullied, research suggests that the effects of being victimized are so pervasive, that support at the time is not enough to decrease the risk of anxiety or depression later on. Girls have been found to be particularly vulnerable to the effects of bullying (Bond, Carlin, Thomas, Rubin, & Patton, 2001). Girls experience anxiety, depression, and depressed self-esteem (Owens, Slee, et al., 2000). For girls who were involved in bullying in any role, eating disorders are a possible outcome (Kaltiala-Heino, Rimpela, Rantanen, & Rimpela, 2000).

Researchers have identified one interesting exception in the bleak picture of effects of bullying on victims. If in early adolescence students are bullied and see others being bullied as well, they tend not to change the way in which they view themselves. At this age, students are able to understand that being harassed or bullied is not personal *when others are receiving the same treatment* by bullies. At the same time, seeing others harassed makes all students uneasy because the school environment that students are dealing with is frightening for everyone (Juvonen et al., 2001).

Victimization and Attitudes toward School

There is a strong relationship between victimization and school attendance. In one study, fifteen percent of children who were frequently absent said that bullying was the reason for not attending school. All types of teasing and bullying have the effect of making the victims feel lonely in school, but only verbal aggression predicts a student's attitude *toward* school. Being *verbally* bullied often results in disliking school. Being *physically* bullied or receiving direct verbal aggression predicts feeling lonely and wanting to stay away from school (Kochenderfer & Ladd, 1996). Victimized children learn to feel uncomfortable and anxious around other children (Hoover & Hazler, 1991). A child might even learn to think that school is dangerous (Ladd & Ladd, 2001).

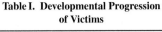

Table I. Developmental Progression
of Victims

Insecure/resistant attachment to parents
Anxious temperament
|
Overprotection at home
|
Tentative interaction with peers
|
Emotional Reaction to mild aggression
|
Isolation/Rejection
|
Reputation Bias

As students age, they are less tolerant of victim behaviors and evaluate victims more negatively (Ray, Norman, Sadowski, & Cohen, 1999). This adds to the pain of being bullied. Peers also reject children who are bullied over a long period of time (Graham & Juvonen, 2001). Children who were previously friendly toward a targeted child will reject the victim of bullying (Ross, 1996). There may be a developmental progression for victims of bullies (Table I).

Degree and Length of Victimization

There is a small group of children who are victimized for a long period of time as they are growing up (Sharp, Thompson, & Arora, 2000). Students who become victims in school by ages eight or nine tend to continue to be teased and picked on by peers (Kochenderfer & Ladd, 1996). For these children lonely feelings continue after bullying stops. However, it is the rejection by peers that appears to be the key variable that predicts difficulties later on in school and in relation to peer interaction (Ross, 1996).

Researchers have followed students who were bullied over a single school year. They found that risk of victimization to vulnerable children increased by one and one half times (Alsaker & Vakanover, 2001). Students who were victimized in one class or at one grade level tended to be victimized again. By the time they reach middle school, the pattern of victimization is well established and may even intensify (Miller & Rubin, 1998; Pepler, Connolly, & Craig, 2000). The degree of victimization can make also difference (Astor, Benbenishty, et al., 2002).

Verbal abuse is as damaging as physical abuse, and often has more serious consequences (Cushman & Johnson, 2000). Students who are bullied because of their ethnic backgrounds feel worse than others when they are victimized, according to some studies (Verkuyten & Thijs, 2001). Rigby (2000), studying students in South Australia, found that being bullied frequently with little support from others was a factor in poor outcomes.

The longer a child is bullied, the more likely that the child will experience difficulties adjusting. The loneliness that results from being bullied increases over time. If the bullying goes on for several years, a student will continue to feel alone even two years after the peer abuse has stopped.

Ladd and Ladd (2001) feel that chronic bullying does more damage than being bullied for short periods, because the stress is fairly continuous. Students who have been victimized over a period of time are at a greater risk for affective illness than their peers. They are also at greater risk for having problems in social relationships in general. Thirty percent of students exhibiting symptoms of depression had been bullied. In addition, they tend to be pessimistic thinkers and explain their plight as due to the hostility of the bully. However those victims who feel that others are hostile, and this is the reason why they bully others, may be able to protect their self-esteem since they are not attributing the victimization to a personal weakness or attribute (Bond, Carlin, Thomas, Rubin, & Patton, 2001; Graham & Juvonen, 2001).

Having been bullied for a period of time results in later symptoms of depression and low self-regard (Olweus, 2001). Being bullied may result in a child losing trust with peers in general. If these feelings are intense, the child may become preoccupied, worrying about whether or not school is safe, and worrying about being alone. This preoccupation may make it difficult to come to school and, also, makes it very difficult to feel 'okay' about school (Ladd & Ladd, 2001).

BUFFERS AGAINST VICTIMIZATION

Friendships may provide a buffer for children who are victimized. Both the number of friendships that a child may have and the willingness of friends to stand up for a child who is victimized make a difference. Sociometric studies show that peer nominations indicating that a child is liked most is the most important protection for a child who is bullied. Peers may offer support, protection or retaliation (Pellegrini & Long, 2002).

Young children are not as likely to continue to be victimized if they ask a friend for help (Ladd & Ladd, 2001). Having a best friend who would be willing to help when a child was bullied is a moderating factor at all ages. In this case, a child would not only be less likely to be bullied but would be less likely to suffer from anxiety or depression afterwards. Children who are bullied and do not have a good friend tend to begin to exhibit behavior problems over a school year (Boivin et al., 2001).

Teachers feel that adolescents who are the object of bullying have difficulty making friendships. They are described by teachers as having difficulty apologizing, as having very few friends, as submissive and perhaps a little 'geeky' (Owens,

Slee, et al., 2001). Although having a friend may serve as protection, one in five students who are victimized have either no friend or just one or two friends available for support or problem solving (Batsche, 1997). This leaves victims without physical or emotional protection.

Coping Strategies

Ross (1996) uses the term coping to include all types of behaviors used by victims whether or not they work. She feels that the most common coping strategy used by victims is avoidance, although a child might direct anger toward himself, or take out feelings on others. Avoidance strategies include blocking thoughts (also described as cognitive distancing), denial, or acting as if the bullying is not happening. Using avoidance as a coping strategy is also described as using an *emotion-focused* strategy (Kochenderfer-Ladd & Skinner, 2002).

In general, victims of bullying tend to react in a more extreme way. They may react quite passively or quite aggressively. Boys who use internalizing strategies feel anxious, lonely or depressed. Boys who try to manage bullying themselves do not experience as many repercussions of having been bullied although if they look for help from others, peers do not tolerate this and isolate them. Girls who seek help for major peer but not minor peer difficulties on the other hand, experienced some protection (Kochenderfer-Ladd & Skinner, 2002).

Coping styles of victims can either de-escalate or perpetuate victimization (Mahady Wilton, Craig, & Pepler, 2000). In addition, the ways in which the child who is bullied copes with the abuse may either lessen or intensify the effects. Children who cope by worrying, feeling badly or feeling sorry for themselves, feel worse. This can be described as an avoidance strategy. If children look to peers to help, they do not feel as lonely. This is called an approach strategy (Ladd & Ladd, 2001).

A SUBGROUP OF VICTIMS

Some studies have shown that more students with special-needs are bullied than other children report. Thirty-three percent of mainstreamed, special-needs children report having been bullied as compared to eight percent of other children (Garrity & Barris, 1996). Children with special needs also reported acting as bullies more often than their peers report. The more involved the learning difficulties, the higher the risk of the student becoming a victim (Whitney, Smith, & Thompson, 1994).

Not all students with special needs are bullied. Only a subset of learning-disabled students appear to have problems with relationships with peers (Tur-Kaspa, 2002). One key variable in determining the risk for having social interaction difficulties due to poor social skills is whether or not the student with learning disabilities also displays the symptoms of attention deficit hyperactivity disorder. The child with symptoms of both disorders tends to be less accepted by classmates, exhibits a higher level of behavioral difficulties as reported by teachers, and exhibits social skills that are less effective when interacting with peers. More specifically, it is the impulsive behaviors that interfere with developing relationships (Weiner & Schneider, 2002).

SUMMARY

Victimization due to bullying is more widespread than is commonly thought. Some children and adults believe that victimization is inevitable. Victims of bullying tend to exhibit behaviors characteristic of children with anxious attachment issues and their parents overprotect them. Victims of bullying are more anxious than their peers and are often less powerful, and more vulnerable to intimidation by bullies.

There are several subtypes of victims. Passive or submissive victims seem to signal insecurity to bullies. Their self-esteem is depressed, and they have difficulty regulating their emotions. This group of victims feels incompetent, does not believe that an assertive response would work and may eventually believe what is being said about them. The effects of having been bullied include anxiety, anger, and even thoughts of revenge in some children. Different types of bullying effect victims in different ways. Peers reject children who have been bullied over time. Girls appear to be more affected emotionally by having been bullied. Children more likely to be victimized include early maturing girls and late maturing boys. Half of the students who are bullied don't tell anyone that they have been victimized.

Children victimized for longer periods of time continue to feel lonely even after the bullying stops. The degree to which a child is hurt emotionally by bullying is related to some extent to how the child thinks about it. If the child believes that the bully is not personally attacking the child, the child will be less seriously affected. Having a friend who will stand by the child who is victimized is a buffer and decreases the emotional damage done by the bully. Coping styles of victims can either discourage bullying or result in bullying over long periods of time. The coping strategies children use to deal with bullying may be a possible starting point for intervention.

CHAPTER 7

Children Who are Both Bullies and Victims

When children who bully others are studied, two groups of bullies emerge. One group can be thought of as socially skilled and the other group socially unskilled. The unskilled group is described as children who both bully others and are victimized by others (Kaukiainen et al., 2002). This unskilled group, which constitute one in five children who are victimized, are described as provoking the teasing and bullying behaviors which they then must endure. The bully-victims can be confrontational with both children and adults. They appear to instigate abuse from peers. They then turn around and bully children who are even less competent than they may be.

BULLY-VICTIMS

Pellegrini (2001a) points out that this group has been called by varying names in the literature including bully-victims, provocative victims, ineffectual aggressors, and/or aggressive victims. The children who are sometime victims and sometimes bullies are the most challenging group of students to support and help in schools. Most investigators feel that this group of children comprises a special category. More attention and study is needed in order to be able to design effective interventions to help them improve their ability to manage their emotions, and also to keep them safe.

If a bullying incident on the playground is analyzed, there will be a bully, a victim, bystanders, and bully-victims. The bully-victim doesn't fit either of the major roles of bully or victim. They appear to ask for trouble and may behave in this way to get attention. It has also been theorized that these children behave in a way so that they can control when, where, and how they are teased (Kayton, n.d.;

Mullin-Rindler, 2001a). They create problems in their classes and are unpopular with peers. At times, they behave as if they enjoy the recognition that they receive being bullied and prefer this situation to being ignored by their peers (Newman, Horne, & Bartomucci, 2000a). Observers feel that they behave in ways that will allow them to seek attention (Bernstein & Watson, 1997).

Provocative or aggressive victims tend to be overactive and have hot tempers. They will react aggressively, even when teasing is not intense or frequent (Wright et al., 2001). Children who both bully and are victims tend to irritate others. They do so with their excessive, attention-seeking behaviors. They are disruptive, argumentative, disorganized, and become easily frustrated and upset when things don't go their way (Perry et al., 2001). The evidence that is available suggests that bully-victims seldom react passively or by withdrawing from situations when there is disagreement (Pelligrini, 2001).

Bully-victims do not feel positive about the school climate. They report that even teachers and other adults in schools 'bully' them (Song & Swearer, 2002). It is their reaction to the interactions of others that seems to start the bullying episodes, or may exacerbate an interaction between several children, which otherwise might not have resulted in bullying.

School staff can easily identify the children who appear to provoke the aggression they receive when they are eight to ten years of age. These students will interrupt an activity as the game is being organized as they attempt to enter the group and obtain a role that they feel is important. They also interrupt the play when the activity involves doing something with others toward a goal (for example, building something), or when there are only two peers involved. They persist in their attempts to participate in peer activities even after their playmates have rejected them (Walker et al., 1995). Persisting once rejected may be related to developing behaviors that would further facilitate rejection and trigger bullying.

A child can be a victim and also the instigator of behaviors from others. The reaction of others who are provoked may in turn exacerbate the individual child's behavioral tendencies (Wright et al., 2001). Individual child variables *interact* with environmental variables and the social situation to produce the bully-victim.

Bully-victims tend to have difficulty reading the social signals which take place when children interact, and have difficulty responding appropriately. They find it hard to control their tendency to respond impulsively, and tend to be both confrontational and challenging with children and adults. This group of children is easily found at the center of incidents on the playground. Everyone can name them. They feel, justifiably so, that nobody is 'on their side'. They personalize situations, lack empathy, and perceive 'put downs', often when no put down was intended. They want to be the focus of the group, but also want to act in positive ways. Some clinicians who have worked with these students suggest that they may have learning problems (Kaukiainen et al., 2002: Mullin-Rindler, 2001a).

INCIDENCE OF BULLY-VICTIMS

Incidence of bully-victims varies from study to study. Provocative bully-victims are found less commonly than passive victims, according to some researchers (Newman, Horne, Bartomucci, 2000a). Olweus (2001b) reported that between the ages of eleven and fifteen bully-victims represent between ten and twenty percent of all students who are victimized. He found more provocative victims among younger students. Canadian and British samples of school children suggest that bully victims make up a smaller group than Olweus identified. One study of fourth, fifth and sixth grade students in the United States showed that children nominated less than five percent of children who would fit the description of bully-victims (Schwartz, 2000).

Canadian studies and studies in great Britain indicate that from two to six percent of students admit that they fit this category when the method to determine prevalence is a survey. However, the percentage of children who fit in the category of bully-victims has not been clearly established. Pellegrini (2001a) reports that the percentage of provocative victims has been reported in a wide range, from two to twenty-nine percent in various studies.

Peer ratings and observations of children by still other researchers indicate that almost fifty percent of children who are victims, are also bullies (Pepler, Connolly, & Craig, 2000). Swearer, Cary, Song, & Eagle (2000) surveyed a group of sixth grade students in the United States and determined that about fifty-one percent of participants described themselves as bully-victims, twenty-nine percent described themselves as victims, and almost two and one half percent described themselves as bullies. These figures may be high because teasing was included in the definition of bullying in this study.

Incidence may depend on the method of collecting data. In some recent studies, which were conducted using questionnaires, in which children rated their own behaviors, the incidence of bully-victims was high. Peer nomination approaches and studies that use several different methods are more conservative. In addition, some of the conflicting results in studies of provocative victims and others who participate in the bully-victim process appear to be related to confusing data around transitions from elementary to middle and middle to secondary school. (Swearer, Eagle, Song, & Cary, 2001; Swearer, Cary, Song, & Eagle, 2001). Grade levels at which transitions occur vary from country to country worldwide, and also differ considerably in the United States.

Using a peer nomination approach, Swartz (2000) identified less than five percent of students in this category, only one of which was a girl. However, when researchers used cut-off scores that compared only same-sex students, they found just as many girls and boys. Varying estimates of incidence differ depending on how the researchers collecting the data define bullying. Estimates also vary depending on the ages of students from whom data is collected. For these reasons, we do not have a clear estimate of the incidence of bully-victims.

BEHAVIORS OF BULLY-VICTIMS

Provocative victims tend to be very impulsive children who are talking or moving before they think. They aggravate their peers with their persistent immature behaviors. According to Pepler, Connolly, and Craig, (2000), these children:

- behave as if they are insecure,
- are less likeable than their peers,
- are easily provoked,
- get angry quickly,
- are at risk for adjustment issues, and
- are magnets for incidents on the playground.

Bully-victims tend to get angry and don't control their emotions such as anger and upset very we ell (Schwartz, 2000). Part of the reason that they respond inappropriately has to do with their tendency to have difficulty reading social signals and controlling impulses (Mullin-Rindler, 2001a). They also may have dominance needs so that they bully children who are weaker than they are. Adults do not typically like them. They exhibit some of the characteristics of passive victims when they are bullied by children who are more powerful (Center for the Study and Prevention of Violence, 2001).

The behavior of bully-victims is irritating and creates tension in the peer group (Olweus, 2001b). Provocative victims may exhibit an *irritable behavioral style*. They escalate social situations. They retaliate when they feel that they have been offended in an angry way. They do not function very well in social groups when there is conflict. Provocative victims can also behave aggressively. As a result of their unsuccessful social interactions they experience depressive symptoms, social anxiety, and don't feel very good about themselves. They know that their peers dislike them. Many have difficulty with concentration. There are more boys in this group than there are girls according to some researchers, while others feel that this is only true if indirect aggression is excluded in questionnaires (Pellegrini, 2001a). Research is ongoing to better understand these children who are both bullies and victims of bullying.

DEVELOPMENT OF A BULLY-VICTIM

There has been some data collected on the home environments of children who are described as provocative victims. In some cases the home life of this group of students seems to be stressful and harsh because of parenting style (Pellegrini, 2001a). Children who respond provocatively tend to have experienced inconsistent parenting (Perry et al., 2001).

Students who fall in the provocative victim group report that their parents are inconsistent, both in regard to child management and to how closely they oversee their child's activities. Communication is an issue in these homes. Bully-victims do not think that their parents show a good deal of positive emotion toward them. They feel that their parents punish them frequently and do not support them very much (Pellegrini, 2001a). They describe their parents in the same way that they describe adults outside of the family, such as teachers and playground monitors.

Olweus describes four variables which he feels contribute to a pattern of aggressive reaction, which is the behavior that is typical of a bully-victim. The variables include a lack of warm and involved interactions with parents, use of power when parents discipline, and family tolerance for aggression. He adds that children who develop aggression as a reaction to situations tend to have a temperamental style, which might be described as hotheaded temperament (Olweus, 1999).

There is also some data to suggest that provocative victims experience more emotional and physical abuse by parents (Duncan, 1999). It appears that at least some of the children who fit the description of the provocative victim have been exposed to violence between their parents, and have been victims of hostility or maltreatment in their homes (Goosens et al., 2002; Schwartz, 2000).

Social Exclusion and Rejection

Classmates say that they do not like bully-victims. Children who are both aggressive and victims are at higher risk for rejection than students who exhibit only one of these behaviors (Pellegrini, 2001). Schwartz (1999) reports that behavior problems in early elementary school may result in peer rejection, which, in turn, precipitates victimization by third and fourth grade. This may be part of the reputational bias that labels some children and places them at-risk.

When researchers study children who have been rejected, they find that there are several different groups. One subgroup is both aggressive and rejected. This subgroup of students does not seem to be as aware of the fact that peers are rejecting them, even though they have the lowest acceptance of all status groups. They may not feel rejected because they have a small circle of friends and they do not appear to take responsibility for the situation when others reject them (Verschueren & Marcoen, 2002). Students in this group show more anger through their facial expressions than their peers may display. In addition, they express more anger verbally. They allow others to see their reaction when they are unhappy during games, particularly when their opponents are doing well. This exposes them as good targets for bullying (Hubbard, 2001).

Reactive and Proactive Aggression

Bullying patterns have been described as 'hot-headed' and 'cold-blooded'. The differences may be related to temperamental variables, such as emotionality or ability to regulate emotions. These temperamental differences, in turn, may explain other differences in empathy and social information processing found in children (Arsenio & Lemerise, 2001).

When an angry and poorly controlled child acts aggressively, in a defensive manner, in retaliation when the child believes that he has been 'put down' or provoked, this behavior is called *reactive aggression*. When the child is purposeful, calm, and aggressive, the goal of the aggressive behavior is to use power to get 'one's way'. This behavior is called *proactive aggression*. It is deliberately coercive (Hubbard, Smithmyer, Ramsden, Parker, Flanagan, Dearing, et al., 2002).

The concept of reactive aggression is derived from the frustration-aggression hypothesis of Berkowitz (1963). The child believes that he has been frustrated on purpose and he reacts aggressively. When the child's goals are blocked or he is frustrated in some other way, he reacts impulsively (Dodge, 1991). The reactively aggressive child believes that someone is out to get him or to prevent him from reaching his goals (Salmivalli & Nieminen, 2001).

The concept of proactive aggression is derived from the social learning theory (Bandura, 1973). The child is aggressive because 'it works'; the child is able to get what he wants. Aggression is rewarded when the aggressive child is able to get his way. The proactive child dominates others and bullies others, and is rewarded for doing so (Dodge, 1991).

Dodge describes the child who uses proactive aggression as troubling *to* others, whereas the volatile child is troubled *by* others (Dodge, 1991, p. 201). Dodge's studies of proactively and reactively aggressive children indicated that eighty-two percent of the aggression in pairs of children of *unequal* power was proactive in the form of bullying which they displayed. Proactive aggression involves dominating others in a coercive manner. Proactively aggressive children may have learned their style of interacting from aggressive models. These children tend to have good control of their emotions and also have the self-control not to react to others' attempts to hurt or upset them (Goosens et al., 2002).

The reactively aggressive child looks like he is out of control when he is behaving aggressively. He is angry and displays temper, reacting very quickly without much thought. In pairs of children who engaged in play that was filled with conflict, forty-five percent of the aggressive behavior would be described as reactive. Reactive aggression is the result of negatively charged social interactions (Dodge, 1991). Teachers and peers are more likely to agree when identifying reactively aggressive students than they are likely to agree when identifying proactively aggressive students (Salmivalli & Nieminen, 2001). The developmental progression for a provocative victim is different than that of a passive victim (Table II).

When in early elementary school, classmates do not like reactively aggressive boys, but they don't reject proactively aggressive boys. The reason that proactively aggressive boys are not disliked is that although proactively aggressive boys may tend to disrupt the group activity, they also have positive traits. Some of these children have leadership ability and some have a sense of humor. Their positive qualities allow their peers to look at them both positively and negatively. However,

Table II. Developmental Progression of Provocative Victims

Inconsistent parenting
|
Poor emotional regulation
Poor behavioral regulation
|
Create tension in the peer group
|
Easily provoked/reactively aggressive
|
Rejected but keep trying
|
Reputation Bias

by the time children are nine years old, peers no longer like boys who exhibit any type of aggression (Dodge, 1991).

Children who are reactive when they are young exhibit more frustrated and rough and tumble behavior on the playground than their peers. Their nonverbal behavior is angrier than their cool headed, proactive peers. Students who exhibit this behavior are more easily physiologically aroused. It is easy for others to get them to react and to provoke them (Hubbard, Smithmyer, et al., 2002).

Children who engage in bullying and are then bullied by others in turn, have been shown to use both proactive and reactive aggression (Camodeca, Goossens, Terwogt, & Schuengel, 2002; Salmivalli & Nieminen, 2001). Both peers and teachers identify bully-victims as the most aggressive group on the playground, given that they are both reactively and proactively aggressive. Pure bullies are not considered to be as aggressive by peers, although observers find them more aggressive than peers' ratings would suggest (Camodeca et al., 2002; Salmivalli & Nieminen, 2001). It may be that their aggression is more hidden because it is planned and the bully is in control.

When teachers rate students as exhibiting reactive aggression, they tend to focus on difficulty regulating anger (Hubbard, 2001). These students have high negative emotionality and underregulate their emotions. It may be that the negative emotions that they experience prevents them from responding appropriately or from feeling sympathy for the children that they turn around and victimize (Goosens et al., 2002). This would explain why a child who has experienced the pain of having been bullied could exhibit the same degrees of aggressive behavior toward others.

For students in grades one through six use of aggressive strategies in reaction to bullying tend to result in bullying continuing or getting worse (Mahady-Wilton et al., 2000). In studies involving students in fifth grade, both proactive and reactive aggression have been connected to bullying behaviors. However, for students in eighth grade, proactive aggression remained strongly related to bullying behaviors, while reactive aggression was significantly less related to bullying behaviors. Age is an important variable that must be taken into consideration when exploring the relationship of aggression to bullying (Roland & Idsoe, 2001).

OUTCOMES FOR STUDENTS WHO ARE BULLY-VICTIMS

Bully-victims tend to be absent from school more often than their peers (Song, Swearer, Eagle, et al., 2000). They experience more depression and more of the physical manifestations of anxiety than either victims or bullies (Pellegrini, 2001a; Swearer, Song, et al., 2001). During middle school, bully-victims report that they experience symptoms of depression. They report higher rates of depression than victims, but lower rates of depression than bullies report, although the differences are not significant (Cary & Swearer, 2002; Cary, Swearer, Song, Haye, & Sohn, 2001).

In general, provocative victims report the greatest psychological problems as compared to others involved in the bullying interaction. In a study exploring the stress felt by individuals in various roles in a bullying incident, the order for students in various bully-related roles according to the degree of psychological issues experienced by each group, was bully-victims highest, then victims, and then bullies (Duncan, 1999).

Among elementary school students, children who were rated by peers as both victims and as aggressors were, also, rated less well adjusted both socially and behaviorally. Bully-victims are more likely to *not want* to attend school than their peers (Pellegrini, 2001a). They do less well in school, exhibit more distress emotionally, and are rejected more than others (Schwartz, 2000). Being rejected by classmates in any way, increases a child's risk for conduct problems (Graham & Juvonen, 2002). Students who took on roles of bully and victim were isolated, did not do well in school, and were involved in problem behaviors in school. Some researchers feel that their behavior appears to come from having been bullied, and they then imitate the behavior that they had experienced themselves by bullying others (Nansel, Overpeck, Pilla, et al., 2001).

PROTECTIVE FACTORS

Just as having supportive friends helps passive victims, Swartz (1999) feels that having a best friend, or a friend to be with, can decrease the risk for bully-victims being victimized in turn by an aggressive cool headed bully. One reason for this may be that children who have friends but who also tend to exhibit externalizing behaviors may be better organized and therefore better accepted than children who externalize but do not have friends. Interestingly, Swartz (1999) found that hyperactive and impulsive behavior in girls, but not boys, was more likely to predate being victimized. Friendships made a difference for immature boys but not as much for girls in preventing or decreasing the risk of being bullied. Unfortunately, relational bullying was not a consideration in this interesting study.

SUMMARY

A special category of children who are victimized is the group of children who both bully others and are also victimized. This group has been variously called bully-victims, provocative victims, ineffectual aggressors, and/or aggressive victims. They are also described as unskilled, irritating, provocative, confrontational, and disruptive individuals in children's groups. They create tension in playgroups. They appear to seek attention for themselves as victims. The incidence of bully-victims is not clear and more research is needed to fully understand the percentage of children involved as bully-victims and their needs.

The behavior of bully-victims is reactive and emotional. They exhibit an irritable behavioral style, and reward those who bully them by getting upset and angry easily. They also tend to be rejected by the peer group which brings its own problems. In play situations some children respond with aggression when they feel frustrated and provoked. Others behave in a purposefully aggressive manner, remaining calm. Bully-victims exhibit both types of aggressive behavior toward peers. This group of children tends to have the worst outcomes.

CHAPTER 8

The Role of Bystanders in Bullying Episodes

Bullying is a result of the interaction between individual students who are involved in the interactions but this is insufficient to explain why it occurs. Not only are the bully and victim involved, but others are involved as well. Bullying occurs in a social context. Once bullying begins, it is maintained by the system. The characteristics of the peer group, and the social context of the classroom, playground or lunchroom, each contribute to the perpetuation of the behaviors (Espelage, 2002). The range of behaviors, from teasing or low-level aggressive behaviors to bullying or harassment, is driven by more than simply aggression.

BEHAVIORS OF BYSTANDERS

Craig and Pepler (1995) have described the various roles of individuals in the bullying sequence or cycle. There are bullies, victims, and bully-victims. In addition, there are students who join in but are not leaders, those who watch but do not join in, those who happen to be playing with either the bully or the victim at the time, and those who try to stop the bullying. These are the bystanders, and they have an important role in the bullying interaction.

Most students in elementary schools, up to ninety-two percent in some studies, have observed incidents of bullying in their school (Henderson & Hymel, 2002). In fact, eighty-five percent of bullying episodes occur in the context of a group (Craig & Pepler, 1995). Students who observe incidents are intimately involved in the bullying system. It is important to understand the role of bystanders, because they may provide clues in regard to opportunities for prevention and/or deterrence of bullying in schools (Henderson & Hymel, 2002).

Several researchers have described the various roles that bystanders may take in a bullying episode. A bystander might become the assistant of the bully and join in, might support and reinforce the bully, might try to help or defend the victim, or may remain an outsider. Students reinforce the bully by laughing or actually cheering on the behavior. The students who watch may instigate an incident, support it, or may join in, and, in turn, model aggressive interactions for others (Craig & Pepler, 2000). Those children who act as if they were outsiders may pretend not to notice what is going on. They may be described by the victim as *cooperating* with the bully because of their nonverbal behavior. Only about seventeen percent of students are willing to stand up for the victim according to some observers (Cowie, 1998; Cowie & Wallace, 2000b; O'Connell, Pepler, & Craig, 1999; Salmivalli, 1999).

BYSTANDERS ON THE PLAYGROUND

Craig and Pepler (1995) videotaped six- to twelve-year-old children on school playgrounds. In their analysis of the videotapes, they determined that bystanders were actively or passively involved in eighty-five percent of the bullying interactions. More than half of the time bystanders were playing the same game as the bully or the targeted child. They reinforced the bully by giving attention to the behavior, by joining in about half of the time, and providing reinforcement through differential attention to the child who was overpowering a victim. Bystanders simply watched in 37% of the incidents. They were playing the same game in 63% of the incidents. Boys tended to be more involved than girls.

Children, who were nearby but not involved, seldom intervened. When bystanders were present, they intervened in only thirteen percent of the incidents. Of the children who attempted to intervene, boys tended to intervene more often than girls, but they did not always intervene appropriately. In seventy-four percent of episodes, children treated the *bully* with more respect. They were more friendly toward the perpetrator in fifty-seven percent of incidents, and appeared to be enjoying the episode in thirty percent of incidents. Observers concluded that classmates reinforced bullying in eighty-one percent of the incidents that they observed, and, therefore, played a critical role (Craig & Pepler, 1995; Craig & Pepler, 2000).

Bystanders tend to give positive attention to the bully, which helps the bully stay in control. Bullies get their power from the children who support their behavior, by paying attention to it. It is not only on the playground where bystanders support bullying, in the classroom bystanders are involved in eighty-five percent of the bullying incidents. Boys who do intervene, do so more appropriately on the playground, whereas girls intervene more often in class (Pepler, Connolly, & Craig, 2000).

Other studies have confirmed the finding that boys support bullying more than girls (Pellegrini & Bartini, 1999). Some boys select aggressive and bossy children as friends (Goosens et al., 2002). Boys are more likely to report that they are excited and frightened when they observe a bully, but girls will say they feel helpless. More boys than girls will say that bullying behavior is fun (Jeffrey et al., 2001).

Not only do bystanders appear to actively and passively reward the bully ensuring that the negative behavior will continue, bystanders may also influence victims' behavior, by joining in or ignoring the behavior of the bully (O'Connell, Pepler & Craig, 1999). Bystanders may teach victims to behave passively by making it clear that they support the bully.

GROUP DYNAMICS

Olweus (1991) used several aspects of group functioning to explain why bullying behaviors are so prevalent on the playground. Two aspects of group functioning, reinforcement and modeling may facilitate and encourage bullying. Reinforcement takes place when bystanders selectively attend to the bully, and modeling occurs when the bully's behavior is imitated by bystanders or when they join in after watching. Craig and Pepler (1995) provided some support for this proposal in their studies of children on the playground in Canadian schools.

It may be that observing aggressive behavior increased the tendency of bystanders to join in, because they don't feel responsible for the bullying if they did not start it. Bystanders' negative attitudes toward victims and respectful attention to the bully reinforce bullying (Craig & Pepler, 1995).

Attitudes toward Bullies

A study in the United Kingdom found that about fifty percent of students were sympathetic to those who were bullied, about twenty-five percent were neutral and twenty-five percent were not sympathetic at all (Smith & Sharp, 1994). Younger children report concern and distress for the victim in a bullying episode (Graham & Juvonen, 2001; Jeffrey et al., 2001). Sixty-five percent of younger elementary school aged girls admitted being upset when they saw peers getting bullied. Even a single bullying event stressed girls for long periods of time. Most of the girls felt that teachers and parents either did not care or were not aware of what was happening (Lampert, 1998). But Jeffrey et al. (2001) found that while only nine percent of fifth grade students expressed a lack of caring about the victim, thirty-six percent of eighth graders were indifferent to victimization of one child toward another. Students felt decreasingly upset about bullying as they passed through middle school. By eighth grade, two times as many boys as girls say that those who are bullied deserve it. It appears that a type of desensitization occurs over this period of time.

Children are affected by the cultural attitudes that demand that an individual should stand up to bullies, or that a person should avoid trouble. These expectations conflict, which makes decisions about how to respond difficult for the victim (McDonald & Moriarty, 1996). These cultural expectations also affect the attitudes of bystanders toward victims. Undoing general cultural beliefs is challenging. Even after exposure to a bullying prevention program which attempted to teach that the intentions of the bully didn't matter, one third of students still believed that the bully's intentions made a difference and took precedence over the feelings of the victim (Khosropour & Walsh, 2001). Anti-bullying programs attempt to teach children that it is the victim's feelings that take precidence. If the victim feels frightened or harassed, the behavior is not innocent.

By early adolescence, at least seventy percent of bystanders stand by and do not try to stop bullying or harassment. Because bystanders blame the victim, they feel angry toward the victim and do not help. More than fifty percent of students in the sixth and seventh grade felt that the victim could control the behaviors for which he or she was bullied. The victim is well aware of the anger of bystanders and withdraws, which contributes to further dislike by the group (Graham & Juvonen, 2001).

Reaction of the Bystanders during Bullying Incidents

Craig and Pepler (1995, p. 89) describe bullying as "the product of the collective", and as "an interpersonal activity". When bystanders watch they are confirming the *power-over* strategies that bullies use so well. Because of the influence of a powerful model, other students may join in. In many ways, the bully is also demonstrating power over *the bystanders* as well as the victim. When students watch an incident, they typically watch the bully, not the victim, and they are influenced and controlled by what they watch.

Classmates tried to stop bullying eleven percent of the time (Craig & Pepler, 1995). Adults try to stop bullying four percent of the time. Students get involved in trying to stop bullying *more often* than the adults get involved (Pepler, Connolly, & Craig, 2000). Although it appears that peers are more likely to intervene, peers are also present when bullying takes place *far more often* than adults are within viewing and hearing range of bullying. If the time present when bullying takes place is taken into consideration, the frequency of peers trying to stop bullying is, actually, low. Given that the students who do intervene are the exception, it would be helpful to know more about these students. If their characteristics and thinking patterns were known, it may be that helping behavior could be taught to other children.

In a study of junior high school students, thirty-three percent of students said that they knew that they should help victim, but they don't. Unfortunately, another twenty-four percent of students said that bullying was none of their concern (Banks, 1997).

Attitudes versus Behavior

Henderson and Hymel (2002) found that more than half of the children surveyed claimed that they used strategies to deal with bullying behavior that would not support it, such as trying to stop the behavior, getting help, or saying something to the child who is bullying. Almost a third of students said they would simply watch the incident or move away. Five to nine percent said that they would join in or encourage the behavior directly. Children in the older grade levels were not as likely to try to stop the bullying or get help, and more often endorsed encouraging the bully. It may be that the aggressive behavior of bullies provides a powerful model for children who are easily stimulated because bullies *get away with* their negative actions. Or, in real life instances, emotions may interfere with thinking, or students may disagree with what they have been told is the right thing to do.

O'Connell et al. (1999) explored the discrepancy between what students report on surveys and what they actually do in a bullying situation. Most bystanders say they would not join in bullying when they are asked using surveys. However, students' responses to surveys *do not match* what students actually do when they are observed on the playground. Bystanders actually join in twenty-one percent of the time. There is also some data to suggest that students who are eager to be part of the group would not stand up to bullies. Because they want to be accepted by the group, and the group does not support making an effort to stop bullying, a bystander may hesitate to attempt to become involved or take any action (Sutton & Keogh, 2000).

REPORTING BULLYING

Lazarus (2001) suggested a number of reasons why students do not report what they know about bullying and threats of violence in schools. His list was fairly comprehensive. The bystander may:

- feel that the bully isn't serious or is only joking,
- be concerned about getting a peer or a friend into difficulty with school authorities,
- fear being ostracized or hurt,
- fear retaliation by the bully, or
- believe that if he or she tells, no adult will take it seriously or do anything about it.

There is a strong code of silence between students in schools, partly because school staff spend considerable time teaching students not to tattle or squeal on their peers, and this is strongly reinforced in the peer group. Past experience suggests that the school administration is not helpful to students who tattle or to students who break rules.

In common with the feelings of some adults, bystanders don't help partly because they feel the victim is learning something or because the victim 'asked for it'. Students say that they believe bullying toughens the victim and helps him learn to behave properly. When asked about bullying, nearly one-third of students will admit to have witnessed the bullying, but seventy-eight percent never report it, and many don't even take it seriously (ABC News, 2002). Craig and Pepler (1995) suggest that if the bystanders took the victim's side, bullying might escallate, and so students learn not to take the victim's side in playground incidents.

There is a strong sanction against informing the authorities. Students have a taboo against telling on others (Crary, 2001). There is a code of honor against tattling. Students do not want to risk being labeled a 'rat fink', a 'squealer', or a 'tattle tail'. They worry that if they tell they would not be protected in the unsupervised areas of the school (Sudermann et al., 1996). It is very difficult to stand up to intimidation by oneself. Bystanders may be relieved when others are picked on instead of them, and avoid the victim. This lack of involvement with the victim makes it easier to walk away. Finally, the 'silent majority' may feel inadequate when dealing with bullies (Goodman, 1999).

BOYS' REACTIONS TO BULLYING VERSUS GIRLS' REACTIONS

Boys are more likely than girls to join in bullying incidents, but they are also more likley to intervene on the victim's behalf. They are more likley to intervene when boys are involved as bullies and victims; girls are more likely to step in when the bully and the targeted child are both girls. When students directed their efforts to stop the intervention against the bully they were more likely to be aggressive in their efforts. When they attempted to help the victim or bully-victim they were not aggressive in their efforts. More than half of the time children were successful when they tried to stop the bullying episode (Hawkins, Pepler, & Craig, 2001).

Boys are more likley to join in bullying a targeted child. This may possibly be because they are more comfortable with rough and tumble play or because they know how to use aggression to establish a peer hierarchy, status, and dominance from their experience in larger, less intimate groups (O'Connell et al., 1999). Boys have had more experience with aggression than girls. It may also be that students are trained by their fellow classmates to engage in bullying.

Boys may also become more excited than girls or more aroused when they watch aggression than girls. This makes it clear that not only is the group influencing the bully and helping him or her perpetuate the negative behavior, but the bully is, in turn, influencing the bystanders (Craig & Pepler, 1995). In essence, the bully gives the bystanders *permission* to act aggressively, by being successful and demonstrating the rewards of bullying.

CONSEQUENCES FOR BYSTANDERS

It is not only the victims that are affected by bullying; bystanders are affected as well. Many children who watch, but don't help, feel guilty for not helping. In addition, when there is a high level of destructive teasing and bullying in schools, bystanders do not feel safe and do not feel as satisfied with school as do children in safer schools. When classrooms are found with high degrees of bullying and teasing, students report that they do not feel as safe as other student and they feel less satisfied with school in general (Skiba & Fontanini, 2000). Students at the middle school level feel even less safe than elementary school students. Most likley because playgrounds are more common at the elementary school level, younger students are more likley than middle school students to feel that their playgrounds are dangerous (Astor, Meyer, & Pitner, 2001). Learning and adjustment is seriously affected when children do not feel safe (Curwin & Mendler, 1997; Kochenderfer & Ladd, 1996).

Many students who watch bullying do not like what they see; they wish it wasn't happening. Bullying and teasing effect the bystanders too because if they cannot control the situation, they aren't safe either. Some worry about being drawn into the bullying because of peer pressure (Asidao et al., 1999; Banks, 1997; & US Department of Education, 1998a). They fear that they might lose their place in the peer group and feel that they need to go along with the group. Some are afraid to respond because they worry that if they get involved, they will be the next victim (McCoy, 1997). When bystanders do not take any action, they can experience feelings of powerlessness just as victims may experience powerlessness; there are consequences for inaction (Cowie, 1998).

It could also be that students don't know what to do, worry that they might do the wrong thing, or worry that they will draw the attention of the bully. The silent majority look away, pretend not to notice, stand at the outskirts, do not make waves, and are quiet (Hazler, 1996). In bullying prevention, the most challenging issue is *to change the behavior of the silent majority*. This is critical because bullies may listen to peers, whereas they are unlikely to listen to adults.

When there are no interventions attempted or when interventions don't work, children who observe bullying and see that it has no consequences for the bully may be more likely to engage in aggressive behaviors themselves. They repress feelings of empathy (Hazler, 1996; Sudermann et al., 1996). Students become increasingly desensitized to bullying when it occurs at a high or persistent level. This becomes clear, because as children grow older they become, increasingly, less likely to help someone being bullied. Bullying causes considerable stress on teachers, complicates school discipline, and has consequences for everyone involved. Bullying can have considerable costs to those involved, to those who witness it, or know about it, and to society in general (Maharaj, Ryba, & Tie, 2000a).

SUMMARY

Bystanders are affected by bullying in various ways. When they observe a bullying incident, they may look away, pretend not to notice, stand at the outskirts, try not to make waves, provide the audience for the bully by watching, become the assistant of the bully, join in, or even try to stop the bullying. Researchers who directly recorded bullying incidents have concluded that students reinforced bullying in eighty-one percent of the incidents that they observed. In addition, bystanders may teach victims to behave passively by making it clear that they support the bully.

Younger students are more empathetic toward the victim, but as students go through the grade levels, they increase fourfold in indifferent attitudes toward victims. There is an inconsistency between what students say they feel and do, and what they actually do when they observe a bullying incident. Although bystanders will say that they would attempt to stop bullying, they intervene to stop bullying in only a small percentage of the incidents that they observe. There are many reasons why bystanders do not intervene when they observe bullying, including cultural dictates, lack of faith in adults to solve the problem, and fear of loosing friends or becoming a target themselves.

During the bullying episode, bystanders behave with significantly more respect toward the bully than they do toward the victim. Boys both support the victim and intervene more than girls. Conversely, they also become more excited, and join in bullying others more often than girls.

Bystanders are clearly affected and influenced by the bully. In the bullying incident, the bully is demonstrating power *over the bystanders* as well as the victim. In addition, the bully gives the bystanders *permission* to act aggressively by being successful and demonstrating the rewards of bullying.

CHAPTER 9

Child-Centered Correlates of Bullying and Victimization

Although bullying is currently thought of as a group phenomenon, it would be unrealistic to say that the individual child makes no unique contribution to the cycle of behaviors that are involved in bullying and victimization. If we think of the bully's behavior, it's easy to see that the individual child contributes to the bullying interaction. It is much more difficult to appreciate the victim's role in the bullying situation. When thinking about a child's contribution to victimization, it is extremely important not to blame the victim. No child should be bullied for any reason. However, there may be individual child variables that increase vulnerability and it may help school staff to understand these variables when designing prevention and intervention activities.

BULLYING AS A STABLE STRATEGY FOR GROUP INTERACTION

Interest in child-centered variables may help explain why some children who bully others continue to bully others. Researchers have been quite interested in why bullying is a stable strategy for interacting with others for some children. Bullying may be stable because

- it is modeled,
- it involves particular temperamental variables,
- it involves a characteristic way in which a student attends to and recalls social information, or because
- it involves the way in which a student interprets the intentions of others (Gottheil & Dubow, 2001b).

An individual child's reaction or lack of reaction to stress appears to be important in understanding the role a child might play in a bullying episode. An individual child's temperament may play a role, as well. Finally, there may be attachment behaviors that help us understand why some children bully or become victims. In thinking about person-centered variables, it is important to keep in mind that behaviors associated with bullying are influenced both by individual child biology and the environment.

CHILDREN'S REACTIONS TO STRESS

Walter Cannon was the first researcher to examine the effects of emotions on our physiology. When a person experiences strong emotions the body reacts as well. Hans Selye described a 'fight or flight' reaction in response to stress. The fight-flight response to stress is an immediate intense stress reaction to a perceived threat. These responses to stress apparently had survival value at one time (Marlowe, 2000).

Once the brain is aroused by something that is happening around us, our bodies experience physiological symptoms and the need to *fight* or *escape* becomes intense (Neimark, 1998). There is a third physiological response to stress. This third response is somewhat akin to being *frozen*. Freezing is simply another survival reflex (Rothschild, 1997). When a 'freeze' response is activated, a person might feel temporarily numb and not respond at all. A child who is bullied may fight back, may try to run away or may be too frightened to react at all to a bully. When stressors are perceived as overwhelming, a person reacts with submission. Children and adolescents who are exposed to stress may react with worrying, losing trust in the adults in their environment, or have problems sleeping. For those five years old and younger, both aggression and anxious withdrawal are common symptoms of stress. Between ages five and eleven, children who are stressed may withdraw, act out, or have difficulty with schoolwork. Physical complaints under stress are common (Bryce, 2001).

Reaction to Arousal

When the 'fight or flight' reaction has been turned on the individual may think that everything is threatening, even neutral situations. The reaction is not under rational control. A person may overreact to neutral or insignificant comments. Worrying is exaggerated, and it is extremely difficult to think. Unfortunately, the cultural expectation is that individuals will handle the stress and exhibit self-control. A child faced with a bully may have no way to avoid the situation because he or she is in school. Fighting back may not only get the child in trouble; it might be dangerous. A child who has been continually exposed to threats of bullying or to worrying about being bullied may start to exhibit physical symptoms related to continuing stress (Neimark, 1998).

Ross (1996) reminds us that the stress that a child perceives may be different from the degree of stress that adults 'think' a child is experiencing or should experience. A child's experience of stress may be related to temperament and to the past experiences that the child has had in other situations in which he or she felt threatened.

Children who are bullied or teased may be repeatedly exposed to threats without being able to stop the painful harassment. Unfortunately the children repeatedly exposed to the threat of bullying may not receive the amount of support that they require, because adults have difficulty seeing the situation from the child's point of view (Ross, 1996).

THE RELATIONSHIP OF TEMPERAMENT TO BULLYING

The behavioral style of a child can be thought of as a child's temperament. Temperament is a trait that is evident from the earliest time and is probably in part, genetically determined. A child's temperament interacts with the many environments into which the child must fit. The temperament of the child must interact with the temperaments of teachers, parents, and the demands of the several environments in which the child functions (Keogh, 2003). Temperament can also be thought of as an emotional style that stays pretty much the same over time (Conner, 2001; Teglasi, 1998a).

While temperament is stable in many ways, it is also context dependent. The speed and degree to which a child reacts, becomes anxious, gets frustrated, or gets excited in a particular situation depends on temperament. Some students are more easily overwhelmed by emotions than peers of the same age might be. Students who are anxious and who react to discomfort by avoiding or withdrawing may not learn to cope in ambiguous or challenging situations. The result is that they feel less capable, more vulnerable, and ineffective. If they experience shame as a result of their reactions, the anxiety may become even more intense, and they may avoid situations more strongly (Rothbart & Jones, 1998; Rubin et al., 1991). Temperament has a powerful effect when a child is under stress, particularly if a child's temperament is more extreme (Keogh, 2003).

A child's temperament affects socialization. For example, temperament is related to the development of personality variables including empathy (Teglasi, 1998b, p. 580). Eisenberg, Wentzel and Harris (1998) define empathy as an emotional response that comes from the child's ability to understand the other person's current emotions that are being felt. In order to respond to another individual with empathy, a student not only must be able to regulate his or her emotions and attention, but also be able to manage his or her reaction to those feelings. Children who are well regulated can act with sympathy toward peers. A child who can shift and focus attention will be able to manage emotions such as fear, and anger, and may be willing to offer help to a peer.

There are several aspects of temperament that may relate to bullying and victimization, in particular. These include a tendency toward withdrawal, self regulation, emotionality, emotional reactivity, and dominance behaviors. Beyond this, attachment influences and coping styles may be related to the bullying interaction.

Tendency to Withdraw

A student's tendency to approach or withdraw in new situations may be related to victimization. A more inhibited temperament predicts the development of difficulties controlling anxiety, because the child experiences fear more readily than others in the same situations. Kindergarten children who are inhibited spend more time alone than their peers (Phillipsen, Bridges, McLemore, & Saponaro, 1999). Henderson and Fox (1998) describe the child who is high in a tendency to withdraw when situations are new and who is also low in self-regulation as a child who will experience anxiety and fear in many situations. This child can be overwhelmed in some situations and unable to use strategies to deal with situations that the child perceives as threatening. If this child were in a threatening situation, teachers or parents could not expect the child to use adaptive strategies, even if the child had mastered them in protected and familiar environments (Henderson & Fox, 1998). Withdrawn children tend to have social goals that have to do with avoidance (Ladd, 1999). A recent finding is that social withdrawal, or inhibition, is one of the strongest correlates of aggression in children (Fischer, Haas, Watson & Carr, 2002; Potier, 2002).

Self-Regulation

The ability to control negative feelings is necessary in order to be able to cope with stress and conflict. A child who can control his or her feelings will be more socially competent and emotionally healthy than the child who has difficulty controlling feelings (Mahady-Wilton et al., 2000). The ability of a child to regulate behavior and emotions is related not only to bullying, but also to reactions when one experiences bullying.

Self-regulation is the student's efforts to increase or tone down his or her emotions in response to a situation that intensifies the child's emotions. A child needs to learn to regulate not only arousal, but also attention, activity level, emotional intensity, emotional appropriateness, and behavior in order to be successful socially (Teglasi, 1998b). Recent research indicates that bullies and victims, alike, have problems with emotional regulation (Shields & Cicchetti, 2001). Students who are poorly regulated during the early school years become victimized by middle school or junior high (Pellegrini, 2001a).

Children who experience negative reactivity, who have low ability to tone down their emotions, and who also use physical aggression in response are at high risk. These children react with tantrums and angry outbursts in reaction to conflict or stressful situations (Farmer & Bierman, 2002). Given that a child's reaction in social situations determines the degree of peer acceptance that the child will experience, a child who is at high risk of over-reacting in conflict situations will have difficulty in social groups.

First grade is a critical point for identifying children who will have difficulty with peers later on. Children who are delayed in their ability to learn to control the degree to which they experienced negative emotions were the same children who exhibited reactive aggression. These children have trouble walking away from situations that upset them. They will have difficulty inhibiting impulsive behaviors and have difficulty coping effectively with their feelings of distress. Classmates rejected the children who were aggressive and withdrew from others in kindergarten by the time that these children were in grade three. Importantly, these children also tend to engage in bullying behaviors (Farmer & Bierman, 2002).

Victims tend to exhibit weak emotional-regulation ability and, in addition, may be reactive when they are stressed. If they feel sad and show their feelings of sadness when they are interacting with peers, the bully feels dominant and rewarded. Interestingly, when one group of researchers observed victims while they were being bullied, the victims often showed surprise. The surprise they felt may have been related to misreading the intentions of the bully. The fact that they showed surprise also suggests that the victims were not controlling their feelings in the bullying situation (Mahady-Wilton et al., 2000). Or, victims may find it difficult to express and communicate their feelings or may even tend to separate themselves from their feelings (Menesini, Fonzi, Ciucci, Almeida, Ortega, Lera, et al., 1999).

Emotionality

Children who have difficulty managing their emotions may be more aggressive, especially if they also feel emotions intensely. Children who are high in negative emotionality act out when stressed. If a child can control his or her emotions, the effects of negative emotionality can be lessened. The intensity with which a child experiences emotions can be buffered by adequate self-control of emotions (Ladd, 1999). Anger regulation is related to aggressive behavior. The relationship is indirect, however, and has to do with the ways in which a child expresses anger nonverbally (Dearing, Hubbard, Ramsden, Parker, Relyea, Smithmyer, et al., 2002). Problems in emotional regulation can be reflected in difficulty accessing the common or appropriate emotion for a given situation, or when one emotion such as anger overrides all other emotions (Menesini, Fonzi, et al., 1999).

Students who were rated by their teachers as very high in emotional intensity were the same children who engaged in bullying behaviors in elementary school.

These students continued to exhibit the same bullying behaviors when they reached middle school. They continued to bully others even after adjusting to the new school environment and making new friends. Bullying others appeared to be the key way these students established status in peer groups (Pelligrini & Bartini, 1999).

Emotionality and overarousal are attractive to other children who have similar temperaments. When boys who are easily aroused choose same-sex friends like themselves, they increase the chance that behavior problems will develop (Ladd, 1999).

Emotional Reactivity

Processing emotion information, and then using it positively, requires more than language ability. Understanding social cues, deciding on social goals and acting appropriately involves both thinking and emotions (Mostow, Izard, Fine & Trentacosta, 2002). Whereas bullies do not have a problem with emotional reactivity, children who are both bullied, and who bully others, have particularly poor control of their negative emotions. They tend to react to provoking incidents with anger and emotional upset. They feel more anxious and depressed than other victims. They typically do not withdraw when negatively stimulated (Schwartz, 2000).

Children who are both bullies and victims fight back when they are targeted, which excites the bully. They usually lose when dominated by an aggressive bully. Some researchers feel that this group has a high level of Machiavellianism and experiences negative self-esteem (Andreou, 2000). Overactive, reactive children become rejected around third grade, because peers will not longer tolerate the behavior of these children who often ruin the game or social interaction (Garrity & Baris, 1996). Anger control is often an issue for children who are both bullies and victims (Newman, Horne, & Bartomucci, 2000a). Children who do not handle anger well tend to be rejected by peers. The children who are quick to feel angry are insensitive toward others, have difficulty taking someone else's point of view and are driven to win rather than working to make friends (Hubbard, 2001). The effect of negative emotions and ability to control emotions have an additive affect on both social behaviors and academic performance (Gumora & Arsenio, 2002).

Dominance

The temperamental variable that is important in bullying is dominance. Dominance is a key personality characteristic of bullies. Bullies use strength and size to gain power over others. They use their status in the peer group. They know each other's vulnerable points and recruit support from bystanders (Pepler, Connolly, & Craig, 2000). Bullies have goals of dominance and reputation or status gained through aggression. The gain from bullying is primary and they do not appear to be concerned about the effects of their actions on the victim (Menesini, Fonzi, et al., 1999). There is a relationship between aggression and dominance hierarchies among young children (Shortly, 1991).

Aggressive children continue to exhibit their own personal, characteristic manner of interacting, and they tend to feel that their behavior is justified. They may also see themselves as victims. Aggressive children do not compare their behavior against the behavior of others accurately and believe that they are well accepted and competent (Coie & Jacobs, 2000). A predisposition for aggressive behaviors includes poor empathetic emotional-mediation of behavior, cognitive misattributions, a difficult temperament, and a concern for power. An aggressive child must also have an opportunity to victimize others and needs victims to be available, along with a strong desire to seek out a victim (Hughes & Giron, 2001; Rosen, 1998).

Studies of aggressive students have focused on aggressive boys until recently. Now, more and more studies of aggressive children are looking at both boys and girls. One of the complications of dealing with girls who are aggressive is that both female teachers and mothers of the aggressive girls are tolerant of their behavior. When behavior is overlooked or ignored, it will continue and could even get worse (Delligatti et al., 2003).

Aggressive children may be popular or unpopular. Aggressive children who are unpopular tend to feel good about themselves in spite of their lack of popularity. They do not seem to use the feedback that they get from their peers, especially if it is rejecting. They have a biased self view in a positive direction (Rudolph & Clark, 2001). Aggressive students believe that they are socially competent. Not only do they believe that they can be successful when they act aggressively, they value having control over others, and feel that it is okay to act aggressively toward others. Gottheil and Dubow (2001b) describe bullies as children who believe that aggression is worthwhile as a strategy for interacting with others and that it pays off. Children who rated themselves or whom others rated as bullies were particularly strong in the belief that aggression pays off. It may be that these beliefs contribute to the stability of bullying behaviors.

During middle childhood, aggressive students either feel extremely positive about themselves or feel extremely negatively about themselves. It is the group of aggressive students who feel extremely positively about themselves who are at greater risk for continued or increasing antisocial behaviors (Edens, 1999).

The boys who are aggressive as a means to an end believe that aggression works for them, and gets them what they want (Ladd, 1999). These boys easily engage in bullying behaviors and are purposeful and deliberate in their bullying behavior.

THE RELATIONSHIP OF EMPATHY TO BULLYING

Empathy has to do with the ability to appreciate another person's feelings both emotionally and cognitively (Funke & Hymel, 2002). It appears to be influenced by modeling and by social reasoning (Shortly, 1991). Empathy is complex. Interestingly, when students are identified as bullies, peers believe that bullies have a very good intellectual understanding of social situations. Peers feel that all children who use indirect aggression are *socially smart*. It takes considerable skill to manipulate others. At the same time, peers feel that students who use all forms of bullying are less empathetic than others. The cognitive and emotional aspects of empathy are split in the case of children who bully (Funke & Hymel, 2002).

In the case of bystanders at the secondary level, Pellegrini and Long (2002) report that boys become less sympathetic for boys who are victimized, but both boys and girls are more empathetic toward girls who are victimized.

COPING STYLES AND REACTIONS TO BEING BULLIED

Victims tend to react in several different ways to being bullied. Mahady-Wilton et al. (2000) described various coping strategies that children might use to deal with being bullied. These included:

- constructive problem solving,
- seeking support from others,
- talking over problems with peers,
- reacting physically or verbally,
- ignoring what is going on,
- distracting oneself,
- denying that anything bad is happening, and
- looking at the situation more positively (p. 232).

In order to respond in a way that will stop the bullying, a child must control his or her emotions, interpret the behavior as bullying, protect one's sense of self, stop the bullying, and do something to keep it from happening again. This is a lot to ask for from a young child.

One coping style when one is being bullied is to become verbally or physically *aggressive*. This coping style has been observed to occur forty-three percent of the time. A student's poor emotional-regulation can become poor behavioral regulation and affect their coping style. Aggressively reacting children who both bully others and are victimized by peers have weak emotional-regulation ability and become angry quickly. Frustration triggers them easily when they are victimized. Once their feelings are aroused, they may act in an extreme way. This has been called *arousal transfer* (Mahady-Wilton et al., 2000, p. 242).

As the bullying takes place, the child becomes very angry, cannot regulate this intense emotion, and acts on his or her feelings. Reacting to bullying with aggression and elevated emotion allows the episode to continue. It prolongues and may even escallate the bullying episode. Mahady-Wilton et al. (2000) found that reacting in this way is unlikely to stop the bullying by a factor of thirteen, as compared to a more adaptive response. The difficulty that a provocative victim has in using an adaptive strategy to deal with bullying appears to be related to a high degree of anger and upset that the child is experiencing during the interaction so that the child cannot problem solve effectively.

Active and Passive Responses to Being Bullies

A victim may react to bullying with a problem solving strategy. Observers in the same study (Mahady-Wilton et al., 2000) reported that fifty-two percent of children's reactions fell in this category. Both active and passive problem-solving strategies were observed.

Within this group of problem-solving coping styles, eighty-four percent of reactions were *passive*. When a victim reacts passively, bullying de-escalates. If the victim also appears to be sad or angry, the bully feels rewarded because the victim is upset. If the victim appears to like the attention, the bully may feel that his or her behavior is acceptable. The behavior of the targeted child signals approval of bullying. The victim is rewarded when the bullying stops. The problem is that the bully will return because the interaction is rewarding. Children who use passive strategies feel frightened because they cannot handle the situation actively. When a child cannot act assertively and instead reacts to bullying by acting submissively, the child is likely to become a victim again. Bad feelings about oneself and symptoms of depression may result (Mahady-Wilton et al., 2000).

Only sixteen percent of the problem-solving strategies used on the playground involved *active* coping with bullying. Students who were able to use this approach had strong social skills. In addition, their classmates supported them. Assertive behavior stopped the bullying, and the victim felt rewarded. The bully failed to reach his or her goals. The victims who could use this strategy felt competent, were accepted by others, and appeared to be emotionally protected from the emotional ramifications of having been bullied (Mahady-Wilton et al., 2000).

Some researchers have described various coping strategies as *emotion-focused* coping versus *problem-focused* coping (Ross, 1996). A student who uses emotion-focused coping feels the situation is uncontrollable. When the student uses emotion-focused copying, the child may decide that he or she deserves to be bullied. Or, the child might decide that being bullied is his or her own fault. This type of coping *reframes* what is happening or changes its meaning. The victim is trying to make the situation less frightening by denying what is happening or attempting to rationalizing it and control it in some way (Menesini, Fonzi, Ciucci, Almeida, Ortega, Lera, et al., 1999). A student who uses problem-focused strategy believes that there is something that he or she can do, to stop the bullying.

There are times when emotion-focused coping may be productive or appropriate. For example, the child who is bullied may decide that the bully is 'immature'. Older students may be in a better position to be able to decide when it is safe to try to stop the bullying and when to accept it for the moment. Emotion-focused coping may allow the victim to stand the bullying momentarily. Whenever a child is able to cope at least momentarily, the child has a chance to get some control in the situation (Ross, 1996).

ATTACHMENT AND REACTIONS TO BEING BULLIED

There has been some exploration of other person-centered variables related to bullying, victimization, and attachment. Attachment theory from the 1970s and 1980s postulates that anxiously-avoidant attached students are more likely than anxiously-resistant attached students to engage in bullying behaviors (Bollorino, 1997).

Studies from the 1980s showed that when students' attachment at twelve months was related to later behavior, it was found that anxiously attached infants tended to behave as bullies or victims four to six years later. Anxious-resistant behaviors correlated with victim behavior, anxious-avoidant behaviors correlated with bully behavior. Bullies who were least attached victimized other bullies in these studies (Bollorino, 1997). In thinking about how pervasive bullying behavior may be, it is important to remember that only fifty-five percent of children are securely attached (Furlong & Smith, 1998).

SUMMARY

Examining child-centered variables that relate to bullying and victimization is important. Children may respond to the stress of being bullied by fighting back, by withdrawing, or escaping, or by freezing so that they are unable to do anything to protect themselves. Consideration of the way in which a given child deals with stress may help practitioners in designing individual interventions. Obviously, telling a child to walk away when bullied would be difficult for a child whose strong tendency is to fight back.

The temperamental variables that may be related to victimization include a tendency in some children to withdraw when stressed. Other children have difficulty regulating emotions and behavior when they are stressed or aroused and may react to bullying by becoming upset. Children who feel emotion intensely, particularly negative emotions may react to stress with anger or aggression. Dominance is the key temperamental variable in bullies. The ability to be empathetic may be weak in bullies.

Coping behaviors need to be understood in individual children. Children need to learn the difference between emotion-focused and problem-solving coping strategies. More importantly, they need to learn when each of the coping strategies is useful. Finally, since attachment issues are so prevalent in children, understanding attachment issues may help practitioners understand individual children and, perhaps, help them react more adaptively to peer stress.

CHAPTER 10

Friendships and Social Groups

The social world in which children function is more complex and intricate than adults imagine. It is important to explore this world, so that the complexity of the phenomenon of bullying can be understood.

MOVING BEYOND THE FAMILY

Children begin to learn about the peer culture while still functioning in their families at home. Older siblings are particularly important in this regard. Family relationships influence the personality development of children which may in turn influence the way that children interact later on with others outside the family (Sarason, Pierce, & Sarason, 1990). Parents who teach their children to initiate and negotiate with others can make a difference in their child's success on the playground when the child enters school (Ladd, 1999).

Once they expand their world beyond the family, children must learn how to behavior in other environments. Different expectations exist in the many environments in which children must adjust. In Western societies peers socialize children once they move into the expanded world. It is in the peer group where children learn to behave in public and learn the cost of nonconformity. Children conform in order to protect their self-esteem and to find their place. Within the peer group they develop individuality as long as they don't stand out too much or are too different. This may occur differently in boys groups as compared to girls groups as long as there are enough children for groups to form based on gender, but the pressure to belong is intense in the cultures which children create (Harris, 1995).

SOCIAL INTERACTION IN PRESCHOOL

Children learn a variety of important lessons as a result of interacting with playmates. Children must learn that a having a friend means sharing an activity with someone else (Corsaro, 1997). They learn that relationships require negotiation. They learn that they will not always get to play or be accepted. They learn that they need to convince other children that they will be fun to play with, and they learn that they need to expect that they may be excluded.

Children learn to use friendship as an excuse to keep others out of the play interaction. Children have very good reasons for this. Interaction between preschool children is temporary. If additional children are allowed to join the play interaction, the play may fall apart and the interaction is over. Because of the delicacy of the interactions between children, preschoolers improve their chances of being accepted into play interactions by spending time with several other children on a regular basis (Corsaro, 1984).

A study of young children showed that when boys play together, the play is rough and involves dominance. The more time that children spend in same-sex groups, the more pressure they feel to engage in specific, gender-based, play activities. Children in these playgroups give strong messages about what is expected, and in doing so, they learn to socialize successfully with their peers (Martin & Fabes, 2001). By age five or six, boys start to prefer to play with boys, and girls prefer to play with girls. This is seen more often among middle-class students (Bigelow et al., 1996).

Maccoby (2000) feels that during preschool, boys tend to engage in large group rough-and-tumble play, but girls who may want to participate cannot easily change these play styles and must learn to roughhouse if they want to participate in the large groups with boys. Maccoby feels that the girls have little influence over the boys. The presence of adults is the only moderating force to hold preschool boys' power-assertion in check. Girls tend to stay near adults when the play is rough. Boys may need the structure of the group more than girls, and they gain a good deal from their experience in groups where they learn about hierarchical relationships. Boys become anxious to hold their status when they are playing in groups with peers (Maccoby, 2000).

Friendship During Preschool Years

Preschoolers will call each other a 'friend' in order to keep others from joining in or to control a play activity. The skills needed for maintaining a best friend are quite different from the skills needed to be popular, which is a group phenomenon. Early on, children learn that they can *exclude* others if they are playing in a restricted space, and they *still remain liked* by others in spite of their decisions to exclude others. Children accept this type of exclusion by the group. Preschoolers also learn that they can use the concept of friendship to get to play with others even after the action has started, simply by claiming 'you are my friend' (Azmitia, Kamprath & Linnet, 1998).

Friendships are considered positive when there is little rejection, teasing, or domination among the pairs of students. Ladd, Kochenderfer, and Coleman (2000) report that boys are more negatively affected by conflict between mutual friends than girls. They argue that boys play in larger groups than girls, but they have fewer close one-on-one relationships, and are, therefore, more affected when these best friend twosomes experience conflict. Close friendships may interfere with academics, because children who are close talk a great deal in class. This has the effect of teachers reacting and separating friends.

ELEMENTARY SCHOOL CHILDREN AND SOCIAL INTERACTION

Once children are in school, they need to find their place in the peer group. Studies show that in the first few years of school, children who behaved as bullies seemed to be trying to *find their place in the peer group* using social power. These children are popular and pick on boys who exhibit victim behavior. The popular boys in grades one and two bully others to establish their place in the group. When these same students reach about nine years of age, or by third grade, the most popular children are no longer the bullies. The peer group has been established, and the boys who bully others are at this point rejected. These bullies continue to victimize boys who are not aggressive (Bernstein & Watson, 1997; McCoy, 1997).

In order to get accepted into a group, a student must behave as the group expects that child to behave. Once the child becomes part of the group, the group controls how aggression is expressed. This explains why children who are aggressive play and hang out with other children who are also aggressive (Cairns & Cairns, 1991). Aggressive boys who spend time with other aggressive boys dislike each other, but hang out together just the same (Bigelow et al., 1996). The most time that these aggressive students spend together, the less they will be influenced by classmates who think differently (Ledingham, 1991).

Making friends and maintaining friendship relationships is not easy. Children with friends are more competent, less troubled, more cooperative, less lonely, and more confident than those children without friends (Hartup, 2000). Social competence is associated with concepts such as empathy, cooperation, altrusim, and prosocial behaviors. Popularity, on the other hand, is associated with dominance, aggression, getting what you want, and power (LaFontana & Cillessen, 2002).

Children who are friends help structure the world for one another by scaffolding the social world (Hartup, 1999). Social support of peers is extremely important for a child. Social support improves a child's general adjustment, the ability to deal with stress around social interactions, and helps the child negotiate school transitions (Cauce, Reid, Landesman, & Gonzales, 1990; Malecki & Demaray, 2002). Friendships also form a safety net, or a safety barrier, against the powerful social hierarchy seen in peer groups (Adler & Adler, 1998).

Boys in elementary school value physical interactions, independence, reliance on oneself, and being cool. Girls are more interested in emotional expression, appearance, possessions, and romance. However, the separation of boys and girls is most common among white and middle class children, whereas, a teasing, bossy style of interaction is more common among Latina, and African-American, young girls. When boys and girls interact, they tend to spend their time chasing each other (Corsaro, 1997).

Social Rules

The social world is extremely complex. The student in elementary school is exposed to and must master the rules of the social world, which involve power, status, and unwritten rules about what is expected (Kutnick & Manson, 1998). Bigelow et al. (1996) describe social rules as ways of acting and thinking about how to relate to others. For some children, the challenge of figuring out what the rules of interaction may be and learning that rules are continually negotiated, is an overwhelming task.

Social rules are different from social skills and are more cognitive than behavioral. They tell a child *how* to act with another child at a particular place in the social hierarchy. However, they are also fuzzy or arbitrary. Rules depend on the relationship the child has with the other children, the age of the child, and the gender of the child. Girls take the rules more seriously than boys. Every interaction with classmates helps a child understand the social order better. Peer rules include controlling feelings and fixing relationships that are threatened (Bigelow et al., 1996).

Self Control

Self-control is more critical among friendships than it is at home with family members. In order to be socially competent, a child must not only control feelings, but also be able to read others feelings and change one's own behavior according to that understanding (Bigelow et al., 1996). Girls' relationships especially require controlling feelings. Girls are more uncomfortable when they challenge other girls or compete with them, than boys would be in their interpersonal interactions with others of the same sex (Benenson, Roy, Waite, Goldbaum, Linders, & Simpson, 2002). Children must learn to consider difficulties in social interaction as temporary, rather than as permanent, in order to maintain self-esteem (Bryant, 1998).

Unless emotions are controlled in children's groups, it would not be possible for play to be coordinated (Bigelow et al., 1996). Children need to understand the costs of expressing emotion in a group. If a child expresses too much, or too intense, emotion more powerful peers will make them *pay for it*. Children learn to control their feelings when classmates are around in order to protect themselves from being ridiculed or losing their place in the social hierarchy. Students learn to show feelings only when best friends are around (Terwogt & Stegge, 1977).

Friendship Contracts

Children establish 'friendship contracts' with others (Azmitia et al., 1998). The responsibility of a friend is to be a playmate, to help, support, and even protect the child. From grade three on, about twenty-five percent of girls expect their friends to keep secrets, and this increases with age. Boys may not feel as strongly about this until the end of sixth grade. Elementary school girls have more trouble handling more than one best friend, and yet triads, which are particularly difficult to manage and generate jealousies, are more common among girls than boys. Girls say that they have difficulty managing more than one best friend and being close to more than one other person at a time. Triads consist of a more powerful girl along with two additional girls who need to share the attention of the most powerful girl in the triad friendship. It is likely that one girl will not feel as good as the other two (Azmitia et al., 1998).

Boys tend to forgive best friends' transgressions. Researchers have found that on average it took one day for boys who are friends to work out problems. It took girls about two weeks to work through a conflict between friends. Three-quarters of girls, but less than half of boys, would end a best friendship if a secret were told (Azmitia et al., 1998). Disagreements may occur more often between two children who are good friends, because friends give friends more freedom to disagree. Children can also be hurt more deeply by friends. Even so, there is less blame when this occurs, because children are focused on maintaining the relationship (Ladd, 1999).

Students will change their behavior in order to get a friend. Friendship success involves both control of one's emotions and a clear focus on one's goal of maintaining the friendship (Kiesner, Cadinu, Poulin, & Bucci, 2002). Correlations between children who have a close relationship are greater for negative behaviors such as bullying (Hartup, 1999).

Popularity

Friendship and popularity are not the same. Popularity has to do with one's place in the peer group. Finding one's place in the peer group, clearly, plays a role in the development of bullying and teasing behaviors. Friendship involves inclusive action, but popularity requires the exclusion of others (Coie, Dodge, & Coppotelli, 1982). Groups train individual behaviors and the training may be useful or deviant (Kiesner et al., 2002). When students engage in cruel behavior toward their peers, they may be trying out aspects of social power. Social power includes the *power to harm* another child (Thompson, O'Neill, & Cohen, 2001). But social power or dominance is not the same as popularity even though they are correlated (Harris, 1995).

Students in early elementary school are concerned about popularity and worry about acceptance. Best friendships become common as early as first grade and protection of those best friend relationships becomes important. The dyads, also, become the base from which loose clubs are formed. The club concept helps children enlarge their group. As some children are not allowed to join, the beginning of stratified groups among the larger group of children is clear (Corsaro, 1997). A child's status in the group is related to *how* the child uses social power (Fine, 1984).

In every classroom there is a status hierarchy, but the hierarchy is different for groups of girls than it is for groups of boys. Children do not choose their status or their roles within the group. More powerful peers decide on each child's status in the group. The group can victimize one or more children in a classroom when a destructive dynamic develops in the group (Thompson, O'Neill, & Cohen, 2001).

As students become more concerned about their own status within the group, they also become more vulnerable to group dynamics. A student's reputation in a group is the perceived popularity of the child, according to the impact that the child has on the group. A child who is *dominant* in the group might be considered by some classmates as aggressive and by others as 'stuck-up'. Popular students use aggression to get what they want. They are at the center of the social group in powerful positions (LaFontana & Cillessen, 2002). The more accepted a child is by the group that they belong to, the more friendships from which the child can choose (Azmitia et al., 1998). Control is one of the basic themes in children's peer cultures according to Corsaro (1997), and one of the things that children try to control is their choice of friends.

Boys will choose popularity over friendship in the third grade. They will join others to pick on boys who don't have equal status. Even the victim's friends join this teasing at the third grade level. Boys tend to spend a lot of energy trying to be accepted by others who do not want to be their friend. It is quite stressful when boys must choose between a best friend who is not accepted by the main group and an offer to join the popular group. Most boys choose to join the group over the friend up through grade seven. Boys tend not to remember the details after a break in friendship. Those who were hurt or rejected say later on that they did nothing about the break up or didn't even let the friend know that they were hurt (Azmitia et al., 1998).

Girls become upset when friends break a promise, tell a secret, tease them in front of others, or exclude them. They are much more likely than boys to consider friendship breeches so serious that they would question the friendship. Girls' friendships are more exclusive and more intense. Girls will choose popularity over friendship by fifth grade and may even manipulate the friendship so that it ends in order to be accepted by the popular group (Azmitia et al., 1998).

Exclusion can spread throughout the class, or grade level, so that a girl could be excluded by *all* of her classmates. Some girls' work so hard on friendship issues that there is little time or energy left for schoolwork. Self-esteem can suffer precipitously when girls have to deal with a friend who is constantly breaking the friendship contract, when a friendship has just ended, or when a new friendship is beginning and the girl is not yet feeling confident that it will catch on. Some girls ruminate about friends' behavior to the extent that they cannot move on or work through ambiguous relationships. They dwell on the meaning of the relationship and the implications (Azmitia et al., 1998).

Azmitia et al. (1998) feel that the strategies that help students become popular and accepted are in direct conflict with strategies needed to develop a best friendship. The 'best friend contract' appears to require an intimate relationship between friends earlier for girls than for boys. Telling secrets was the most frequent cause of break ups for both boys and girls in early elementary school. Corsaro (1997) points out that there is a great deal of jealousy if one member of a best friend dyad plays eith someone else which results in quarreling and conflict.

Rejection

Rejection is tough in elementary school. Five to ten percent of children at this age are without a friend (Asher & Renshaw, 1984). However, if you asked students who do not seem to have a friend if they have a friend, they would name someone (Hartup, 1998). Children who are not accepted by peers ask adults for help when there is conflict and cannot make good suggestions, or offer aggressive ideas when interacting with others (Asher & Renshaw, 1984). Rejected children may have casual friends. Students who are socially left out feel that their friendships are less supportive than other children tend to feel (Ladd, 1999). Children who are rejected by fourth grade may be able to change their social status by fifth grade, if they participate in sports or other activities and are aggressive (Sandstrom & Coie, 1999).

Students in American schools believe that it is okay to exclude others because of their gender, but not their race. Rejecting a child on the basis of race is not accepted, for the most part. However, peers can effect classmates' judgments in regard to excluding others. Girls are more tuned in to issues of exclusion than are boys (Killen, 2002).

Empathy

Children also learn empathy from peers. The goal of empathy is keeping the peace. The price for hurting a friend is very high. Real emotions must be hidden, because this is the norm. In addition, hiding feelings avoids embarrassment and makes tolerating being teased easier. Hiding emotions avoids conflict and allows a child to maintain a positive sense of self. Hiding one's feelings supports relationships (Bigelow et al., 1996). Hiding feelings can be motivatyed by empathy or may be motivated by avoiding conflict.

Separation by Gender

The powerful and popular boys seem to be in control of the degree of separation of boys and girls. They may instigate teasing and chasing girls, but they do not consider girls friends. When there are issues between groups, they label each other as having 'cooties' or they may ridicule others in a very hurtful manner (Adler & Adler, 1998, p. 102).

Social Status

As students go through elementary school, rules are enforced depending on a child's status within the group. Children in out-groups must learn to accept that the fact that the rules are not enforced for everyone (Fine, 1984). A good example of this is seen in playground games such as four-square. In this game the ball must be bounced into one quardrant of the square. A child who is part of the in-group will be given the benefit of the doubt when his or her ball touches the perimeter of the square. A child who is part of the out-group will be called 'out' and told to leave the game if his or her ball hits the line. This is important for adults to understand who are observing children at recess. Children liked by the group are given breaks that other children are denied and rules may be invented on the spot to control who is 'in' and who is 'out'.

Children learn social rules by watching interactions of their peers. Rules are invented and changed during the course of interaction, and the use of rules, as well as who uses them, is part of the interaction. This is why negotiation skills are so important. Some of the cruelty of children toward other children may have to do with protecting oneself, rather than an attempt to victimize the other child (Fine, 1984).

Cliques

All social groups form hierarchies of members who work hard for status in the group. The status of individuals in groups affects how they feel about themselves, how well they understand social interactions, and their emotional adjustment (Anderson, John, Keltner, & Kring, 2001).

Cliques have a hierarchical structure. The leader or leaders of cliques use their popularity to control the group (Adler & Adler, 1998). Popular children are prosocial, as compared to other children, their postive behavior may help them hold their place in the group (Greener, 2000). If the leader of the clique likes a child, that child may be brought into the group. The closer to the leader that a child may be, the more popular that child. However, status in the clique is unstable and can be threatened. Other children who are close to the leader subsequently challenge the new member of the group. The process is fluid or dynamic. A child is first accepted, and then put down. Clique leaders may manipulate and rearrange the hierarchy by extending favor on a particular child who is lower in the hierarchy. Leaders hang on to their power by manipulating the feelings and status of other children. Leaders also manipulate clique members into bullying others, and then withdraw themselves so that others take the blame (Adler & Adler, 1998).

In schools, where there are over eighty students at a grade level, students stratify into a popular group, a group of 'wannabes', a middle group (which is composed of many small groups), and children who are isolated from all of the groups (Adler & Adler, 1998, p. 75). By fourth or fifth grade, the popular clique has grown each year until it includes one third of all students at the grade level. This group controls the school climate and has a lot of power, which must be protected. A popular clique might have one or two leaders surrounded by several circles of students with progressively less power. The followers competitively move up and down in status at the whim of the leaders. The hierarchy and power of the leaders makes it difficult for students to support friends and generates a lot of uncertainty and anxiety.

The wannabes constitute ten percent of students at the grade level, and these students imitate the behavior, language, and dress of the popular clique. The wannabes have their own small groups of friends, but would prefer to be in the popular clique. The children in this group have the lowest self-esteem, even though they have high status (Adler & Adler, 1998). Corsaro (1997) has described activities that delineate the boundaries between groups, which he calls 'borderwork'. One example of 'borderwork' is chasing games, another is describing a group as having 'cooties' (when a group is derided in this way researchers call this a pollution ritual). A third example is the 'invasions' children make to disrupt games. In these several ways, children try to cross the boundaries of a group that they might like to become part of or they attempt to attract attention from members of the group with the hope of developing a relationship with members of the group.

The middle group of students, which makes up half of a class, is made up of small friendship groups. A student in this group has a few good friends. Students in middle groups accept others, tend not to try to belong to the popular groups, and tend to have closer, less competitive friendships. However, they do not admire the popular children and are critical of the wannabes. Children in this group are not as anxious as children are in the more competitive groups.

The isolated children, constituting ten percent of a class or grade level, have no real friends and are excluded. They may have casual relationships, and they may get to play if another person is needed in a game. They may establish relationships with younger children. When teased or picked on, no one supports them. Unfortunately, they reject one another (Adler & Adler, 1998).

Children in late elementary school are learning about power, conformity, in-groups and out-groups. They are learning about status based on power and popularity. They are learning what is accepted behavior and what happens when they do not fit the norm (Adler & Adler, 1998).

MIDDLE SCHOOL SOCIAL INTERACTIONS

Positive relationships with others help students adjust to middle school, especially when the friendships are outside of school as well as in-school (Hirsch, Engel-Levy, DuBois, & Hardesty, 1990). If children are asked how supportive their friends are shortly after entering a new school, this can be used to predict how popular they will be later in the year and what their attitudes will be about others (Hartup, 1998).

As students move from elementary school to middle school, peer relationships are less stable for girls than boys (Hardy, Bukowski, & Sippola, 2002). In middle school, popularity tells how the student is seen in the hierarchy. Popular peers may not be liked by all of their classmates, but instead are dominant in the group. They are talented in both positive and negative behaviors. They get what they want one way or the other. Girls associate popularity with negative behavior more than boys do, and the association between popularity and negative behavior reaches its strongest point in sixth grade and remains at this high level through seventh and eighth grades (LaFontana & Cillessen, 2002). Aggressive boys are liked. They hold higher status and may be leaders of some groups (Cadwallader, Farmer, Cairns, Leung, Clemmer, et al., 2002).

Armitia et al. (1998) report that through seventh grade, boys continue to choose popularity over intimacy. If they must choose between an unpopular best friend and the popular crowd, they will choose the crowd and feel badly about it. Boys may reach out to others who are left out, if the person left out is at least as popular as they are. Boys will feel quietly stressed when friends tease them in public about something that they care about in themselves. Boys, especially as they get older, see advantages in avoiding conflicts with best friends and will tolerate a violation of the 'best friend contract' when their chief desire is to keep the friendship.

Girls will recruit other girls to 'freeze out' a friend who has violated the friendship contract. Freezing out a girl is a power play. Girls may pass around 'slam books' in which a group would write cruel comments about the excluded girl. Girls may single out even the most popular girl in the group to exclude (McCoy, 1997). Another manipulative technique girls use involves inviting a girl to a sleep over and 'helping' her by telling her how she needs to behave to be accepted by the group (Armitia et al., 1998). Bullying can be particularly painful at the middle school level (Harris & Petrie, 2002).

Same-sex cliques change to become mixed-sex cliques in middle school. Dating is not the chief focus at this point, although some students date. Students who are unpopular and the students who are popular in the extreme tend to become involved with the opposite sex (Connolly et al., 2000). Children learn appropriate ways to approach the other sex from their peers.

Popular middle school boys are either the best athletes or have a particular interest in sports and tend to challenge authority, which gives them status. Popular boys are often controlling and manipulate others. They are interested in popular girls. For girls, socioeconomic status, having more freedom than peers, and attractiveness make a girl popular (Adler & Adler, 1998).

SECONDARY SCHOOL AND SOCIAL FUNCTIONING

Social groups among adolescents have gate-keeping regulations which assure that new members are selected because they are similar to others who already belong to the group. The group helps the individual student establish identity and helps meet the individual's needs to belong, but at the same time the group controls the student's behavior particularly the expression of aggression. Group memberships change from year to year because of shifting alliances. Students move up and down in status within the larger group, but do not change from one large group to another. Once a new member of the group is allowed to participate, further socialization takes place. Students learn the values of the group and take on the social problems of the group. The individual student increasingly has fewer choices socially among peers, as he or she moves from childhood to adolescence (Cairns & Cairns, 1991).

Boulton, Trueman, Chau, Whitehand, and Amatya (1999) found that teenage students who agreed that they were best friends were less likely to be bullied. Those most likely to be bullied were without a best friend over time. By adolescence, students will avoid conflict in order to keep friends. More boys than girls see the advantages of avoiding trouble with close friends, and may never discuss the problems they experience in their most important relationships. Boys and girls are in the same general groups in adolescence.

Students in high school who are considered by others to be popular are accepted by other popular students, are confident, and win arguments. Students describe adolescent girls who are popular as individuals who 'think' that they are important and who are very choosy about their friends. By this age, students are popular with peers who are like them. Students form groups among students who achieve at about the same level and who feel the same about schoolwork (Gorman, Kim & Schimmelbusch, 2002).

Adolescents will argue that the functioning of the group takes precedence over including others (Killen & Stangor, 2001). Girls with low self-esteem ruminate about relationships and can't seem to move on when there is conflict. They search for answers trying to understand what the difficulties might mean for them (Azmitia et al., 1998). Peers are influenced by a classmate's status when they decide whether or not to support another person. Popular adolescents actually get the least support from peers, possibly because their classmates don't think they need it (Ross, 1996).

SUMMARY

In order to develop a more complete picture of the bullying interaction, it is important to understand what is really going on in children's social groups.

Children learn to exclude others from the group as early as preschool, where it may be necessary to exclude a child who wants to join in in order to maintain the social interaction. Peers socialize with their classmates. Friendships and popularity become evident from the preschool years.

Once children enter elementary school, status hierarchies' form and children vie for a place in the peer groups. Some children learn to use bullying in order to find a place in the group, and this occurs at no cost, because bullies are popular. Maintaining friendships is challenging, as children must master the complex social rules that have to do with relationships. They must learn how to act with other children at each level of the social hierarchy. Both behavioral and emotional control is critical if friendships are to be maintained. Children must accept friendship as a goal and sacrifice other goals such as winning. Social power is seen in the cliques that students form. Popular students have learned to use social power to maintain their status in the groups.

Students will choose popularity over friendship up through middle school. The popular clique controls the school climate, and often, it is the powerful and aggressive boys who are in control and hold the highest status. Students learn that rules are negotiated and are not applied equally to everyone. Even during secondary school, perceived popularity is extremely important to students as their social choices become more and more restricted.

CHAPTER 11

School Wide Interventions

In order to decrease bullying successfully in schools, interventions must reach every area of the school and the community in which the school is located. The culture of the school must be altered. School culture refers to the expectations of all of the stakeholders involved as well as the norms, values, rituals, and history of the particular school. The culture of the school influences the ways that people in the school think, how they feel, and how they behave. School culture is the way things are done in the school and what individuals believe is important. Each school has varying willingness to change (Peterson, 2002).

THE DIFFICULTY OF MAKING CHANGES IN SCHOOLS

Sarason's writings (1996) have helped school personnel understand the challenge of making changes in schools and school culture. The key resources needed to make changes in schools are human resources. He suggests that *power* in schools has to do with building social support for change. Building constituencies takes considerable time. Individuals must *own* the change while they also function as *the object* of change. Teacher support is critical if change is going to take place in a school.

When attempting to change the school culture, it is critical to change attitudes of teachers if they are not supportive. This does *not* have to be accomplished before beginning to implement prevention programs including bullying prevention programs. Research suggests that changes in practice can precede changes in attitude and beliefs. Studies show that teachers will change their feelings about policy when they realize that changing a previously accepted practice works (Gersten, Chard, & Baker, 2000).

INVOLVEMENT OF FAMILIES AND THE COMMUNITY

Parents and community members must be involved as well. Families must recognize bullying behaviors and become more aware of the extent of the problem in their homes. Parents as well as teachers need to confront bullying behaviors. Families may need some help in developing clear rules against bullying in their own homes. Families also need to protect their children if they are bullied (Swearer & Doll, 2001). Bullying has to do with the attitudes that some students have in regard to other students. These attitudes are taught in families, or are part of the local culture (Maharaj, Ryba, and Tie, 2000b). Schools must eliminate bullying and promote tolerance in order to prevent violence (Phillips, 2000, p. 28).

PREVENTION RESEARCH

Prevention research has delineated 'best practices' as they are currently conceived. In order to truly make a difference, programs that extend over several years or are ongoing are most likely to make a difference (Carney & Merrell, 2001). It is important that prevention programs begin as early as possible, certainly in kindergarten and better still if they are started in preschool. It is important that programs are complex rather than simple, addressing support systems as well as negative behaviors. Programs must be aimed at changing the whole system as well as changing individuals. The best prevention work involves primary efforts aimed at the whole school community, along with secondary prevention efforts and treatment for those most in need within the system that is being addressed (Greenberg, Domitrovich, & Bumbarger, 1999).

Schwartz (1999) cites the strategies that are most effective which schools can use to address violence. These include a social competency curriculum, which may not be effective when used alone. They include a positive school environment with explicit behavior standards and clear rules. The establishment of codes of conduct and norms involving safety can help reduce negative behaviors. These variables work when there is adequate supervision and modeling of positive behavior by staff. Consequences are *not* as strong as *norms* that expect children to respect one another. Teacher training is critical and work with parents is necessary, as well as ongoing training of new staff that may enter a school each year (Sharp & Thompson, 1994). Schwartz (1999) points out that the public has not as yet supported comprehensive approaches to reducing school violence.

Rigby and Slee (1999) conceive of strategies that schools take to deal with bullying as moralistic, legalistic, or humanistic. When a school community describes bullying as inconsistent with the school's values, this would be an example of a moralistic approach. When bullying is carefully defined and clear consequences for bullying behavior have been set, this is an example of a legalistic approach. When counseling is the designated method that schools use to deal with bullies, this might be described as a humanistic approach. Bullying can also be viewed as a component of efforts to prevent violence in schools.

RISKS INVOLVED IN MAKING CHANGES IN SCHOOLS

There are risks involved in addressing bullying in schools. Because the focus in the media has been on bullying in schools, the public may see the school as the *cause* of bullying and as solely responsible for stopping it. Unfortunately, many schools react to bullying when it occurs as an isolated instance rather than addressing bullying systemically (Soutter & McKenzie, 2000). Ross (1996) suggests that the passive approach of schools toward bullying incidents allows bullying to flourish in some schools. Children have already learned to bully when they start school, so the responsibility of schools is to develop primary prevention programs. Addressing multiple risk factors through school programming is more powerful than addressing bullying as an isolated issue.

WHOLE SCHOOL APPROACHES TO PREVENTION OF BULLYING

Our current understanding of bullying behavior is that it depends on the whole school community in order to exist. If this is the case, prevention programs must be school-wide (Curwin & Mendler, 1997). The best-researched intervention is the Bullying Prevention Program designed by Dan Olweus. Implementation research around this program has been considerable. The importance of a multi-pronged approach has been made clear through Olweus' work. Olweus (1991) emphasized systemic factors as compared to individual interventions in his writings. He felt that individual interventions cause school staff to underestimate the extent of bullying and misunderstand the basic social or group process that is involved in bullying. In addition, when school staff look only at single instances they tend to develop interventions that are child centered or victim centered. Interventions should focus on working with adults, recognizing that victims are not able to stop bullying alone.

The chief components of whole-school bullying prevention projects include policy development, implementation, and evaluation. Initially, it is critical to increase awareness of the extent and effects of bullying in schools in order to increase motivation for making changes in existing policy. The whole school community needs to be involved in creating a specific policy to address bullying. In order for change to occur, training is necessary for everyone involved along with regular reminders to keep the policy in the front of everyone's minds and to keep bullying prevention a high priority.

A Norwegian study, lead by Roland (reported in Sharp & Thompson, 1994), determined that bullying increased in those schools which did not maintain their already established anti-bullying policies. Students, staff, and parents need continuing reminders of the policy and expectations. In addition, the reminders need to be very specific in spelling out the behaviors that must *not* occur explicitly. This is different from the common practice in many schools in which the behaviors identified to be changed are phrased positively; for example, instead of saying don't call others bad names, the rule would be to treat others with respect. Continued support is needed from school administrators and from influential community members or parents outside the school (Sharp & Thompson, 1994).

Mellor (1999) feels that we do not yet have the ability to totally prevent bullying or to eliminate it completely, but we do have sufficient knowledge at this point in time to reduce bullying and to do so significantly. School psychologists and other mental health workers in schools must take a leadership role in assisting stakeholders in developing policies around prevention of bullying behaviors. Cultural expectations that victims must be able to 'take it' or 'fight back' need to be countered (Sullivan, 1999). Schools must also use effective practices when bullying occurs and make certain that parents and community members are part of the solution rather than making the situation worse. Parents can make things more difficult when they attack the school for not immediately solving problems or for not solving problems as parents believe that the problems should be solved. Schools must assume responsibility when bullying occurs on school property.

Two fundamental beliefs must be established. First, bullying *is* a serious problem in most or all schools. Second, the situation *can* change, and the school is in the position to do something to stop bullying and harassment (Khosropour, & Walsh, 2001).

The Bullying Prevention Program: A Model Whole School Program

In 1996, the Center for the Study and Prevention of Violence in the United States with funding from the Colorado Division of Criminal Justice, the Centers for Disease Control, and the Pennsylvania Commission on Crime and Delinquency initiated a new project. The goals of the project were to identify ten violence prevention programs that met a very high, scientific standard of program effectiveness. The goal of this effort was to begin a national violence prevention initiative in the United States.

A key objective was to identify truly outstanding programs which would be described in the form of 'blueprints'. Blueprints were designed to provide *practical* descriptions of effective programs, which would allow states and local school systems to become aware of 'what works'. Ten Blueprints Model Programs were selected from a review of over 450 violence prevention programs that were examined. The criteria for selecting the Blueprints programs established a very high standard. The criteria included a strong research design, evidence of significant and sustained program effects, and, replication at multiple sites. Only *one* bullying prevention program was selected as one of the ten model programs, from all of the programs evaluated. This is the program designed by Dan Olweus, who is considered by some practitioners to be the principle expert in bullying in the world and whose initial studies are both large, complex, and far more extensive than studies done elsewhere.

Olweus (1993, 1999a) has reported that some elements of the Bullying Prevention Program are more critical than other elements. One identified, critical component is the process of *raising awareness* of bullying and involving the adults in prevention both within the school itself and also in the community. At the individual school level, a survey or questionnaire is critical, as well as a school conference day, to teach district rules and establish sanctions against bullying. Increased adult supervision is a critical component, especially in lower structure areas of the school. Firm, but not hostile, consequences for bullying must be implemented consistently. The Bullying Prevention Program includes establishing and enforcing specific classroom rules against bullying. The Bullying Prevention Project suggests rules that include making a commitment not to bully others, helping students who are bullied-including ALL students who are easily left out, and reporting bullying (Elliot, 2000).

Regular classroom meetings are a critical component of the Bullying Prevention Program. Holding discussions with children seated in a circle is strongly recommended. Class meetings become a kind of 'social control' through which classmates and teachers attempt to influence the behavior of bullies. At the individual level, serious talks with the specific children who have engaged in bullying behaviors and the individual children who are victimized are critical components. The goal is that the program will become a permanent part of the school culture (Elliot, 2000).

Evaluation of the Model

The "Bullying Prevention Program" designed by Dan Olweus (1993, 1999a) was originally systematically evaluated as part of an intervention project involving 2,500 children in forty-two schools from the city of Bergen, Norway, during the two and one-half year period from 1983 through 1985. Since that time, there have been numerous replications of the program, both within Norway and in several other countries. Most recently, a new large-scale intervention project involving 3,200 students in thirty schools was initiated in Bergen, Norway (Elliot, 2000).

In evaluation studies of Olweus' program, researchers use both self-reports and peer ratings in which students need to estimate how many classmates they consider bullies and how many classmates may be victims. Data is also collected from teachers. Research assistants collected the original data from children, because Olweus wanted to reduce teacher influence. The behaviors that were measured were clearly described, and the time lines during which observations were to be made were clearly specified. Data was collected at two points. Although it might have been expected that reports of bullying would have increased over the period between the two data collection points primarily because students became more aware of bullying after training, reports of bullying decreased (Olweus, 1991).

The Bullying Prevention Program using quasi-experimental designs has been demonstrated repeatedly in every country in which it has been implemented, to result in a substantial reduction (50% or more) in boys' and girls' reports of bullying and victimization. Effects were more marked two years later, as compared to one year later, with significant reduction in students' reports of general antisocial behavior such as vandalism, fighting, theft, and truancy. Studies demonstrated that there were *significant* improvements in the "social climate" of the schools that participated in the program. Importantly, there was no displacement of negative behaviors to other environments such as on the way to school or on the way home, and both primary and secondary prevention results were identified (Elliot, 2000; Olweus, 1993; Olweus, 1999a).

Olweus continues to evaluate the data first collected in 1985. Recent analysis of the 1985 data showed that two percent of students reported having been bullied by their teachers. In eleven of the classes surveyed, students reported that one student in the class was bullied by the teacher. Olweus (1999a) feels that bullying by teachers deserves more attention from researchers. He feels that some individual teacher behavior may exacerbate bullying by modeling it in the classroom and by identifying potential victims for bullies.

The Bullying Prevention Program has been implemented in elementary, middle, and junior high schools. Results depend on the degree with which the core components of the program are implemented. Students report somewhat stronger effects than do teachers (Olweus, 1999a). The Bullying Prevention Program is considered the most effective, anti-bullying school level program of *all* programs that have been developed to date (Barone, 1997).

Attempts to Implement the Program

The Bergen Study by Roland, also conducted in Norway, did not replicate the strong effects of the original Olweus study. In fact, the results were partly negative. Olweus (1999a) feels that the reasons for this were differences in preparation, differences in the quality of the data collected, different timing of the measurements taken, and the lower amount of support provided for the school staffs in the Bergen study. In the Norway intervention project, a good deal of support for school staff had been provided by consultants, which may account for differences.

In the United Kingdom, there have been two intervention efforts to address bullying using components of the Bullying Prevention Program. The Safer Cities Project in Wolverhampton and the Sheffield Project each used components of the Olweus program (Sharp & Thompson, 1994). Reductions in bullying were small in the secondary schools in the Safer Cities Project (Smith, 1999). In the Sheffield Project, primary schools showed decreases on average of fifteen percent in bullying, with some schools showing much greater reductions. Success in secondary schools was quite varied. Students said that they were more likely to tell teachers if they were bullied after the interventions, especially in secondary schools. This was an increase of thirty-percent as compared to attitudes before the program was implemented (Whitney, Smith, et al., 1994).

There were reductions in all types of bullying on playgrounds. Researchers concluded that the greater the effort to make change, the better the outcomes. The Sheffield project did not obtain the degree of reduction in bullying that Olweus demonstrated, although the reductions were greater than those found in Canadian studies reported in the 1990s and reported below (Whitney, Smith, et al., 1994).

The differences between results of interventions in primary as compared to secondary schools were hypothesized to be due to the fact that greater effects were found in smaller schools. Most primary schools are smaller than secondary schools. Another difference between the English and Norwegian schools was the transition age between primary and secondary schools. Transition periods generally show increases in bullying; so when data is collected, the data becomes skewed for the first year in a new school. The changes in secondary schools in the Sheffield project were described as more in attitude and in the school culture, as opposed to the actual behavior of students (Sharp & Thompson, 1994).

In Canada, the Toronto Board of Education conducted an intervention in four elementary schools modeled on Olweus' program. The teachers were given the responsibility to develop the intervention, identifying preferred interventions in their respective schools (Pepler, Craig, Ziegler, & Charach, 1994). Eighteen months into the intervention, students reported an eighteen percent decrease in having been bullied in the past five days and a seventeen percent decrease in the percentage of students who said they would join in bullying others. However, more students said that they were bullied because of their race, more admitted that they had bullied others, and there was no decrease in numbers of students who felt badly when they saw others bullied after implementation. Researchers felt that it may take as long as three to five years to fully realize changes using a whole school approach (Pepler, Craig, Ziegler, et al., 1994).

The Toronto pilot study, using components of the Olweus' program, showed a thirty percent reduction in reports by students of victimization in schools after the first six months of the intervention. Eighteen months into the intervention, fewer students reported that they thought about joining in the bullying and more students reported incidents. In spite of these changes, the percentage of bullies increased as did racial bullying (Harachi, Catalano, & Hawkins, 1999a).

The Flemish Anti-bullying Project also utilized Olweus' program. Research on the Flemish attempt to implement the program determined that *moderate* implementation in primary schools was sufficient to get positive results, but the same amount of implementation in secondary schools did not result in the same degree of success. The difficulty that schools had in implementing the program at the secondary level was attributed to the attitude of adolescents that rules are *changeable* agreements between people. Sanctions against bullying appeared to set up a conflict between teachers' needs for order and students' needs to gain social rewards from peers (Stevens, Van Oost, & De Bourdeaudhuij, 2001).

The Olweus program was implemented in South Carolina in the United States. After seven months of the program, students who received the program reported a decrease of 25% in bullying and a slowed rate of engagement in other antisocial behaviors. Elliot (2000) reports that the program appeared to slow the degree to which negative behaviors typically rise in schools in that area of the country. Cumulating studies suggest the success of the Bullying Prevention Program depends on how well the core components of the program are implemented. Olweus (2001a) feels that there are 'dosage-response effects' when the program is implemented. When more components of the program are included, there are better results.

The Bullying Prevention Program has been implemented in Canada, England, Finland, Germany, Holland, Norway, and the United States (Elliot, 2000). When Olweus' program has been implemented elsewhere in full or when adapted to fit the particular area, it appears that school personnel are able to implement the key components of the model adequately. Researchers who have reviewed the adapted models feel that it is important to set objectives that fit the target school's population, to include parents, to develop family interventions, and to pay attention to how processes are adopted for the particular school in question (Stevens, DeBourdeaudhuij, & Van Oost, 2001).

It appears that it is more difficult to implement the program at middle and secondary schools. Teachers at these levels find it difficult to provide the amount of supervision of students needed and to hold the classroom meetings that are so important for shaping attitudes. The demands on teacher time are difficult to meet at these levels as well as the demands for ongoing training of staff (Elliot, 2000).

The Expect Respect Project

The Bullying Prevention Program is not the only school-wide program used by schools. The Expect Respect Elementary School Project is an example of another comprehensive prevention project. The Expect Respect Elementary School Project is a prevention program that utilizes a curriculum developed through the Center for Research on Women, at Wellesley College, in the United States. The curriculum focuses on negative attitudes such as the acceptance of bullying in school communities. This project was funded by the U.S. Centers for Disease Control and Prevention for three-years in six elementary schools in Texas (Khosropour, & Walsh, 2001; Sanchez, Robertson, Lewis, Rosenbluth, Bohman, & Casey, 2001).

The Expect Respect project is a whole-school intervention model. Early findings from an evaluation project of the program at grade five indicated that indirect bullying was reduced. Observers noted that teachers dealt with girls bullying more than they addressed boys bullying (Khosropour, & Walsh, 2001). Effects were identified in increased awareness of bullying and its effects, in knowledge about sexual harassment, and in regard to students' attitudes toward helping a student who was being bullied. The program did not fully dispel the concept that the bully's intentions do not matter. This had been one of the principle concepts covered by the curriculum. In addition, it was difficult to teach the concept of 'bullying' to Spanish speaking children, because there is no Spanish equivalent for the concept of bullying (Sanchez, et al., 2001).

BULLYING PREVENTION AROUND THE WORLD

Rigby (2002) completed a meta-analysis of studies designed to address bullying in eight different countries, including the United States. The areas in which programs were similar were staff training and the involvement of all stakeholders, to include not only students but also teachers and parents. Programs were similar in curricula that addressed social skills for young students and conflict management for older students, as well as bullying. In addition, improved monitoring and supervision during recess, teaching students who are victimized to ask for help, and a specific plan to deal with bullies were common among the variety of programs. The main differences in programs had to do with how to address bullying when it occurred.

Most studies reported reductions in bullying of around fifteen percent. These effects were found primarily among younger children. Greater changes occurred in reduced numbers of students being victimized, than in reductions in numbers of bullies. The more time and effort that staff invested the better the results. Rigby (2002) could *not* determine whether or not approaches to bullying that used problem solving worked better than approaches that set firm consequences for bullying, although the former approach does have good support.

SUMMARY

Prevention programs in schools need active leaders and careful planning. They need to begin in the early grades and extend over time, involving the entire school community.

An outstanding example of a whole school intervention program designed to address bullying is the Bullying Prevention Program. The Bullying Prevention Program, designed by Dan Olweus, is the best-researched intervention available. It involves a number of core elements and supplementary elements. Replications of the Bullying Prevention program have determined that success depends on the degree to which core components of the program are included and the amount of time and energy school personnel are willing to give to efforts to reduce bullying behaviors. It is more difficult to implement bullying prevention programs at the middle school and secondary level. In general, bullying prevention projects have been able to reduce bullying by about fifteen percent in schools in which programs have been implemented.

CHAPTER 12

Interventions for the High and Low Structure Areas in Schools

The classroom is considered a high structure area in schools. When students are in class, teachers are more likely to address unwanted behaviors. Embedding a curriculum within the general curricula which addresses the ways in which students interact with one another is an accepted approach to reducing bullying in school. Two important low structure areas in schools are the school lunchroom and the playground. It is in the low structure areas where there is a higher likelihood of non-professional supervision. Of course, the lunchroom and playground and are not the only unstructured areas in schools. Increasing adult monitoring in hallways and around lockers is also very effective in reducing bullying (Conoley, Hindmand, Jacobs, & Gagnon, 1998).

LEADERSHIP IN INTERVENTION WORK

Mental health workers, such as school psychologists, may be the ideal individuals to take a leadership role in attempts to change schools. School psychologists are trained in conflict resolution, program planning, program evaluation, and communication. School psychologists can help select curricula with research support and can participate in teaching curricula covering bullying issues, facilitating discussions with students or teaching lessons. They can take leadership roles involving the training of teachers and supervisors who will monitor students. They can bring expertise to the challenge of planning, implementing and evaluating anti-bullying interventions in both the high and the low structure areas of schools.

INTERVENTIONS FOR THE CLASSROOM

The most effective whole school programs designed to reduce bullying in schools include the use of a specific curriculum implemented at the classroom level (Swartz, 1999). There is general agreement that prevention programs should address students' attitudes. When students are taught positive beliefs and are given standards which teach them to reject negative behaviors of peers, the risk of violence may be reduced (Hawkins, Herrenkohl, Farrington, Brewer, Catalano, Harachi, & Cothern, 2000).

In reviewing the different approaches that could be used in classrooms, the Centers for Disease Control and Prevention have determined that social-cognitive approaches are particularly useful when school staff want to try to prevent violence in schools. These approaches take into consideration children's thoughts and beliefs as well as their behaviors and the influence of the environment. In fact, these approaches are currently considered to be 'best practices' (Thornton, Craft, Dahlberg, Lynch, & Baer, 2000). Unfortunately, programs currently on the market use only some of the components of the social-cognitive model.

Issues around Prevention Interventions

More than 300 violence prevention interventions have been published, but many have not been evaluated scientifically in regard to their effectiveness (Swearer, Song, et al., 2001). Researchers agree that few of the hundreds of programs that have been developed have been evaluated thoroughly. (Clayton, Ballif-Spanvill, & Hunsaker, 2001).

Most of the research on the effectiveness of school-based interventions has only correlational support (Boxer & Dubrow, 2002). Many programs do not monitor the integrity of their programs. They do not monitor whether or not the specific intervention generalizes and do not use sound designs to determine outcomes. They do not use a variety of methods to measure outcomes or whether or not those who use them feel that they are effective. A recent study of thirty-four broad programs found that *none* were efficacious and *only five* were 'possibly efficacious'. In addition, teacher manuals are often difficult to use (Leff, Power, Manz, Costigan, & Nabors, 2001; Zaff, Calkins, Bridges, & Margie, 2002).

Beyond this, few evaluations have even looked at whether or not the programs were implemented properly. This is critical in any evaluation, in order to determine if the various aspects of the program actually caused the changes seen. When determining whether or not implementation was successful, the training of staff, the actual performance of staff, and support for the program each need to be examined (Zaff, Calkins, Bridges, & Margie, 2002).

School-based professionals need some way to determine whether or not these programs might be effective in their school and when they decide to implement a new program, curriculum, or intervention (Swearer, Song et al., 2001).

THE PROGRAMS USED BY SCHOOLS

Researchers, school psychologists, and other mental health workers have developed a variety of programs to reduce bullying and prevent school violence. These include peer mediation programs, affect control training, violence prevention curricula, social competency programs, and bullying prevention programs. A complication of attempting to categorize programs is that a number of programs combine several approaches, such as peer mediation and conflict resolution.

Peer Mediation

Peer mediation has been implemented in some schools, because it has been determined that even elementary school-aged students can learn to mediate conflict (Bowman, 2001b). Peer mediation is not specifically designed to address bullying. Conflict resolution curricula is often paired with peer mediation programs (Skiba & Peterson, 2000).

Violence Prevention Curricula

There are several general categories of *violence prevention* curricula: conflict resolution curricula, social problem-solving curricula, and specific violence prevention curricula.

The Hamilton Fish Institute worked with researchers from the University of Maryland to identify violence prevention programs that met the criteria of broadness. They selected programs that were only one component of wider efforts within a given school or district. The programs identified by the Hamilton Fish Institute have been evaluated. They each include a curriculum guide. Each program has been examined in terms of intervention effects. Included in their list of effective programs are the Anger Coping Program, BrainPower Program, and First Step to Success (Hamilton Fish Institute, n.d.).

Clayton et al. (2001) also reviewed the large number of curricula and programs with the goal of identifying those that were specifically designed for elementary schools. They looked for curricula that taught conflict resolution and that had been validated as effective or have been identified as promising. This effort resulted in thirty programs thought to be promising or effective. Six anti-violence programs, three conflict-resolution, and nine peacemaking programs were deemed to be effective using their criteria.

Leff, Power, et al. (2001) reviewed thirty-four violence prevention programs. They set criteria for judging the programs efficacious or possibly efficacious. They looked for strong research designs and strong intervention procedures. They felt that both staff training and monitoring how interventions were implemented were critical. They looked for varied measures of outcomes using instruments with at least adequate reliability and validity. They required follow up of outcomes for at least six months after the intervention and replication by independent scientists in order to consider the programs 'established'. *None* of the programs that were reviewed were able to meet *all* of the criteria set in regard to efficacy. Five programs met sufficient criteria to consider them 'promising'.

The five programs that were felt to be promising included Promoting Alternative Thinking Strategies (PATHS) and Second Step, which are designed for all children in a school. In addition, the First Step to Success, the Anger Coping Program, and Brain Power Program were considered promising but these are small group interventions designed specifically for aggressive students. Common to most programs, an independent evaluation of outcomes was the missing piece which prevented programs from demonstrating efficacy (Leff, Power, et al., 2001).

Social Competency

There are a number of broad programs that have been built around the development of social competency and/or academic competence. Most social competency programs are skill-based. Social competency programs may or may not include specific lessons designed to reduce bullying behaviors. Finally, there are specific programs for bullying prevention.

EVALUATION OF THE VARIOUS APPROACHES

Research on conflict resolution programs in general shows that students learn the mediation process as a result of training. However, there has been no solid evidence of reduced violent behaviors in the schools using the programs demonstrated to date (Shapiro, Burgoon, Welker, & Clough, 2002). Questions have been raised about peer mediation programs in regard to efficacy. Practitioners must consider whether or not a program that they might want to implement has been independently evaluated (Leff, Power, et al., 2001). Some researchers feel that peer mediation is a poor solution to bullying problems. A victim cannot mediate with a bully because there is a power difference. If the mediators selected by the school staff are the popular students, at some grade levels, these may be the students who are also involved in bullying behaviors which would make it very difficult for victims to trust them in a mediator role.

Conflict-resolution curricula add the skills training children need to deal with conflict when it occurs and are typically designed for all children in a school. However, these programs do not always include teaching prosocial skills. Edwards (2001) identified a critical problem with programs based on conflict resolution. These programs place responsibility for control of violence on student-to-student communication with the assumption that student-to-student dialogue can solve the problem. Edwards also indicates that it is inappropriate to call conflict resolution, peer-mediation, and anger management programs, '*prevention*' programs, because they are designed to deal with behaviors *after* they occur. On the other hand, Boxer and Dubow (2002) feel that aggression-reduction school programs *are* helpful. They have modest-to-moderate effects with younger children, where they are have been shown to work to some degree.

Anti-violence programs appear to be successful in teaching skills to aggressive children to avoid getting involved in inappropriate behaviors, but these program do not include skills training to deal with conflict when it occurs. Peace programs address resiliency for all children in the school community. Some peace programs also address the needs of at-risk children, in addition to the basic peace curriculum (Clayton et al., 2001).

SELECTING OR DESIGNING THE PROGRAM
FOR A GIVEN SCHOOL

Boxer and Dubow (2002) recommend that schools conduct needs assessments and design interventions around the specific concerns raised by staff and parents in a given school. It is important, from their point of view, to begin training in the first three grade levels. Consequences for negative behavior must be clear, consistent, and then implemented in all areas of the school and in all grades. Programs should be designed to deal with teasing, disruptive behavior, and verbal put-downs, which are precursors of more harmful behaviors. The major concepts of the program need to be incorporated into the general grade level curricula. The ecology of the school must be taken into consideration, and the extended community must be involved if the program is going to be successful. It is critical to measure outcomes and take a long-term view, so that the program becomes embedded in the school culture. Spending time on social issues is important.

It is critical that any program that might be implemented in the classroom be evaluated for effectiveness. It is also critical that prevention efforts be extended beyond the classroom to make sure that they generalize to the unstructured areas of a school. When implementing programs, integrity checks are needed along with multiple measures of outcomes. Measures of both negative and positive behaviors should be made and long term effects must be planned for in advance. Checks to determine whether school staff and parents are satisfied with a program are important (Leff et al., 2001).

It is also important to make sure that a program that is selected is culturally relevant (Leff et al., 2001). Multi-cultural concerns and culturally relevant material are extremely important to consider when choosing a program. A curriculum also needs to match the developmental level and interests of students. Programs need to be comprehensive and appropriate for *all* children. Teacher training is extremely important so that the programs are implemented correctly. Teachers benefit from learning to interact differently with students so that the school culture is changed.

A key goal for program success may include strategies to help children feel better about themselves (Clayton et al., 2001).

Any curricula chosen by practitioners should meet the specific needs of the school involved and should be part of a more comprehensive prevention/intervention program. Unfortunately, many programs do not monitor integrity of implementation, do not use a variety of methods to measure outcomes, and are difficult for teachers to use. Each of the several types of programs described has strengths and weaknesses. When considering programs specifically for prevention of bullying, programs selected need not only to *reduce* aggressive behaviors but also need to *increase* prosocial behaviors among students and must change student attitudes. In theory, the programs that directly address bullying would seem to be best yet these programs are the *least well* researched and are the newest category of curricula.

INTERVENTIONS FOR THE LOW STRUCTURE LUNCHROOM

Part-time workers or monitors are often placed in charge in lunchrooms in public schools in the United States. These individuals are not typically trained to manage discipline issues. Lunchroom monitors are not often supported in their dealings with students and rules are often lax.

The Sheffield Project in England included work with lunchtime supervisors in several schools. Schools were offered assistance with training of lunchroom monitors and with ways to improve the status of lunch supervisors. The project also addressed improving relationships between students and between lunchroom supervisors and teachers. Training sessions involved morning meetings to teach lunch staff about bullying behaviors, and strategies for preventing and decreasing these behaviors (Whitney, Rivers, Smith, & Sharp, 1994).

School psychologists and other school mental health workers can become involved in training lunchroom staff and in facilitating relationships between lunchroom monitors and teachers. Students need specific instruction in treating all adults in the school community with respect.

INTERVENTIONS FOR THE SCHOOL PLAYGROUND

It has been shown that there is inadequate supervision on playgrounds, as well as in other low structure areas in schools (Asidao et al., 1999; Barone, 1997). Olweus found that as the number of playground supervisors increased bullying decreased. Supervision is expensive. The cost of increased supervision is not a priority in school budgets. Not only do staff need to watch students carefully, they need to get out on the playground on time (Craig, Pepler, & Atlas, 2000). Even in schools where trained teachers have recess duty, teachers cannot reduce bullying when they are expected to manage large numbers of children. Schools may need to find ways to train paraprofessionals or volunteers in order to solve the problem of needs for increased supervision on playgrounds.

Interventions to Reduce Aggression on the Playground

Although not designed to address bullying specifically, researchers at the University of Missouri-Columbia, in the United States, attempted to decrease problem behaviors on the playground using two interventions. First, they assisted a school team in designing lessons around behavioral rules for the classroom. The lessons defined rules, provided examples, modeled behavior, provided practice, and tested learning. A group token economy system was set up for recesses with wrist loops given to students who were behaving appropriately. Loops were collected after recess and teachers talked about behaviors with their classes after recess. Each class could vote on a reward when the container of loops was full. Students who chronically exhibited negative behavior continued to do so. Yet, across three recess periods the average number of problem behaviors dropped from thirty to twelve (Lewis, Powers, Kelk, & Newcomer, 2002). An intervention of this type may have the potential to be helpful in reducing bullying on the playground.

Role of Adults on the Playground

Since three-quarters of bullying takes place on the playgrounds, it is important to explore a variety of ways to reduce aggressive behavior on school playgrounds. Some practitioners have suggested that adults take part in children's games as a way of controlling the behavior of the group. Adult participation in games appears to prevent aggression. However, children cannot construct a social order with adults present. They are less likely to find a friend or learn to deal with conflict when adults take control of their games. Children already have very little free playtime in their highly structured lives filled with adult managed sports activities and various lessons. It may be that if adults organize activities and then step back, the negative effects of adult involvement could be prevented. This is particularly important in the case of special needs children who might otherwise not get to play with the group.

A great deal of the outside play in schools is active and rough. Boulton (1994) provided training tapes for playground supervisors to help them distinguish between rough and tumble play, and aggressive behavior. When fighting is playful, it is restrained. Roles are frequently reversed. Boulton's training emphasized that adults need to remain calm, listen to all sides, and avoid critical responses when mediating disputes. Labeling *behaviors* as unacceptable, rather than labeling the *child*, was stressed. Playground staff also needed a list of increasing consequences and they needed to manage students causing trouble without calling for the child's teacher to mediate because this immediately reduces the status of the playground supervisor with children.

One school used a system of cards for children who had engaged in inappropriate behavior on the playground. A yellow card was given to a child who had bullied others on the playground. This card needed to be signed by the recess supervisor at the end of each play period if the child exhibited good self-control. Once the child had five signatures, the child was free and clear of the card system. However, if a child received three yellow cards over time, the child was issued a red card. The red card indicated that parents would be notified and the child would not be allowed to attend school lunch or recess for one week (Boulton, 1994). Oakden (1997) added to this intervention by suggesting that the activity that the child would engage in on the playground be written on the card. This helped the playground supervisor know where the child would be playing. If the card was 'lost', the consequence was that the next two recesses were also 'lost'.

In the Sheffield Project, supervisors were introduced to children through an assembly with an explanation about the authority of the supervisors and how to address them. School staff was defined by the administration as *all* adults. Supervisors participated in some classroom activities, so the children would get to know them. Supervisors spent time with teachers, and teachers observed supervisors without taking over when there was a problem. When supervisors had been trained before working on the playground, interviews indicated that that there was a decrease in all types of playground bullying as reported by students. The longer the intervention the more positive the outcomes. The drop in bullying was forty to fifty percent over four terms (Boulton, 1994).

Supervisory staff need to learn to intervene immediately rather than waiting for serious incidents or until someone is hurt according to Olweus (1993). Inconsistent punishment for negative behaviors may be *worse* than not responding at all (Goldstein, 1999). Goldstein (1999) includes teasing and bullying in the category of low-level aggression. When teasing, bullying, and other manifestations of low-level aggression are tolerated or not handled very well, higher levels of aggression often follow. This occurs because as the frequency of low-level aggression increases, students are actually practicing aggressive behavior and becoming disinhibited with practice. Ignoring low-level aggression in the form of bullying facilitates its development in frequency and intensity.

Teaching children the rules of the playground explicitly is important. In discussions with students, Walker et al. (1995) recommended making lists of the rules of the playground, directly teaching the rules once they have been determined, and using incentives to make certain that they are obeyed. Boulton (1994) suggests that activity areas can be set up with passive games or reading areas for students when recess must occur indoors. Indoor recess is another period during the school day when supervision can be lighter. Older students might be recruited to help supervise, play with, or read to younger students. Recess in elementary schools is typically scheduled so children who are in adjacent grades are on the grounds together. Innovative schools have changed this tradition, mixing older with younger students at recess. Older students were trained to interact with younger students using peer mediation techniques (Brooks, 2002).

One obvious intervention is to provide sufficient equipment and space for games (Ross, 1996). Adding more organized activities and more interesting activities to playgrounds has been suggested by several researchers working on reducing bullying (Swearer & Doll, 2001). Adding organized, cooperative games at recess can reduce aggression by more than 50% (Embry, 1997). It is also particularly helpful if an adult at each grade level or at each recess/play area is designated as the person to whom students can report incidents and know that they will be heard (Lazarus, 2001).

Students indicate that bullying occurs in the hidden areas of playgrounds or around corners where adults cannot easily see what is happening. Some playground equipment hides bullies from view. The combination of not enough to do and many hidden areas is an open invitation for low-level aggressive behaviors to occur. In schools where the play period is quite long, there is more aggression toward the end of the lengthy lunch period (Swearer & Doll, 2001).

It is also important to understand that some of the practices that schools have put in place to deal with aggressive behavior may actually *increase*, rather than decrease, the frequency of bullying. If playground monitors are told to 'find bullies', this can increase the focus on bullying and cause it to increase. Competitive games on the playground increase aggressive behavior. Frequent calls to parents to report the negative behaviors of their children may increase negative behavior and the negative feelings of the student toward school (Embry, 1997).

Playground Equipment and Design

The Sheffield project provided additional equipment for the playground. The process that schools used to improve the equipment was complex, in that students were involved in the design and choice of equipment. Three of four schools improved their playgrounds. One school with high levels of student and parental involvement in improving the playground was second of the twenty-three schools in reducing the frequency of bullying. This school had the lowest percentage of children who said that they were bullied on the playground (Higgins, 1994).

SUMMARY

School psychologists, and other mental health workers, are in a position to become involved in classroom lessons and in the training of teachers and supervisors who monitor students. Their training in program development and program evaluation will be valuable assets to schools.

Although practitioners have many programs from which to choose when considering classroom curricula to support bullying prevention efforts, many programs on the market do not have adequate support. Many programs do not monitor integrity of implementation, do not use a variety of methods to measure outcomes, and are difficult to use. Each type of program has strengths and weaknesses. When considering programs specifically for prevention of bullying, students need not only to reduce aggressive behaviors, but, also, need to increase prosocial behaviors and change the attitudes of children and adults in the school. Anti-bullying programs are the least well researched and the newest category of curricula available for teachers and mental health workers to use in the classroom. Any curricula chosen by practitioners should meet the specific needs of the school involved, and should be part of a more comprehensive, prevention/intervention program.

Staff training for lunchroom and recess monitors is extremely important. The status of these important members of the staff must be elevated if they are going to be able to reduce bullying. Not enough to do and areas outside the building that are unsupervised are key facilitators of bullying. Cooperative games, on the other hand, reduce aggressive behavior on the playground by fifty percent. Involving children in the redesign of playgrounds to reduce bullying would not only would increase their awareness of bullying but may help them understand that all children's needs must be considered and are important.

CHAPTER 13

Teasing and Low Level Aggression

School personnel tend to look at bullying incident by incident. Teachers deal with teasing one incident at a time. Teasing is pervasive in our culture. In the same way that bullying occurs worldwide, teasing is a problem in every school everywhere.

ATTITUDES TOWARD TEASING

We tend to think of teasing as play or fun. We teach toddlers to tease in a game-like manner. Most children will tease and call others silly names by age three or four. Although most children experiment with teasing and name-calling by three or four years of age, they are more likely to do so if the children or adults around them engage in and model these behaviors. Teasing is clearly evident in groups of children by age five. Most children do not tease because they are angry or want to hurt others at the preschool level (Butler & Kratz, 2000). Four-and five-year-old children do engage in destructive teasing and taunting behaviors and are rated negatively by both teachers and peers. In fact, children who tease are rated even more negatively than children who express anger during peer conflicts (Miller & Olson, 2000). Teasing is pervasive among young children and continues to increase through the middle school years.

School personnel tend to consider children's complaints about being teased as minor incidents. Adults often address teasing in an offhand manner. Humor can become teasing and bullying quite easily. Students need to be taught the rules about making jokes about others. When making a joking statement, a student's comment needs to be exaggerated so it cannot be misinterpreted. When a child becomes upset by comments or jokes, the child is being teased or bullied (Bryant, 1998). These concepts need to be taught to all students in schools.

Teasing is a two-sided behavior. On one side, the person doing the teasing is having fun *with* the other person. On the other side, the individual who is teasing is making fun *of* the other person. When people tease each other, intentions can be quite mixed. When a bigger child teases a smaller child, when a teacher or parent teases a child, or when a smarter, stronger or more quick-witted peer teases a less competent child, the teasing becomes a *power* play. The child being teased is in the 'down' position. Some experts feel that teasing might be a strategy to deal with feelings of shame in oneself. Although this may fit some situations, teasing is also a strategy to trigger feelings of shame *in* others (Kayton, n.d.).

THE COMPLEXITY OF TEASING BEHAVIORS

We have far fewer few studies of teasing behaviors as compared to studies of bullying behaviors. Teasing is a more complex behavior than bullying because whether or not the behavior is considered to be teasing depends on whether or not the teaser intends to harm and/or whether or not the child being teased interprets the behavior as mean and hurtful. Teasing is challenging for this reason. Children must be able to perceive the intent of the teaser and interpret whether or not the intent is to harm (Seward, n.d.). Goldstein (1999) indicates that the identification of low-level aggression is subjective, but this should not dissuade adults from dealing with it.

Teasing is currently thought to be an aspect of bullying, part of the sequence of bullying, or a milder form of bullying. Bullying involves repeated verbal or physical mistreatment when there is an imbalance of power (Wiler, 1993). It may be that intent is important in distinguishing between teasing and bullying. Smith, Cowie, Olafsson and Liefooghe (2002) suggest that there is no intention of harming the other person in a situation where teasing is friendly. However, some teasing crosses the line and the intention is not friendly.

Children are socialized into teasing early on. Teasing behavior may be one of the ways that children learn about peer relationships and group culture (Goodman, 1999). Boys use teasing to interact safely with girls in elementary school. This behavior increases in middle school. Some writers feel that this is a way for boys to begin courting behavior. Unfortunately, teasing can lead to bullying and to sexual harassment (Pellegrini, 2001b). Teasing can be damaging to some children who are unable to handle it (Goodman, 1999).

Lumsden (2002) includes a number of aggressive behaviors in her definition of bullying that includes teasing. Teasing has been considered to be a *subtype of bullying* in some current studies. Verbal aggression and teasing are related constructs (Seward, n.d.). Some researchers feel that teasing differs from bullying only in degree. Teasing is part of the continuum of behaviors that some children use to hurt others (Froschl, Sprung, et al., 1998).

Olweus currently includes behaviors such as saying mean things, making fun of others, and name-calling when he specifies the behaviors of concern. He specifically indicates that mean and hurtful teasing *is bullying* when it is repeated and is hard for the victim to defend him or herself. Olweus would not consider teasing bullying when it is friendly and playful. Adults must be able to tell the difference between malignant and friendly teasing. He admits that the *perception* of the victim may determine the difference in whether the behavior is teasing or bullying (Olweus, 1999b; Olweus, 2001b).

Teasing is a common behavior in schools. More than twenty percent of children in a British elementary school said that experienced teasing behaviors every day. Nearly all of the children interviewed felt distressed about being teased (Crozier & Dimmock, 1999). In a study conducted in an urban school district in the United States, about one third of staff at the elementary, middle, and secondary school levels felt that teasing and/or bullying along with verbal threats were serious concerns. Teasing was a serious concern at *all* school levels (Massey, Armstrong, Boroughs, Santoro, & Perry, 2002). In urban schools in Florida, teasing among students was the strongest of three fairly equal concerns at the elementary school level. At the middle school level, teasing among students was the greatest concern of the top four issues. Teasing was the fourth greatest concern at the high school level. Authors concluded that teasing was a significant problem among students at all schools (Massey et al., 2002).

Ross (1996) points out that teasing is independent of bullying, and is a problem by itself. It can occur as part of a bullying incident or it can occur alone. Teasing has positive aspects. It can help build warm relationships in the family and can teach social skills in some corners of American culture. When teasing is positive, it is impersonal (Skernen, n.d.). However, teasing is often at the expense of the other person and is ambiguous.

Many individuals in our schools do not consider teasing serious. Teasing by a peer can be accepted by a student or not accepted. Acceptance of teasing depends on who is involved, the context, and whether it is clear that the teasing is part of the game. Children who think that teasing is positive are often the children *doing* the teasing. Teasing among older students is often more cruel and targets the other persons vulnerabilities (Ross, 1996).

Whether or not the teasing is positive, students don't feel positively about children who get upset when they are teased and do not feel sympathy for the child who is teased. Children seem to feel differently when making judgements about a child who is teased than they feel when they are teased themselves (Landau, Milich, Harris, & Larson, 2001).

Most of the teasing between eight to ten year olds is mean and provocative, more so for boys than girls. Teasing among boys involves intimidation, power, domination, control, humiliation, and threats. Girls can be socially mean, manipulating others. A group accomplishes most of the teasing at ages eight to ten against one child. Response to teasing is emotional at this age, but the children who have a tantrum in reaction to teasing or who are not socially skilled are *most* likely to be teased. Eight to ten year olds believe that they know how to stop teasing, but the strategies they use either don't work or increase the teasing (Walker et al., 1995).

INCIDENCE OF TEASING

Survey Data on Teasing

Shapiro, Baumeister, and Kessler (1991) found that ninety-seven percent of third and fifth graders admitted experiencing negative emotions including anger and embarrassment when they were teased. When teachers were asked how children should handle teasing, teachers said that they should ignore it. However, thirty-nine percent of the students said that they would respond in a hostile manner if they were teased.

In another study eighty-nine percent of students in grades two through five said that they had been teased with thirty-one percent of students admitting that they were teased on a daily basis. Students reported that they were teased in every school environment. Five percent of students said that they often or always teased others. Seventeen percent of students felt that teasing is a "big problem," and twenty-eight percent said, "teasing is never okay." Although 90% of students said teasing should stop, a high percentage felt that it depended on circumstances. Students in second grade reported being teased more than other grade levels. This is consistent with findings from the international research on bullying, possibly because this is the lowest grade level with which survey data is used. Being teased by brothers was strongly correlated with teasing others (Macklem, & Kalinsky, 2002).

DEVELOPMENT OF TEASING BEHAVIORS

Teasing in Families

It is more likely that children will tease others if the adults and children around them engage in teasing behaviors (Butler & Kratz, 2000). Clark (1987) feels that the interactions of family members play a key role in teasing behaviors. Affectionate teasing in families is confusing for children who have difficulty understanding the behavior, because of the mixture of ridicule and warmth.

Children imitate what happens to them at home. When their parents tease them or when older sisters and brothers tease them, children learn teasing behaviors and in turn tease others outside of their immediate families (McCoy, 1997). In a small study in United States, the strongest correlation found around teasing behaviors was that students who teased others in schools were teased at home by family members, particularly by their brothers (Macklem, & Kalinsky, 2002).

Why do Children Tease?

Teasing may be related to an odd kind of learning such as learning about differences or learning about what it feels like to be included or excluded. Some students may tease classmates because they are trying to understand what makes a particular child different or special. They tease children who are not as competent academically or who are handicapped. Children who are identified as needing special education services tend to get teased a good deal in some schools where there is no sanction against teasing (Freedman, 1999).

Some children tease to get negative attention. A common saying is that 'negative attention is better than no attention' at all. Some students tease because it is 'cool'. These children think that the more popular children might accept them if they join in teasing others (McCoy, 1997). Many students share that they teased others so that they fit into or find a place in the group, even though they knew the other child was stressed (Bernstein & Watson, 1997).

Goldstein (1999) suggests that teasing is associated with children's attempts to force peers to fit in with the group if they are different in any way. In addition, teasing may be a strategy that children use to express aggression in a safer way or even to communicate affection in a way that does not embarrass the child who is doing the teasing.

Children's Beliefs about Teasing

Interviews with fifth graders in the United States suggested that students think of teasing as a subtype of bullying. When they talked about teasing, students were really talking about verbal aggression which is currently considered a type of bullying. In fact, this is the type of bullying in which children engage most often. The word 'teasing' appears to be used by some children for all behaviors that are not physical. About half of the boys interviewed defined bullying and teasing in very similar terms. When thinking about interventions it may be very important to use children's definitions initially in a school discussion or program (Khosropour, & Walsh, 2001).

Responses to Being Teased

Individual views of teasing range widely. A student's views about teasing depend on the child's teasing history and the roles the child has played in the teasing interaction (Kowalski, 2000). The effects of having been teased can be serious just as the effects of having been bullied are serious. Studies indicate that the consequences of having been teased can include anger and thoughts about retaliation. Students report that teasing is hurtful to a greater extent than their parents believe. Being teased is likely to result in humiliation because it is so public. Children have significantly less ability than adults to get away from or to stop their persecutors (Landau et al., 2001).

Ross (1996) feels that teasing can be as damaging and as cruel as bullying for some children. Students teased as children may experience effects into adulthood. The children who have a strong temperamental trait of *emotional reactivity* are more sensitive to the shame involved in teasing (Kayton, n.d.). These children react quickly. They may cry or fight back, both of which may instigate more teasing. Teasing by itself can result in embarrassment, feelings of intimidation, worrying, and loneliness. Teasing alone can trigger retaliation, so teasing can be dangerous. The peer group looks at the target of teasing as timid and unpopular. Those doing the teasing are considered very visible and popular by the group. Targeted children become devalued just as children who are repeatedly bullied become devalued (Landau et al., 2001).

Landau et al. (2001) suggest that teasing can *not* be considered harmless and instead must be considered a type of bullying. They feel that teasing must be taken seriously. Goldstein (1999) feels that aggressive statements can be more harmful to an individual child than being hurt physically. Studies generally show that fifteen to twenty percent of all students have experienced a degree of teasing that could be considered to be damaging at school (Kayton, n.d.).

Children are teased for a variety of reasons. For example, girls who do not follow the dress norms for their group are teased (Schofield, 1984). Children who are overweight are frequently targeted for teasing (Neumark-Sztainer, Falkner, Story, Perry, Hannan, & Mulert, 2002). Almost one-quarter of the girls at junior and senior high schools teased by *both* peers and family said that they had attempted suicide. Twelve percent of boys teased by both sources said that they had attempted suicide. Being teased may be more damaging than is popularly thought (Eisenberg, Neumark-Sztainer & Story, 2003).

ADULT PERSPECTIVES ON TEASING

Landau et al. (2001) found that preservice teachers did not understand how stressful being teased was for children. Ross (1996) agreed that adults, in general, do not appreciate that worrying about being teased can be a major fear of young school-aged children. It is not surprising that adults do not know how much anger students' experience in association with being teased. Ross (1996) felt that lack of knowledge about the emotional reactions of students is a key reason why school administrators do not take action to stop it. Adults are unaware of the fact that being embarrassed in front of peers is a major fear of children in elementary school (Landau et al., 2001). This is likely to be the case among older students as well.

Teachers need to address even low levels of negative behavior. When low-levels of negative behavior such as name-calling teasing or shoving are tolerated in schools, behaviors will escalate. Teachers, however, need support when they try to enforce policies. They need support because children who bully are very powerful. Teachers may have to interact with them alone with no other adults to support them or to model effective interventions for them, which can be challenging (Garrity, Jens, et al., 1994).

STRATEGIES FOR HELPING CHILDREN DEAL WITH TEASING

Dorothea Ross (1996) provided information about several programs to deal with teasing. The programs taught children to ignore teasing or gave them a list of strategies using verbal responses to teasing. Both ignoring teasing and developing verbally assertive skills is challenging for victims of teasing. When training children to deal with teasing, it is important to teach strategies to stop teasing that take into consideration how the child will be perceived by classmates (Landau et al., 2001). Children must be taught to determine the motivation of the student who is teasing to avoid personalizing the events (Barker, n.d.). If the teasing isn't taken personally it is easier to respond unemotionally, which is also a challenge for targeted children.

Training Students to Deal with Teasing

When considering interventions for children who are teased, the individual child's temperament is important, as is the child's age and verbal ability. The best strategies for a given child fit that child's situation, age, skills, temperament, and the seriousness of the teasing incidents. Anti-teasing strategies cannot be simply described, they need to be mastered and practiced if the child is going to be able to use them successfully. Students need to be taught about personal safety, to stay with friends, and to avoid places that are hidden from adults.

When studying entry behaviors into children's groups, Corsaro (1979) found that children needed to attempt strategies repeatedly when they wanted entry into groups. In fact, when children made *three* attempts, they were most likely to be able to gain entry into a group. Anticipating that the same principle might be involved in other behaviors or situations, the goal in teaching strategies to deal with teasing might be to select several strategies that the child feels he or she could manage. The first strategy that a child attempts in a teasing situation, after assessing how dangerous the situation may be, ought to be the most comfortable strategy. Eventually, students might be able to develop a personal package of strategies that fit them well. Landau et al. (2001) suggest that children who are teased frequently require feedback on how well they can 'pull off' the strategy.

Training needs to begin by teaching the student to interpret whether or not a situation is safe enough to try out a strategy. Students need to understand that if they have requested that the teasing stop and it does not stop, it is okay to tell a trusted adult. It is also necessary to teach students that when teasing doesn't stop, involves touching, is threatening, or when it is extremely hurtful it is necessary to report the teasing to an adult. In this case, the situation is dangerous and the behavior may no longer be teasing (Macklem, & Kalinsky, 2002). Students need to be taught that it is most likely that several strategies will be needed and the strategies will need to be repeated until the child doing the teasing is convinced that teasing isn't fun anymore. Lists of strategies for dealing with teasing are readily available (Freedman, 1999; Kayton, n.d.; Lindgren, 1996). Organizing and matching the strategies to the student are another matter.

Taking Temperament into Consideration when Teaching Strategies

Training needs to take a child's temperament into consideration. Children who are inhibited are easily stressed in novel situations (Rubin et al., 1991). If a child tends to withdraw when stressed the child's goals are avoidant. Discussions around goals may be helpful so that the child's revised goal is to problem solve rather than withdraw. Internal 'pep' talks may be helpful so that the child can keep the level of emotion that is expereinced within limits. Children who experience intense emotions and are highly reactive will need to learn to hide their reactions from the bully. They need to avoid sending nonverbal stress signals to the bully which would be rewarding. Anger control training is needed for children who might behave aggressively when they are angry.

Self-control strategies must be mastered before more specific strategies are taught. Self-control strategies include staying calm under pressure and using well-known techniques such as deep breathing and/or counting backwards. Assuring oneself that the teasing can be handled requires concentration. Visualizing oneself in a quiet place also requires concentration, as does positive thinking. Simply distracting oneself may be useful when teasing occurs. All of these self-control strategies must be practiced or the child will not be able to call on them in an anxiety-provoking situation (Macklem, & Kalinsky, 2002). Assertive, nonverbal body language should be practiced. Children need to practice standing up tall, looking directly at the person who is teasing, relaxing one's body, and tightening one's facial muscles. The remaining strategies can be grouped according to the degree of emotional control required to use the strategy.

Children who are younger, who have limited emotional control of their anxiety, have disabilities, or who get upset quickly because they are reactive, need strategies that are brief or are focused internally. Simple strategies include avoidance of areas where there is little to no supervision and reacting in a neutral way to the teasing. If a child is going to look as if he or she is not responding to teasing, the child needs to look away from the other child and appear disinterested. A slightly more active and quick technique that does not require responding very much involves a quick shrug and walking away.

The next set of strategies requires a momentary confrontation and should not be used until the student can control himself or herself at least for a minute or so. These strategies include looking at the peer who is teasing and saying "so?," This is followed with a smile, a shrug, and walking away. Leaving assertively takes more self-control and involves looking directly at the person who is teasing, turning around, and walking away. For those who can manage to make one quick assertive statement, a statement can be made such as 'Leave me alone' or 'Find something else to do' before walking away.

If the student has more control, can remain calm, and can think while being teased, making a distracting statement about a nearby activity or stating the obvious, such as 'you're standing in the way', can be useful strategies. Making a statement over and over, such as 'Enough already, enough already', with a slight smile, can decrease the teasing.

Students who have a little acting ability and are in good control can use more sophisticated strategies. These include responding with a compliment, agreeing with the facts, or asking the teaser to repeat what he says over and over. When students are whispering, the target student could ask 'Do you have something to say?' Or, if peers are teasing, the child might say 'I don't see what's so interesting about that' or 'Makes sense to me'. These strategies need to be used without emotion or they will not be successful. Only children who are able to control their bodies, facial expressions, and tone of voice will be successful with this group of strategies.

Assertive strategies require confidence and experience. Assertive strategies include desists, fogging, come-backs, or reframing. Desists are strong statements such as, 'I'd appreciate it, if you'd cut it out'. Fogging is the technique of agreeing with everything the person says who is teasing. Come-backs involve mimicking, sayings, or comments such as 'Get a life'. Reframing is a strategy which turns the comment into a compliment, 'Thanks for noticing . . . '. For skilled and fast thinking, middle school-aged students, responding with humor works well. Adults use 'I feel' statements. Older students might use this technique but it doesn't typically work for school aged children unless there is a sympathetic adult within earshot.

These strategies have not been systematically evaluated for effectiveness but may give counselors some ideas for small group training in dealing with teasing. School psychologists can also help students by educating teachers and non-professional school staff about how stressful and upsetting teasing can be. School staff need to take teasing seriously and become as intolerant of hurtful teasing as they are of physical aggression (Landau et al., 2001).

SUMMARY

Teasing is both accepted and pervasive in our culture. Teasing is a complex behavior, because it depends on the reaction of the person being teased and the intention of the person who is doing the teasing. Teasing is most often considered a subtype of bullying or a low level of bullying. Students say that they don't like teasing but they are not sympathetic with children who react negatively to being teased. The effects of having been teased over time can be very serious, more so for some children than others.

Students need to determine if the situation is safe before they attempt to deal with teasing themselves. Strategies for helping students deal with teasing involve making judgements about the safety of the situation, learning self-control strategies, and then mastering several strategies to use when being teased that match one's emotional maturity, temperament, and age. Strategies must be practiced so students can use them under stress.

CHAPTER 14

Interventions for Bullies and Bully-Victims

There are a number of different approaches that professionals have taken to stop aggressive behaviors in schools. In addition to considering interventions for children who are generally aggressive, specific interventions are needed for bullies, and to some extent, different interventions are needed for children who both bully others and are also victims of bullies.

INTERVENTIONS FOR AGGRESSIVE STUDENTS

Aggressive behavior on the part of one child against another begins in the family. A child's siblings become the *trainers* for aggressive behavior, teaching verbal aggression first and then physical aggression. The highest levels of aggression and conflict observed between siblings have been found in families with older brother-younger sister dyads. The younger girl with an older aggressive brother is at risk for behaving aggressively if the difference in age is three years or less (Aguilar, O'Brien, August, Aoun, & Hektner, 2001).

Parents also teach aggressive behaviors when they do not follow through with requests for compliance when they tell the child to do something. Once a child is successfully noncompliant, the child experiences a sense of power; and this becomes the child's motivation in their interactions with other children and other adults. The child learns *not to respond* to the anger or disapproval of others (Goldstein, 1995).

Parent training is considered the most promising way in which to decrease aggressive behaviors in younger children. Unfortunately, parent training does *not* generalize to school relationships (Forehand & Long, 1991). Parent supervision is also important so children are not able to spend so much time with deviant groups (Dishion, Patterson, & Griesler, 1994). The goals of parent training should include changing what happens in the family when the child both behaves and misbehaves and teaching parents to stop the cycle of coercion (Coie & Jacobs, 2000). Parents and teachers can control aggressive behaviors somewhat, by limiting children's passive exposure to aggression. When time spent watching television and videos is reduced, aggressive behavior can be decreased in school (Robinson, 2001).

Since boys are involved in three times the incidents that girls are involved in, it is important to decrease aggressive behavior in boys when they are young (Froschl, Sprung, et al., 1998). The accepted approaches to intervention for aggressive children target both the family and the child. Parenting interventions with aggressive children have been *moderately successful* in preventing long-term, aggressive behaviors, especially when they focus on noncompliance. Peer relationships must be targeted also. Aggressive behavior that *works* with peers may contribute to the aggressive child's belief that aggression is a positive solution and a positive tool (Coie & Jacobs, 2000).

Teachers also have a role in reducing or maintaining aggressive behavior. In the school environment, teachers need to reward the behavior that they want consistently. They need to intervene when they observe behavior that they do not want, rather than letting it go (Coie & Jacobs, 2000). Approaches to dealing with aggressive students, (although they have not yet been demonstrated to be useful specifically for students who engage in bullying behavior), include behavioral management strategies, emotional control strategies, training in prosocial skills, training in social information processing, and training in perspective taking.

There is less research available on emotional control strategy training and social skills training than there is on behavioral management in helping aggressive students (Coie, Underwood, & Lochman, 1991). The most promising way to assist school-aged aggressive children is to increase their positive interactions with others in the class and to set up classroom interaction patterns, so that they spend time with prosocial children. This approach involves classwide involvement, such as cooperative learning. The networking of students in the class is the target of this type of intervention approach (Dishion, Patterson, & Griesler, 1994). Increasing positive interactions must be paired with consequences for aggressive responding. Dodge (1991) recommends consistent punishment for aggression and teaching the bully that aggression has negative ramifications. He also feels that cooperative behavior must be rewarded if it is going to continue.

There are a number of programs that have been designed to reduce the aggressive behaviors of school aged students. Any program that is implemented with small groups of students, particularly aggressive students, must be carefully controlled so that negative behavior is not rewarded by peers and so students cannot gain negative attention and approval for inappropriate behaviors (Leff, Power, et al., 2001).

INTERVENTIONS FOR HELPING BULLIES

A variety of interventions designed specifically for bullies have been proposed in the literature. These include: changing the environment by teaching peers to disapprove of bullying, increasing consequences when students engage in bullying, and working individually or directly with the bullies (Gottheil & Dubow, 2001b).

Consequences for Bullying

Bullies must have consequences for their behavior that are both immediate and long term. Immediate consequences are important because bullies have no reason initially to change their behavior (Gagnon, 1991). The longer-term consequences might be thought of as *formative* consequences, which offer opportunities to learn skills and insights. Beyond consequences for the immediate and specific incident that has just occurred, Pepler and Craig (2000) recommend that the bully be taught the difference between positive and negative power, beginning with impersonal examples from stories, books, movies or television. Training in perspective taking and empathy could take place during recess. Counselors and school psychologists need to explore ways to build on strengths with students and help them gain positive attention. Bullies might role-play being the victim and/or observe prosocial behaviors in others during recess with an adult acting as a coach. Finally, work with parents is critical.

Catching bullies in the act is difficult. Bullies tend to inhibit their behavior once they get what they want unlike other aggressive children and provocative victims who have difficulty with their emotions and cannot stop easily once they have become upset (Gottheil & Dubow, 2001b). Ross (1996) suggests using video cameras in school areas that have reduced adult supervision. This approach is controversial, but closer supervision and increasing external controls is extremely important. Bullies need to be told that the behavior must stop, that they will be watched closely, and that there will be consequences. Recess monitors need to let bullies know that they are being watched.

Remedial Efforts

Another important consideration is the thought that there may be a need for different interventions depending on which subtype of bully the intervention is attempting to change (Swearer, Song, et al., 2001). For example, the interventions that may assist bullies with strong self-control may not be appropriate for bully-victims. Efforts to reduce bullying must decrease both opportunities and rewards for the bullying behaviors (Ericson, 2001). Goldstein (1999) reminds us that in order to reduce bullying there must be interventions at the classroom level, the school level and the community level, as well as at the individual child level for children who are bully-prone.

Establishing Group Interventions

When establishing group interventions for children who bully others, it is important for school psychologists and other mental workers to plan the group experience carefully. When groups are formed of students who think alike, the effect is group polarization of attitudes. Negative beliefs will become more negative. Students will support negative comments overtly or covertly because participants in groups prefer to make *belief-supporting* comments. When no contrary voice is expressed, beliefs become exaggerated (Brauer, Judd, & Jacquelin, 2001). When the entire group has similar issues, the problem behavior becomes the group norm (Johnson, 1996). It is difficult for an adult to mitigate the effect of peers in homogeneous groups. Younger students do not seem to be as effected by deviancy talk nor do groups which include at-risk as well as typical students who are not interested in this type of discussion (Dishion, McCord & Poulin, 1999).

Peers influence each other to the extent that they can be thought of as *trainers in deviancy*. Correlational studies show that some adolescents use deviant talk as a way to develop friendship groups. Students' negative talk is subtly reinforced when peers laugh or show interest by attending to the negative model. Lower achieving students with behavior problems were more affected than others, so it is important not to group together lower achieving students with behavior problems (Dishion, McCord, et al., 1999).

Designing groups for children in schools in a practical sense is extremely difficult because of school schedules and other priorities. In small schools there may be situations in which a single child who bullies may need a group experience. Johnson (1996) reminds mental health workers that if the group is not safe for one child, even if that child is the bully, it is not safe for any member of the group. Placing one person in a group, who does not fit because that person is quite different from others, may set up that student as a scapegoat.

It is not only boys who bully, girls needs must be addressed as well. Rubin et al. (1991) suggested that aggressive girls may respond well to a social-cognitive intervention. Teachers have been found to be as skilled as peers in identifying girls who demonstrate relational aggression or indirect bullying when they are given clear and comprehensive definitions of bullying (Crick, 1996). It is important that teachers' and students' understandings of bullying include social aggression (Boulton & Hawker, 1997).

Because bullies have strong confidence in aggressive solutions to social difficulties, they may benefit from learning about and being rewarded for practicing and using nonviolent solutions to conflict situations (Haynie et al., 2001). Aggression Replacement Training (Goldstein, Glick, & Gibbs, 1998), the Anger Coping Program (The Hamilton Fish Institute, n.d.) and the Earlscourt Social Skills Group Program (Pepler, King & Byrd, 1991), may be useful in reducing aggressive behaviors including bullying in schools.

Helping Bullies Meet Dominance Needs

Bullies have needs just as other children have needs. One important consideration for bullies is school performance. Academic tutoring is important for children who are aggressive or rejected to help them find positive ways to succeed (Coie & Jacobs, 2000).

Dominance is a characteristic style of behavior or a temperamental quality (Rummel, 1975). When dominance is a strong trait in children, it can be observed in disobedience, teasing, insensitivity, bossy, and even bullying behavior. Bullies are power seekers. They exhibit unemotional, instrumental aggression. The goal of the bully is to get something that the child wants such as the 'upper hand' so that he or she is powerful socially. For bullies for whom power is a motivating source, personal goals need to be 'reframed'. Instead of acting in order to be socially dominant, bullies need to be taught to work for *social prestige* (Coie, Underwood, et al., 1991). Social prestige can be earned by being a positive leader if students are provided with opportunities to head group projects, to tutor younger students, to assist adults in problem solving or to sit on student councils. The dominant child with a tendency to bully others needs to learn to behave in ways that will allow the child to be well thought of or admired for positive contributions to the group.

This important intervention for some students who bully others involves teaching bullies alternative ways for getting their dominance needs met. Meeting dominance needs can be done in other ways as well, such as through assertiveness training. Keep in mind that students are taught to respect themselves and others, equally, as part of assertiveness training programs. Aggressive students behave as if their rights have a higher value than others rights and needs. A change in thinking is accomplished through assertiveness training. Through assertiveness training student will continue to feel powerful without stepping on others rights.

Teaching Empathy

Bullies are different from the broader group of aggressive children, in that they *intend* to cause the victim distress. Their goal is to overpower the child they bully, and they go after the same target again and again. Peers rate bullies as socially intelligent. The bullies who use indirect aggression are considered especially bright. Bullies need a good amount of social cognitive ability in order to manipulate others without getting caught (Sutton, Smith, & Swettenham, 1999). Verbal and physical victimization of peers, on the other hand, is not associated with social intelligence (Funke & Hymel, 2002).

Bullies, generally, are not sympathetic toward victims (Menesini, Eslea, Smith, Genta, Giannetti, Fonzi, et al., 1998; Sudermann et al., 1996). Empathy and aggression are not compatible (Newman, Horne, & Bartolomucci, 2000a). One strategy to consider for changing the behavior of bullies is empathy training.

Empathy training includes training students in perspective taking and instilling responsibility. Teaching approaches would include learning to label emotions in oneself and others, increasing awareness that people have different points of view, role-playing, and use of stories and literature. Trainers need to make it clear that empathy is a school value (Stetson, Hurley, & Miller, 2001).

Specific studies of bullies suggest that they may not be totally without empathy. There appear to be two aspects of empathy: an emotional aspect and a cognitive aspect. Emotional empathy is the aspect of empathy that is lacking in aggressive students. These students may have competence in regard to cognitive empathy because they have adequate social cognition and social intelligence, but they may lack the emotional component (Funke & Hymel, 2002).

MANAGING BULLYING INCIDENTS

When a bullying incident occurs, school personnel need to send the victim away from the situation to the protection of a teacher or school mental health worker. Once reported or caught, bullies need to be separated from the group. When bullies are confronted, it is critical that they don't have any more opportunities to gain peer attention. They need to be dealt with privately with as little attention as possible (Ross, 1996; Schwartz, 1999).

The bystanders need to be interviewed confidentially, and a record needs to be made of the incident. The bully is interviewed later and can be required to write an account of the incident. This account can be kept on file or mailed to parents, depending on the severity of the incident. Further involvement of parents depends on the severity of the incident and whether the incident is part of a pattern of incidents. Although school administrators may prefer to deal with behaviors in-house, at times parents should be informed (Elliot, 2000). Once the consequence is over, the incident is over (see Ross, 1996, pp. 107–108 for more detail). Sudermann et al. (1996) suggest that responses to bullies should be carefully designed. Harsh punishment can backfire in that bullies will become vindictive.

DeBruyn and Larson (1984) warn practitioners that there are several common errors school personnel make in managing bullies that may perpetuate bullying.

- Telling a bully that people won't like them and will get upset with them may backfire, particularly if the bully's motivation is to get attention.
- Publicly 'putting down' a bully will backfire as well.
- Making threats to try to get the bully to change his behavior has little to no effect.
- Responding inconsistently to a bully will not stop the behavior.
- Getting into arguments with bullies or their parents will not stop the behavior from occurring again.

INTERVENTIONS FROM THE LITERATURE

The literature on interventions for dealing with bullying includes several interesting possibilities, including bully courts, the No-Blame approach (Mains & Robinson, 1992), and the Method of Shared Concern (Pikas, 2002). Practitioners in the United States are not as familiar with these interventions as they may be with other interventions.

Bully Courts is an intervention that has been attempted in some schools in Europe. There is very little research on the use of bully courts in schools. The few studies available showed decreases in bullying but those studies that have been conducted are confounded, because there were other changes which could have accounted for reductions in bullying (Ross, 1996).

The 'No-Blame' approach is a counseling procedure. It was designed to avoid the possibility that punishment might result in enhanced status of the bully and place the victim at risk (Smith, Cowie, & Sharp, 1994). A group meeting is held with a group of students. The teacher presents the victim's view to trigger feelings of empathy in the group. Independent replication with more specificity about how to effect change of attitudes is needed before this intervention strategy is used widely. The No-Blame approach has been used in the United Kingdom (Demko, 1996).

The Method of Shared Concern for children older than nine was designed by Pikas in Sweden. Students discuss solutions for bullying in a series of meetings, and talk about how to make and maintain changes (Ross, 1996; Smith, Cowie, & Sharp, 1994). The 'Method of Shared Concern' differs from the 'No Blame Approach' in regard to who is talked with first. Pikas emphasized talking with bullies first, so that the victim has no need to 'tell on' the bully. He feels that it is important to speak individually with each child involved, so that stories can be safe from group influence (Ross, 1996).

Olweus has been critical of the 'Method of Shared Concern' because he feels that it relies on bullies feeling guilty. The research does not support that bullies are likely to feel guilty. Olweus describes the 'Method of Shared Concern' as 'manipulation' on the part of the adult to win the cooperation of the bully (Smith, Cowie, & Sharp, 1994). On the other hand, Smith, Cowie and Sharp (1994) have used the approach in their work and they feel that the fact that it does not require the bully to admit to anything is helpful.

Pikas (2002) in turn, is critical of whole school programs to counter bullying. He feels that the data to support a reduction in bullying in whole school programs is derived from attitude changes alone. He does not think that the attitudes of bullies will change through an attitude formation program nor will bystanders be affected if they feel innocent and uninvolved. In addition, Pikas is critical of simply increasing policing in low structure areas. Pinkas feels that only a consensus with students on preventing bullying through conflict mediation is likley to have a long-term affect on bullying.

INTERVENTIONS FOR BULLY-VICTIMS

The child who both bullies others and is bullied in turn needs special consideration, because this group of children is challenging to help. These students will require considerable time and effort on the part of school staff if interventions are going to be successful. In the case of bully-victims, forgetting that the bully may need protection, at times, acts against changing the child's behavior (DeBruyn & Larson, 1984).

Interventions Taking Temperament into Consideration

Bully-victims or provocative victims tend to have specific temperamental characteristics. These include poor self-regulation, high reactivity, sensitivity to negative stimuli, excitability, and impulsivity. When a child is highly reactive to challenging or threatening situations and *is also* poorly regulated, the child is less likely to respond effectively to being teased or bullied. It will be more difficult for this child to think of effective strategies to respond and to deal with the very strong feelings involved when the child is bullied (Teglasi & Epstein, 1998).

When a child has difficulty shifting his attention away from the stressful situation and remaining in control so that he doesn't react impulsively, he is likely to be delayed in the ability to regulate negative emotions. This, in turn, can result in reactive aggressive behaviors and bullying, which will cause peers to avoid or reject the child (Farmer & Bierman, 2002). In a potentially threatening, or even in an ambiguous interaction, the emotional context is the variable that controls how deeply a situation is processed (Ledingham, 1991). Reactive students are not problem solving very well when they are under pressure. Because emotions effect the processing of social cues, a child who experiences negative emotions might perceive another child's motivation as hostile (Seward, n.d.).

When a child experiences one negative emotion, additional negative emotions are likely to be triggered as well (Teglasi, 1998a, b). Negative emotionality is closely related with acting out (Furlong & Smith, 1998). Bully-victims assume that others have negative intentions when situations are not clear (Coie, Underwood, et al., 1991). Provocative or bully-victims tend to be restless, irritable, and end up losing in power plays with bullies (Garrity, Jens, et al., 1994).

Interventions that are appropriate for provocative victims include teaching emotional control strategies, teaching students how to process social-information, social skills training including how to enter groups and how to deal with teasing, compliance training, and anger control training. Provocative victims need to understand the consequences of engaging bullies and learn to identify their own motivations when they choose to interact with peers (Newman, Horne, & Bartolomucci, 2000a).

Training in Self-Regulation or Emotional Control

Bully-victims need to master emotional control strategies (Coie, Underwood, et al., 1991). They need to learn how to express feelings in a socially appropriate way. Training in self-regulation is important and difficult to master. Bully-victims need to learn to control both positive *and* negative feelings (Hubbard, 2001).

Cognitive Retraining

Social information processing interventions for bullies are important, because aggressive children have overly positive beliefs in regard to how well they are accepted by peers. This is likely to be a defensive, self-enhancing bias in the case of provocative victims. Interventions that focus on helping these students acknowledge mistakes and tolerate negative feedback are important. Accurate feedback in the context of acceptance is critical (Hughes, Cavell, et al., 2001). Work with bullies in regard to social information processing must be done in the early grades in school. Beliefs about the value of aggression begin to stabilize around fourth grade. Once these beliefs are stable, intervention would be far more challenging (Gottheil & Dubow, 2001b). Cognitive retraining is needed to help bully-victims understand that the motivations of their peers are often neutral rather than aggressive.

Social Skills Training

Walker et al. (1995) have identified several social skills that bully-victims need to master. These include how to join a group without disrupting the ongoing activity, dealing with being provoked, and compliance with adult demands. Provocative victims also need prosocial skills such as friendship making skills and 'reality-checks' in order to learn how their behavior affects others (Mullin-Rindler, 2001a).

Provocative victims' behavior appears to be a reaction to avoid looking help-less. They want to present themselves as if they can't be 'pushed-around'. They need to learn to 'win' by not letting others 'get to them'. Arguing with bully-victims when they are caught will not help. However, mobilizing peer disapproval of aggression is helpful in fostering self-control in bully-victims (Ross, 1996).

Compliance Training

Provocative victims need templates for compliance. Training should be sys-tematic, combined with coaching. Students need to learn the skills of negotiation and need to learn to give reasons for refusal in an appropriate tone of voice, if they are going to refuse to comply. This skill may prevent a confrontation with an adult. These students need to learn to negotiate for some leeway in the rules.

In addition, provocative victims need to learn about the expectations for behavior in unstructured and low structured areas. They need to know the recess rules, which often are unstated or differ from teacher to teacher. Rules need to be taught explicitly using positive and negative examples for each rule. Additional teaching techniques might involve discussion, role-play, coaching, and debriefing or dialoguing (Walker, Colvin, et al., 1995).

Anger Control Training

Gagnon (1991) reports that work with rejected children shows that time spent on control of anger makes a difference. Provocative victims need anger control training (Coie, Underwood, et al., 1991; Dodge, 1991; Gagnon, 1991). Anger control training involves the substitution of positive thinking for negative thinking. It teaches students to recognize body cues that will let them know themselves that they are angry (Haynie et al., 2001).

Behavioral Management

Only *after* training has made a difference in the behavior of the bully-victims, should contingency management be added to guarantee that students use their new skills (Walker et al., 1995). There is a tendency to use behavioral management techniques with provocative victims. Behavioral management tends to fail with provocative victims if it is used initially. Ross (1996) feels that students must be first taught that control is possible, and that control can be gained using strategies other than aggression. Assertiveness needs to be taught to replace direct aggression.

REPUTATIONAL BIASES

Sufficient investments of time and effort in addressing the needs of bullies and bully-victims so that they make changes in their behavior may not be enough. If school psychologists or school counselors are successful in helping a student to change his or her behaviors, the need for intervention may not be complete. The peer group may not accept a student who has made changes in his or her behavior as a result of interventions. The social status of the bully or bully-victim does not always improve, even when the child has been able to make significant changes in behavior. The group may continue to dislike the student who has developed a negative reputation (White, Sherman, & Jones, 1996).

Reputations, once developed, are communicated both verbally and nonverbally in children's groups. The child's reputation persists even after behavior improves (White et al., 1996). The child will continue to require support, and the peer group will continue to need attention from mental health workers.

SUMMARY

Procedures and processes for intervention with bullies have attracted considerable attention in the literature. Parent training is used in schools with some success to decrease aggressive behavior in young children. The cool headed bullies require external controls and close supervision. Specific interventions for bullies include teaching empathy, cognitive restructuring, aggression replacement training, anger coping, and social skills training. Several of the process approaches include Bully Courts, No Blame, and the Method of Shared Concern, but more research is needed for these approaches.

Since interventions for bully-victims must differ from interventions designed for bullies, the needs of these children are considered separately. Bully-victims need compliance training, training in anger control, training in prosocial skills, empathy training, and after progress has been made, contingency management is needed. A considerable complication in helping aggressive students is that bullies—particularly, bully-victims develop reputations. Reputational biases interfere with the likelihood that a child will be accepted by the peer group even after the child has gained control of his or her behavior and has made changes.

CHAPTER 15

Specific Interventions for Victims of Bullying

Just as group interventions are used as strategies to help children who bully others, victims can also be helped by group interventions. In the case of victims of bullying, just as in the case of aggressive students, groups must be designed with care for the protection of every child who participates. Students will not contribute in a group unless they feel valued. Students need to believe that they can contribute to the group and that they will personally benefit. It is also extremely important for each child in a group to have someone in the group that they like, is interested in them, or accepts them. This is, especially, important for victims of bullying (Johnson, 1996).

Groups that consist only of victims are just as difficult to influence, as groups that are designed for students who act out. These students will reinforce each other's beliefs in the same way that aggressive students influence one another's thinking. Victims have particular worldviews and attitudes toward dealing with their more powerful peers.

PROCESS FOR INTERVENING WITH VICTIMS

In order to help victims, children need to share that they have been bullied. Rigby and Barnes (2002) found that between seventy and eighty-two percent of students who had been bullied told someone about it at least once. Ten percent of those who told said that telling made it worse. When school staff either do nothing to help or react so strongly that the child who tells is placed in a difficult or dangerous position, students will not report bullying in schools. Adults must be prepared to react in ways that will protect students from negative outcomes.

There has been significantly less research conducted on programs specifically designed for children who have been victimized than for students who are aggressive bullies. Schools tend to concentrate on the bullies rather than focusing on the children who have been victimized. The victims have not received much attention (Miller & Rubin, 1998). It is extremely important to be responsive when a child reports being teased or bullied. If a victim's reports are discounted or the adult does not respond with empathy, the child is victimized twice (Newman, Horne, & Bartolomucci, 2000b).

Pepler and Craig (2000) point out that it is imperative that adults attempt to see the situation from the victim's point of view to prevent themselves from minimizing the plight of the victim. It is very important that school personnel do not tell the victim to solve the problem himself because by the time that the student tells a staff person, everything that the student could have done will have been tried unsuccessfully. Victims fail in attempts to deal with bullies because of the power imbalance in bullying. When an adult becomes involved after a bullying incident, the victim needs to be interviewed first. The victim needs assurance that the situation will be taken seriously and that he or she will be protected.

SPECIFIC INTERVENTIONS FOR VICTIMS

The several ways in which a student may respond to teasing and bullying have to do with the student's past experiences and temperament. Children who are extremely sensitive and children who are highly reactive need special consideration. Playful teasing and especially exclusion by peers can have a dramatic effect on a child with a sensitive temperament. Children who are inhibited can be stressed very easily (Rubin et al., 1991). Highly reactive children learn to avoid stressful situations (Carey, 1998). Evaluating a child's temperament can help school psychologists select specific strategies to teach to children to deal with bullies.

The primary responsibility for protecting the victim *lies with the school*, rather than with the student. Suggestions from the Bullying Prevention Program for helping children who are victimized include helping the student develop talents, helping the student make new friends, and giving the child physical training to help with coordination, increase confidence, and decrease body anxiety (Elliot, 2000; Olweus, 1993). More formal interventions include cognitive interventions, social skills training, training in self-regulation, training students to report bullying, and assertiveness training. Students need training in self-regulation so that they can remain calm in the face of bullying (Mullin-Rindler, 1998).

Support Groups

Children who experience a good deal of stress at school tend to respond both passively and ineffectively. However, students who believe that they have peer support, tend to use active strategies and look for help from friends (Elting &

Demaray, 2002). Emotional support is vital for students who are very stressed by bullying. Informal support is more useful than formal support (Bryant, 1998).

Cowie and Wallace (2000b) suggest that peer support is an effective approach to assisting students in schools where bullying is a problem. When a variety of peer support interventions were evaluated eighty-two percent of students found it 'very helpful' or 'helpful' but eighteen percent of students did not find them helpful. The benefits reported by students included having someone to talk to, feeling supported in efforts to deal with the situation, and knowing that someone cares about them. Helping the victims of bullying develop strengths and friendships is important.

School psychologists and counselors can help by forming informal support groups around a child who has been victimized. Establishing activities during indoor and outdoor recess and by asking teachers to seat victimized children near peers who may include the child is helpful. Support groups help students with a variety of needs to learn to behave like their peers, become accepted, and experience a sense of belonging. Ross (1996) suggests that groups should not be too large. Group size such as six students at the elementary level, ten students at the middle school level, and twelve students at the secondary level work well. She suggests that same-sex groups are best for victims to avoid embarrassment. The support groups can also be used to provide skills training.

Canadian studies suggest that because children who are victimized have more issues than children who are bullied more intensive interventions are needed for victims. Victims who receive social support along with training in coping strategies, seem to do better than those who do not receive such training. Programs designed to include *both* of these factors directly or indirectly will be helpful to the victims of bullying (Craig, Peters, et al., 1998).

Cowie and Wallace (2000b) suggest that 'Circles of Friends', an intervention first developed to support mainstreamed handicapped students, can be used to support young children who are victimized. For children ages seven through nine years of age, cooperative group teaching approaches, non-evaluative classroom discussion periods, and 'befriending' are peer support methods to be added to the Circle of Friends internvention. Befriending might also involve after school clubs. For nine through eleven-year-old students, all of these peer support approaches are useful along with conflict resolution and peer mediation approaches. For students eleven through secondary school, peer counseling, peer tutoring, and peer mentoring can be considered. And, if a student has been bullied for a long time the school psychologist or school counselor will need to work with the student intensively.

Social Skills Training

Social skills training might be an obvious intervention for children who have been victims of bullies. Social skills training increases a child's acceptance by peers but does *not* influence friendship choices. About half of students who are trained in social skills groups do *not* change their behavior, however, as a result of the training. These students who are not successful with their peers after training might feel that they have failed rather than looking at their difficulty as a temporary problem (Bryant, 1998).

Social skills training that addresses very specific behaviors and, also, addresses *attitudes* may be more helpful. There are two specific behaviors that school psychologists and counselors will want to include in their training sessions: the ability to quickly look for a sympathetic peer and responding in a non-emotional manner. Victims of bullying need to be taught what to do if they are trapped. When bullied by several students, victims can be taught to pick out the student in the group who looks most uncomfortable as the student most likely to help (ABC News, 2002, comment by Michael Thompson).

Girls who are bullied tend to react with helplessness or nonchalance. Boys tend to react with aggression or nonchalance. Nonchalance is the better strategy for stopping the bully, and children need to practice this reaction (reported in Bjorkquist & Osterman, 1999). Using role-play, videos, literature, and actual experiences of being bullied can be used to teach skills. Skills training should include training in both nonverbal and verbal strategies. Students need to practice strategies to prevent the bully from being rewarded and need training in how to protect themselves from bullying. Victims need to learn how to change the bully's focus away from them (Mullin-Rindler, 1998). Children who are most likely to accept a child who may be somewhat isolated should be included in groups.

Peers reject victims over time. Rejected children remain rejected from third grade on (Gagnon, 1991). Because rejections and exclusion are the forms of bullying that can result in feelings of shame, students who are still victimized by grade six need to be evaluated for depression and provided with cognitive therapy for depression (Cushman & Johnson, 2000; Swearer, Cary, Song, & Eagle, 2001). Psychoeducation and other interventions for depression can be targeted for sixth and ninth grade students who are about to deal with school changes, because these are stressful times for students who are bully-victims or who are passive victims (Swearer, Cary, Song, & Eagle, 2001).

Submissive children rate submissive strategies for dealing with bullying as the most likely to be successful. In play situations, some victims exhibit passive play that shows little flexibility. These children rarely initiate prosocial play behaviors. They present as overly needy and seek approval even when they have just been rejected (Bernstein & Watson, 1997). Training can be targeted to change these behaviors and improve social problem solving.

Assertiveness Training

Victims need to be directly trained to speak up and tell a parent, teacher, counselor, or friend when they have been bullied. Children who are victims need to be taught the difference between tattling and getting help to stop the bullying

(Mullin-Rindler, 1998). Staff who will listen must be identified in schools, so students feel that it is safe for them to report problems with being bullied. It may also be helpful to establish a way for students to report bullying anonymously. If this approach is used, students need to be directly taught to give enough information so that it will be possible for adults to place themselves in areas of the building or grounds so bullying cannot take place and they can observe what the student is reporting. School psychologists and school counselors need to convince students that they will handle the information that they are given appropriately, and that the victim will be protected (Crary, 2001).

When a student is bullied verbally, the child is given direct messages about himself or herself. When bullying is repeated over time, the child may begin to believe the messages. It is important for those who are trying to assist the victim to look at the content of the messages (Kochenderfer & Ladd, 1996). These messages may need to be countered in some way or reframed, so that the student can think about himself or herself more positively. A complication in providing help for victims is that mental health workers may want to help victims understand how their peers may perceive them. Counselors may feel that this would give a victim a sense of control over the situation. This would need to be handled very carefully because the child and his or her parents may feel that this approach is 'blaming the victim' (Newman, Horne, & Bartolomucci, 2000a).

Assertiveness training improves self-esteem, decreases anxiety, increases a child's coping strategies, increases self-confidence, and increases peer acceptance when children use the skills (Sharp & Cowie, 1994). Assertiveness training may be helpful for some students, but probably not all students victimized by bullies. Some students' temperaments may not allow them to learn to be assertive very easily. At the same time, it is critical to increase victims' feelings of competence, because victims are at risk for eventually believing that they deserve to be bullied. Bullying has been compared to a form of brainwashing that eats away at a child's self-esteem. Victims need to understand that it is not their fault that they are bullied. The Sheffield Project in Great Britain included assertiveness training. Students who were trained gained support from others in the training group and reported a sixty-eight percent decrease in being victimized (Sharp & Cowie, 1994). Booster sessions are important after training has been completed. Booster sessions are often neglected in school programs even though the data is strong in support of them.

In some extreme cases, when a child's reputation as a victim does not change even after the child has learned and is using new skills, a move to another school may be necessary and may be the only choice left to the child and family (Swearer & Doll, 2001). This may not work as well as parents hope, however. Olweus has demonstrated that victim behavior is relatively stable even after the child changes schools (Olweus, 1994). Another option is to change classes within a school. However, several studies show that victimization continues even when there have been changes in classrooms (Gottheil & Dubow, 2001b).

INTERVENTIONS FOR STUDENTS VICTIMIZED OVER TIME

If a child has been victimized over a period of time and is exhibiting symptoms of depression, a more intensive intervention may be needed. An important risk for victims of bullying is mood disorders. Mood disorders may be treated *and prevented* through programs that have a cognitive-behavioral focus (Craig, Peters, et al., 1998).

The Penn Prevention Program is also known as the Depression Prevention Program. This intervention was built around cognitive-behavioral principles. There are two main components: a cognitive component and a problem-solving component. In addition, there is a coping skills component. Students are taught to think of optimistic explanations for what happens to them and to use behavioral positive coping strategies as well (McWhirter et al., 1998).

Gillham, Reivich, Jaycox, and Seligman (1995) found that children who participated in the program reported a reduction in symptoms of depression. Effects of the program were noticeable two years later. More replication studies are needed and it is important to determine whether this approach would be relevant, specifically, for victims of bullying because this has not yet been explored (Greenberg et al., 1999). Students in sixth and ninth grades face school transitions. These are stressful periods for victims and interventions to help students with depression should be planned for these periods (Swearer, Cary, Song, & Eagle, 2001; Swearer, Eagle, et al., 2001).

Because students seldom tell adults when they have been bullied, peer counseling may be useful in helping students report having been bullied to school counselors (Sharp & Cowie, 1994). Ross (1996) is less supportive than others might be of peer counseling as an intervention for victims of bullying. She feels that students may be given too much responsibility and may assume the role of adult professionals without the training or experience of adults.

Parents of victims are generally frustrated, angry, and worried. Parents of victims also need to be supported by school staff. School counselors can help parents understand that the school can be a mediator, rather than suggesting that parents try to deal with parents of bullies themselves (Pepler & Craig, 2000). Parents can be encouraged to facilitate friendships outside of school. Experts advise parents to talk to children about all sorts of serious issues, much earlier and much more frequently than they are doing at this time. Parents need to let their children know that they can talk with them about being bullied. Children need to know that their parents will remain calm when they report being victimized. Children may be ashamed to report that they are frightened or that they cannot manage bullies. Parents must teach their children that they are not expected to be able to manage peers who have so much power.

Olweus (1994) reminds school staff that the target of interventions should be the *environment*, not necessarily the victims. The fact that victims remain victims is not because of their personalities, as much as it is due to the fact that the social world in which they must exist does not change. The responsibility for controlling bullying and keeping children safe belongs to adults.

SUMMARY

Group interventions are particularly important for children who are victims of bullying. Groups must not be formed of victims alone, however, as this would not result in changes. Although victims are not at fault and cannot be asked to stand up to bullies, they can learn strategies that may afford them some protection. Several intervention strategies that may be helpful include forming support groups, specific skills training, cognitive therapy, assertiveness training, and prevention programs to help victims avoid depression. Finally peer counseling and parent training may be helpful and are important.

CHAPTER 16

Interventions for Bystanders

Now that most researchers feel that bystanders are the *key* variable in decreasing bullying, research has begun to explore the behavior of bystanders and their role in bullying behavior with the goal of developing interventions. Lines, Plog, and Porter (2002) suggest that bystanders are a resource to help school psychologists and counselors address bullying in schools. They suggest that it is important to let bystanders know that their anxiety around bullying situations is normal.

INFLUENCE OF THE LARGER GROUP OF CHILDREN

Interventions designed to reduce bullying must include the peer network. Peers control the reinforcement contingencies of the group. Bullies and other aggressive students must learn that aggression results in social disapproval. If bullies understand that this is the case, they may be willing to change their goals (Coie & Jacobs, 2000). Craig and Pepler (1995) advocate helping the larger group of students acknowledge their discomfort around bullying and condemn the harmful behaviors.

Bystanders are *expected* to so something, because there is strength in the numbers of students they represent. In order for this approach to be successful, students will need both strategies and reinforcement for their positive actions. Cleary (n.d.) makes the point that all children in schools have a responsibility to support victims of bullying. Bystanders need to be trained to 'say something', when they observe bullying behaviors.

Cairns and Cairns (1991) recommend school transition periods as the best time to provide interventions for bystanders. Coie and Jacobs (2000) identify the two major transitions: the first time a child attends school in kindergarten and the grade level at which students switch to middle school. If school psychologists become engaged in teaching students about bullying and in training students to deal with bullying behaviors at these transition periods, they may be able to prevent or at least reduce bullying duirng these stressful periods.

BASIC UNDERSTANDINGS OF BULLYING

Craig, Pepler, and Atlas (2000) suggest that school staff develop school-wide programs for young students to shape attitudes against bullying behaviors and to help students become empathetic toward the victim, rather than rejecting the victim. It is particularly critical to *re-sensitize* students to negative behaviors in schools where bullying has previously been ignored. In some schools, the general student population will need help in identifying bullying. Bullying may have become so pervasive and so accepted that many students do not even recognize behaviors as bullying when they see it occur. Students can be taught to attend to the victim rather than the bully during aggressive episodes which may trigger an empathetic response (Craig & Pepler, 1995). This work must begin with young children because sympathy for the victim decreases as students go up in the grade levels (Craig, Pepler & Atlas, 2000).

Raising Awareness

A cognitive approach to raising awareness of bullying is to teach students to use a series of questions that they can ask themselves when observing incidents. This set of questions can be framed as 'Bully Tests' (Macklem & Kalinsky, 2002). These questions may help students to discriminate behaviors that are getting out of control or are harmful and which the group can decide together are bullying behaviors (Table III).

Behaviors that Support Bullying

Bystanders also need to be especially clear about the behaviors that might be considered to be supporting bullying. Students can generate a list of behaviors with the help of a school psychologist or counselor. For example, behaviors such as passing on harassing notes, passing on rumors, or forwarding e-mail messages reinforce bullying, just as laughing at negative behavior is rewarding for the bully. It is important to change the misperceptions of bystanders that the victim deserves what he gets and to stop spreading misperceptions such as the idea that the victim asked for it. It is also important to increase awareness of the effects of bullying on the victim (Craig & Pepler, 1995). Teaching the group to support any student or students who stand up to bullying is important because it is the group that holds the power rather than the individual student. Students need direct instruction in what they need to do when they observe interactions between students that may fit in the category of bullying behaviors (Table IV).

Table III. Identifying Bullying When you See it

The Bully Tests are a series of questions that students can ask themselves when thinking about, observing or discussing situations in which bullying may be taking place.

Bully Tests

1. **Do both students like the behavior?**
2. **Did the student being teased ask the person doing the teasing to stop?**
3. **Has this happened more than once?**
4. **Can the person change what he or she is being teased about?**
5. **Is there an audience?**
6. **Are the students involved equals?**

These six questions can help students answer the questions "How Can we know that what we are watching is really bullying?"

- If both students involved in the teasing are not feeling good about the behavior, then it may be bullying.
- If the student being teased asked the person to stop and he or she did not stop, then it may be bullying.
- If the person who teases continues to tease or teases again and again, then it may be bullying.
- If the teasing is about something that the student cannot change (height, glasses, weight, reading ability, athletic ability) then it may be bullying.
- If there are other people standing around watching, giggling, encouraging or joining in, it may be bullying.
- If one person is stronger, less emotional, smarter, more popular, older or more powerful in any way, it may be bullying.

Table IV. Strategies for Bystanders

1. Refuse to be the audience, walk away.
2. Say something that lets the other students know that the behavior is not okay.
3. Label the bahavior bullying.
4. Distract the bully by talking about something else.
5. Tell the bully to leave the person alone.
6. Say "We don't like this."
   Say "This isn't funny."
7. Call attention to the behavior so that any adult who is available will pay attention.
8. Tell the student who is being bullied to come with you, and walk away.
9. Threaten that you will report the bully if the behavior doesn't stop.
10. Go and get help.

Empowering Bystanders to Report Bullying

Empowering bystanders is thought to be one of the most effective ways to decrease bullying, because bystanders often feel as if they are in a no-win situation. Bystanders need to learn that they have the potential to significantly reduce bullying by being proactive in their response. Students can learn to *refuse to support* bullying. They can learn to report it. Reporting bullying must be distinguished from tattling. The difference between tattling and reporting may have to do with motivation. In tattling, a child's motivation might be to get the other person in trouble. Reporting is motivated by a need to get help for oneself or for the victim. Bystanders can help victims by not isolating them from the power of protection of the group on the playground or in the cafeteria. Students must learn to express disapproval because a bully's power is limited when his or her status is affected and no attention is given to reward the behaviors (Cavendish & Salomone, 2001). Craig, Pepler, and Atlas (2000) remind practitioners that children need to be given the language that they need if they are going to be expected to speak up against bullying.

Each individual bystander acts as part of a group and for this reason bystanders should be worked with in a group. This will help them feel the strength of the community. Group discussion techniques help bystanders understand that they generally feel the same way about bullying behaviors. An environment needs to be created where peer abuse is condemned, and students know how to intervene when someone is being abused (Hazler, 1996). If students understood that bullying is a group process that includes all children, they would be more likely to understand how their own responses to bullying behaviors contribute to the problem. They need to appreciate how group processes pressure individuals to do things that they don't approve of and wouldn't ordinarily do if they were alone (O'Connell et al., 1999).

BYSTANDERS REACTIONS TO BULLYING

When a child is bullied, the bystander's initial reactions may include a feeling that the victim might have been him or her. The child who watches may feel strong negative emotions. If the child who watches the bullying incident tries to help but fails, the potential helper may be frustrated and may feel negatively toward the victim. The child who has been victimized is aware of the other children's uncomfortable feelings, so the victim may try to hide his or her feelings. This may further heighten the bystander's own uncomfortable feelings (Silver, Wortman, & Crofton, 1990).

As the bullying is repeated, the victim continues to be stressed and the other children reject the victim. If the child who is victimized expresses his or her resentment, potential supporters will be even more uncomfortable. If the victim appears as if he is trying to deal with the bullying, the bystanders may not reject him and may support him. The victim may be faced with the need to communicate both distress and coping in order to get support from bystanders (Silver et al., 1990). Both students and adults have difficulty when children are upset, which is a likely occurrence when a child is victimized. If the bystander tends to deny or minimize the upset child's behavior, the child will feel even more isolated (Bryant, 1998).

Supporting the Victim

Bystanders need to learn how to help victims. Students need to learn how they can denounce the bullying behavior without denouncing the person. Students who develop a list of ways that they can support victims themselves may be willing to do so when they have agreed upon a strategy during group discussions. Students need to become aware that they isolate victims. Students may need to hear specific steps that they can be take to support victims such as spending time with them, talking with them, including them in games and inviting them to play regularly. Bystanders need to know when to ask adults for help, and which adults they can trust to manage the situation carefully. Students who report bullying do not want adults to make the situation worse or make the reporter vulnerable. Students need to decide as a class that they will not be silent about bullying (Hazler, 1996).

TRAINING BYSTANDERS TO ACT

When considering interventions for bystanders, practitioners need to include a variety of training opportunities to improve the likelihood that most children will be able to respond appropriately. Bryant (1998) recommends not only helping students recognize bullying when it occurs, but he feels that empathy training, self-regulation training, praise for responding appropriately, and evoking guilt when bystanders do not respond appropriately are important interventions. Children who are more sympathetic than their peers are more likely to help when a peer is being victimized (Laner, Benin, & Ventrone, 2001).

Education around Emotions

A child's ability to react to others with empathy depends on a child's level of emotionality and the degree to which the student can control his or her emotions. If a child is able to regulate his or her emotions, this child typically reacts with sympathy when another child is upset. Boys who frequently experience negative emotions and who feel emotion intensely exhibit low levels of situational empathy and low levels of sympathy. If a child's attention can be improved, the child may react with more sympathy toward others. Children who have difficulty controlling emotions need to learn to control emotions first, and then learn to respond empathetically. (Eisenberg, Wentzel, et al., 1998).

Whether or not a child will act to help others appears to be associated with the specific emotions that the child anticipates after acting. If the student anticipates that he will feel *pride* for behaving in a particular way *or* if the student anticipates that he will experience *guilt* after behaving in a particular way, he will make the decision to behave responsibly. Feelings of either pride or guilt experienced after a child responds to a given situation support helping behaviors. On the other hand, if the student anticipates that he will experience *shame or fear*, he will respond irresponsibly (Bear, Telzrow, & deOliveira, 1997). Shame is related to violent behavior towards oneself or others (Cushman & Johnson, 2000). This is why it is so dangerous to evoke shame in victims or in bystanders for that matter. Praise for responding appropriately to bullying incidents as well as evoking guilt but not shame when students have failed to act may be helpful in decreasing bullying. Students need to understand the plight of the victim both intellectually and emotionally.

When working with bystanders, it is important to help students realize that they can act on their own in the unstructured areas of the school *if* they act together. Bullying is maintained on the playground by the attitude of the students who watch or reinforce it by tolerating the behavior. Students will not act against bullying until they have learned to appreciate how they contribute to it. Students need to disapprove of bullying and they may do so if they are taught to identify with the child who is bullied (Craig & Pepler, 1995).

Antibullying Curricula

Antibullying programs and curricula help children become more aware of the issues involved in bullying. They attempt to make bystanders more willing to report the behaviors that they observe. They also teach students that adults will support and protect them when they do report. Specific antibullying programs as well as programs that include peer mentoring and conflict management may help change attitudes (Craig & Pepler, 2000). Several of the antibullying curricula make the group responsible for reducing bullying, along with attempts to increase empathy.

Research indicates that eighty-three percent of students feel unpleasant after watching a bullying incident. If students feel uncomfortable they need to learn to listen to their feelings. But at the same time they need strategies for intervening safely. Students need to learn non-aggressive strategies to stop bullying so that they themselves are safe (O'Connell et al., 1999).

Peer Mediation

Sharp and Cowie (1994) recommend collaborative conflict resolution with both mediation and peer counseling to help bystanders become involved in stopping bullying behaviors in schools. They suggest that all students need training in conflict resolution and learning to negotiate win-win solutions.

Stacey (2000) describes mediation as an approach which allows those involved to describe the problem as they see it and to express their feelings and needs. In addition, the process helps students listen to others needs and emotions so that they really hear the other person's point of view and to agree on what to do about it. The process of peer mediation has been quite popular in the United States and has spread widely to other countries. There have been a few formal attempts to evaluate the technique. These efficacy studies show that mediation can have a positive effect on the level of bullying incidents that take place in schools. A complication is that the technique is sophisticated and if it were implemented poorly it might fail.

Ross (1996) reminds us that there is no solid data to indicate whether or not conflict resolution is helpful with very young children although many practitioners feel that it can help students even at the elementary level. Students at upper elementary school grade levels can be taught to take the role of conflict managers. It may even be possible to place a bully in a leadership position, because it would allow the student to be in charge in a positive way and to act as a peacemaker. Mediators should be trained to work in teams of two so that the behaviors of the mediators are controlled. This would be especially important if a former bully were placed in the role of mediator. The partnership aspect of this arrangement would provide a positive role model for a child who had bullied others in the past. Because there is a power imbalance in bullying, if mediation is used in a school, each person should bring a friend to mediation. A limiting factor is that peer mediation only works if both parties involved in an incident agree to mediate the issues and agree on a solution (Cowie & Wallace, 2000a).

Quality Circles

The Quality Circle, which was originally designed for use in industry, has been adapted for use with students. Ross (1996) described how it could be used for bullying situations. Using the Quality Circle format the group would begin to deal with bullying issues using a *why-why* and *how-how* analysis. Initially 'why' questions are proposed and answered by the group. Then students address 'how' questions. The group develops a plan to solve a problem with the facilitator making sure that the plan can actually be implemented. Ross reports that use of a Quality Circle in a school setting has been evaluated positively (Ross, 1996 p. 143).

THE INFLUENCE OF THE GROUP

Children form groups because it is rewarding to do so. All groups have norms, which explain the group standards to the individual members of the group. Social norms are the beliefs that individuals have about which attitudes and behaviors are considered normal or are accepted by the group. Social norms can include the behaviors that are expected by the group as well (Ritzel, 2002). Expectations are communicated to members of a group by means of socialization. Members of a group have assigned roles. The roles determine the status or relative standing of each person in the group. Those who do not belong to the group may be treated differently than those who are accepted by the group as members. Membership in a group effects self-esteem. Group influence has to do with how the group controls the behavior of every member of the group (Parks & Sanna, 1999). Peer influence through group interaction variables is stronger than family and other influences certainly by middle childhood.

Given that bullying is a group phenomenon, group interaction variables can be used to understand the behaviors of students during a bullying incident. When students are participating in groups responsibility for taking positive action is equally distributed among *all* of the children present. If an individual student is one of five people to witness an event, such as bullying, that student will feel only twenty percent responsible to take action against it. This is the principle of *diffusion of responsibility* (Parks & Sanna, 1999). This concept has been helpful in understanding bystander behavior. Principles of group dynamics suggest that when a student is in a group he or she may not feel personally responsible for stopping bullying.

Group Dynamics

The more people available to help, the less likely that an individual student will take action to stop bullying. An individual student may reduce effort and cooperation as the size of the group increases. This is the phenomenon of social loafing. In addition, the larger the group, the more pressure that the group has on any single individual and the less influence each person has on the group (Pettijohn, 1998). The individual student is more likely to act responsibly if alone than he or she is likely to act in a group when witnessing bullying. Researchers have found that when they are in a group, children take cues in regard to how to react to bullying from other members of the group (Salmivalli, Huttunen, & Lagerspetz, 1997). Since the group is less likely to take responsibility for responding to bullying and the individual child is influenced by the group response, it is not likely that an individual child would take action.

Bystanders watch but do not act because they think or hope that someone else may take responsibility for standing up to the bully. The student may think that others are not concerned about the behavior that the group is watching, even though the individual may be concerned him or herself. This is the phenomenon of *pluralistic ignorance*. Pluralistic ignorance also explains how an individual would behave in ways that do not match his or her personal values (Prentice & Miller, 1993). The student watching bullying does not attempt to stop it and may even support it because of the belief that others think it is okay to support it.

Principles of group dynamics have already been proposed as helpful in understanding the bullying phenomenon. The group mechanisms that Olweus (1991) has explored include the principles of social contagion, disinhibition, diffusion of responsibility and changes in perception. Olweus (1999) feels that insecure and dependent students who do not have much status in the group but who would like to have status are attracted to bullies. They are susceptible to the phenomenon of *social contagion*. Social contagion has to do with the spread of emotion and/or behavior from one person in a group to others (Lindzey & Aronson, 1985).

Aggression is enhanced when students believe that it won't be punished. This occurs through disinhibition (Feshbach & Feshbach, 1998). Boys in particular are attracted to aggression and find it exciting. Arousal spreads through the group as if the emotion were contagious (Craig & Pepler, 1995). Olweus (1999) feels that modeling is also involved when peers see the bully rewarded. He feels that children who are typically 'nice kids' can get drawn into bullying when they are in a group, because they feel less responsible for what is going on. Social contagion occurs because children behave more aggressively after they observe others acting aggressively, especially, when the aggressor is considered tough, without fear, or strong. Students who are insecure bullies or who have low status in the peer group, but who want to be accepted may be most susceptible. As the group size increases, students who support bullying or who join in will feel *less guilty* later on. As a particular child is repeatedly victimized, the group begins to look at the victim as someone who deserves what he or she gets (Olweus, 1991; Olweus, 1993).

Most often there is an audience when a child is being bullied. Bullying is visible behavior on school playgrounds to the children, if not to the adults. Children who value aggression may think that bullying is actually *accepted* by their peers. Once a misperception occurs, it is contagious and can spread in a school community. Bystanders may join in when they observe bullying behavior, even though they might not ever think of bullying themselves if they were alone.

Students who frequently bully others may believe that others engage in bullying behaviors to the same degree that they do. Students who only occasionally engage in bullying behaviors may assume that others tease and bully even more than they do. This phenomenon is the *false consensus effect.* The false consensus effect suggests that individuals might think that their own behavioral choices or judgements are common and appropriate, whereas, other choices are inappropriate (Ross, Greene, & House, 1977). The bystander may feel pressured to conform to the majority behavior. Beyond this, the more powerful students will control the behavior of the group, and in very large groups a single voice raised to stop the bullying may be disregarded.

Research on bystander behavior suggests that most people want to do something to assist a person being victimized, but they don't act for several reasons. One of those reasons has to do with social influence. The principle of *social influence* suggests, because others are not helping the victim, there really isn't a serious problem involved. In addition bystanders may worry that if they try to do something to stop the victimization and fail, they may be embarrassed. This is the principle of *audience inhibition.* The principle of *audience inhibition* is that the probability that a person will help someone in need is reduced when the person is in a group, as compared to when the person is alone (Harrington, 2001).

Investigation into how the principles of group dynamics might relate to bullying is a recent interest of researchers particularly around Olweus' (1991) use of several of the principles to explain bullying. Craig and Pepler (2000) analyzed videotaped interactions of children on elementary school playgrounds. Teachers and peers each identified students who were aggressive and students who were competent socially. Both groups of students were observed during forty-eight hours of playground play at recesses. The goal was to determine if evidence for the several hypotheses of Olweus (1991) could be substantiated. Bystanders reinforced bullying most of the time. Researchers felt that this allowed the bully to hold power over the child being victimized and maintained the status of the bully (Craig & Pepler, 2000). This study represents important initial attempts to demonstrate that the principles of group dynamics can be applied to bullying episodes.

SOCIAL NORMS THEORY AND BULLYING

Social Norms Theory proposes that behavior is influenced by the individual's perceptions about how others in a group think and act. These beliefs or perceptions may not be accurate (Ritzel, 2002). Social Norms Theory can be used to explain situations in which students believe that the attitudes of their peers are different from their own attitudes. When students witness bullying or other negative behaviors, they may misperceive what is going on. Misperceptions begin and spread when individuals see a minority of students behaving in highly visible ways. In this way students observe bullying on the playground by a single bully or a bully supported by one or two others that is ignored by adults and they perceive that it is acceptable behavior.

Researchers have applied *social norms theory* to studies of adolescents' alcohol use and abuse, to tobacco use, violence between adults, and academic performance (The National Social Norms Resource Center, 2003). According to *social norms theory*, students typically overestimate the degree to which their peers support negative behavior. When students overestimate the support of their peers, they are more likely to join in that behavior. If a child who is easily excited believes that the group supports destructive teasing or bullying, that child is likely to support the behavior or join in.

Social norms interventions are targeted on the influence of the group. Peer pressure or influence has been identified as even more influential on individual behavior than temperament, family values, or other influences (Berkowitz & Perkins, 1986). The goal of social norms interventions is changing misperceptions and therefore changing behavior. Social norms approaches connect the behaviors desired to the majority group so that individuals will change their behavior (Charnchoochia, 2000). Peer leaders are used to spread accurate information and to model the new behaviors. Rewards for using the new behaviors are thought to be helpful, especially praise from a valued peer. Both observational learning and modeling are each used to influence behavior change. Individuals must feel pressure from peer leaders in order to change their behavior (Andreasen, 1995). Mixon (2001) emphasizes that it is important to use a limited number of positive social norm messages on a common theme and to send the messages through many channels to affect behavior change.

Criticism of the Social Norms Approach

A complication and criticism of the social norms approach is that some groups of individuals do not actually misperceive the norms, of their group. Their norms are unhealthy and they already know it. The approach would not be likely to affect these individuals (Reisberg, 2000).

Some students who join in bullying others may know that they are behaving inappropriately and these students would not be affected by learning that others do not approve or are upset by it.

Another complication is that social learning theory might be used to explain bystander behavior in another way. Social learning theory suggests that when a situation is ambiguous, individuals might purposefully imitate the behaviors they observe (Bandura, 1971, 1986). Children on the playground observing bullying that is not stopped by playground supervisors might be unsure how to react because approval or disapproval of the behavior is not clear. If they see others join in, they may consciously join in as well.

Designing Interventions Using Norms Based Interventions

No attempt to use social norms approaches to address bullying behavior in schools with elementary aged children or secondary level students has been published as yet but norms based interventions for preventing or decreasing bullying may be useful. Using social norms theory, along with research on group behavior and applying it to bullying behavior, interventions could be aimed at changing perceptions. Information about the incidence of bullying could be made public, along with the ways in which most students feel about bullying obtained from surveys of student attitudes in a given school. Students need accurate information about the percentage of students actually engaging in bullying behavior, and even more importantly, they need information about most students'*attitudes* toward bullying.

Those who engage in a great deal of bullying need to know that bullying behavior is not perceived by the majority of peers and perhaps, by significant or high status peers as 'innocent fun'. Providing feedback and correct information for those engaging in bullying behaviors may be helpful in decreasing behaviors for some children who engage in bullying and particularly for those students who join in or stand by and passively support it.

Students who watch bullying but don't participate need to understand that they *are* participating, albeit passively, by the way they watch and *talk about* bullying behavior. They may participate by spreading the misperception that the victim 'asked for it' to others. Social norms theory suggests that is not that the majority of students believe that bullying behavior is okay or that the victim is responsible for his or her own misery, but rather the majority of students believes that most students think bullying is okay or cannot be prevented or stopped. Prevention recommendations coming out of social norms theory involve educating students about their complex role in bullying.

Social norms theory suggests if we can correct student misperceptions around bullying, students will either reduce their role in engaging in or will no longer support bullying behaviors.

Bystanders underestimate the effects of bullying on the victim or rationalize the bullying behavior. At the same time, they discount their own uncomfortable feelings about the bullying behavior. The social norms approach to changing perceptions may help bystanders understand the affects of bullying on the victim. Interventions would be aimed at *decreasing tolerance* for bullying behavior.

Standing by without helping might be countered by the elements that have been proposed to reduce the phenomenon of social loafing. In order to counter this phenomenon, individual children and the group as a whole must expect that they be judged. The children would be helped to set a goal to act next time so that they would avoid personal consequences and incentives would be established for taking action. If students believe that they can make a difference it is more likely that they would make an effort to act in a group. For example, it might be possible to increase a student's willingness to step forward to help if each student is helped to feel that doing so is critical to reducing bullying.

Students could be asked to set personal and class goals to reduce bullying or at minimum to 'say something' when they see a child being bullied or to report it. Incentives, such as approval from the peer group, might be established for bystanders who are willing to report or to say that bullying is 'not okay'. After an incident has occurred where a child has been bullied and others have participated as the audience, a consequence might be appropriate. Appropriate consequences might involve discussions with bystanders and requests for a commitment to take some appropriate action next time that would be safe in the given situation. When aggression appears to be accepted by bystanders, students will act aggressively (Cairns & Cairns, 1991). On the other hand, students who provide support for victims can affect school climate as a whole positively (Cowie, 2000).

Using Principles of Group Dynamics to Desgin Interventions

Strategies for helping bystanders take action include teaching them to pay attention to the victim rather than the bully and teaching them to interpret bullying negatively. In addition, bystanders need to see bullying as a problem and need to understand how others feel about these inappropriate behaviors. Bystanders must understand how bullying affects them personally and begin to understand that they can be part of the solution. Bystanders need to learn about the influences of group dynamics so that they realize that they can be affected by them.

SUMMARY

Interventions for bystanders are critical, because the 'real' power lies with the bystanders even though they may not realize this. In designing interventions for bystanders, it is important to address the biases of bystanders toward victims. In addition, empathy training and using both pride *and* shame will improve the chances that bystanders will intervene to help victims of bullying. Interventions for bystanders include: bullying prevention curricula, conflict resolution programs, peer mediation, and quality circles. It is critical to deal with and dispel the biases that bystanders have in regard to bullying.

There are a number of group phenomena which have been proposed to explain the behavior of individuals in group situations that might be applied to bullying situations. When students are in a group and observe a bullying incident, they may be reluctant to act due to the effects of *audience inhibition*. *Diffusion of responsibility* helps the individual child excuse his or her lack of action with the thought that someone else will take action or responsibility. Because of *pluralistic ignorance*, bystanders might feel that others may not be as concerned about bullying as they themselves are, and this may inhibit any tendency they may have to help the victim. A *false consensus effect* might make a bystander feel pressured to conform to the inaction of the larger group. At the same time, because of the effects of *social contagion* some students may join in bullying interactions even when they would not otherwise act in an aggressive manner toward their peers. Social contagion effects have been specifically studied in association with bullying behaviors and there is some early data to support the idea that this phenomenon is involved.

Finally, *social norms theory* suggests that bystanders may be influenced by beliefs about the victim which are misconceptions, such as the victim 'asked for it' or deserves the bullying in some way. These changes in perception are group phenomenon. Bullies may believe that most children approve of their behavior or that others are just as or more aggressive than they are. Social norms interventions have been used to address a variety of social behaviors that practitioners would like to change. The approach involves correction of misperceptions and the spread of a more accurate view of the behavior that needs to be addressed. This approach may be useful to consider as part of a broad effort to address the problem of bullying in schools. School psychologists and other mental health workers must take advantage of the help that bystanders can provide for reducing bullying given their critical role in the bullying process.

References

ABCNEWS.com online chat (2002, February 19). Popularity wars: The "in crowd" and social cruelty; http://www.abcnews.go.com/sections/community/DailyNews/chat_thompson021902. html.

Adair, V. A., Dixon, R. S., Moore, D. W., & Sutherland, C. M. (2000). Ask your mother not to make yummy sandwiches: Bullying in New Zealand secondary schools. *New Zealand Journal of Educational Studies, 35*(2), 207–221.

Adler, P. A., & Adler, P. (1998). *Peer power: Preadolescent culture and identity.* New Brunswick, NJ: Rutgers University Press.

Agnew, R. (1994). The techniques of neutralization and violence. *Criminology, 32*(4), 555–568.

Aguilar, B., O'Brien, K. M., August, G. J., Aoun, S. L., & Hektner, J. M. (2001). Relationship quality of aggressive children and their siblings: A multinformant, multimeasure investigation. *Journal of Abnormal Child Psychology, 29*(6), 479–489.

Aidman, A. (1997). *Television violence: Content, context, and consequences.* Champaign, IL: ERIC Clearinghouse on Elementary and Early Childhood Education. (ERIC Document No. ED 414 078).

Alsaker, F. D., & Vakanover, S. (2001). Early diagnosis and prevention of victimization in kindergarten. In J. Juvonen & S. Graham (Eds.), *Peer harassment in school: The plight of the vulnerable and victimized* (pp.175–195). New York: The Guilford Press.

American Academy of Child & Adolescent Psychiatry (1997). Bullying. *Facts for Families,* 80; http://www.aacap.org/publications/factsfam/80.htm.

American Association of University Women (1993). *Hostile hallways: The AAUW survey on sexual harassment in America's schools.* Washington, DC: Author.

Andershed, H., Kerr, M., & Stattin, H. (2001). Bullying in school and violence on the streets: Are the same people involved? *Journal of Scandinavian Studies in Criminology and Crime Prevention, 2*(1), 31–49.

Anderson, C., John, O. P., Keltner, D., & Kring, A. M. (2001). Who attains social status? Effects of personality and physical attractiveness in social groups. *Personality Processes and Individual Differences, 81*(1), 116–132.

Andreou, E. (2000). Bully/victim problems and their association with psychological constructs in 8-to 12-year-old Greek schoolchildren. *Aggressive Behavior, 26*(1), 49–56.

Arce, R. CNN Producer (2001, March, 8). *Study: Kids rate bullying and teasing as 'big problem'*; http://www.cnn.com/2001/US/03/08/violence.survey/.

Archer, J. (2001). A strategic approach to aggression. *Review of Social Development, 10*(2), 5.

Ardelt, M., & Day, L. (2002). Parents, siblings and peers: Close relationships and adolescent deviance. *Journal of Early Adolescence, 22*(3), 310–349.

Arsenio, W. F., & Lemerise, E. A. (2001). Varieties of childhood bullying: Values, emotion processes, and social competence. *Social Development, 10*(1), 59–73.

Ashby, N. (Ed.) (2002, October 1) Close-up: No child left behind: School safety. *The Achiever.* Jessup, MD: ED PUBS.

Asher, S. R., & Renshaw, P. D. (1984). Children without friends: Social knowledge and social-skill-training. In S. R. Asher & J. M. Gottman (Eds.), *The development of children's friendships* (pp. 273–296). Cambridge, UK: Cambridge University Press.

Asidao, C., Vion, S., & Espelage, D. (1999, August). *Interviews with middle school students: Bullying, victimization, and contextual factors.* Paper presented at the Annual Convention of the American Psychological Association, Boston, MA.

Astor, R. A., Benbenishty, R., Marachi, R., Haj-Yahia, M. M., Zeira, A., Perkins-Hart, S., & Pitner, R. O. (2002). The awareness of risky peer group behaviors on school grounds as predictors of students' victimization on school grounds: Part I—elementary schools. *Journal of School Violence, 1*(1), 11–33.

Astor, R. A., Meyer, H. A., & Pitner, R. O. (2001). Elementary and middle school students' perceptions of safety: An examination of violence-prone school sub-contexts. *The Elementary School Journal, 101*, 511–528.

Azmitia, M., Kamprath, N., & Linnet, J. (1998). Intimacy and conflict: The dynamics of boy's and girl's friendships during middle childhood and early adolescence. In L. H. Meyer, H. Park, M. Grenot-Scheyer, I. S. Schwartz, & B. Harry (Eds.), *Making friends: The influences of culture and development* (pp.171–187). Baltimore, MD: Paul H. Brookes Publishing Company.

Baker, J. A. (1998). Are we missing the forest for the trees? Considering the social context of school violence. *Journal of School Psychology, 36*(1), 29–44.

Baker, J. E. (n.d.) Sticks and stones will break my bones, and names hurt too. New Jersey; http://www.aspennj.org/baker.html.

Baldry, A. C., & Farrington, D. P. (2000). Bullies and delinquents: Personal characteristics and parental styles. *Journal of Community & Applied Social Psychology, 10*(1), 17–31.

Bandura, A. (1973). *Aggression: A social learning analysis.* Englewood Cliffs, NJ: Prentice-Hall.

Banks, R. (1997). *Bullying in schools.* Champaign, IL: Clearinghouse on Elementary and Early Childhood Education. (ERIC Digest, EDO-PS-97-17).

Barker, G. (n.d.). National Bullying Awareness Campaign (NBAC). National Education Association. Washington, DC; http://www.nea.org/schoolsafety/bullying.html.

Barone, F. (1997, September). Bullying in school: It doesn't have to happen. *Phi Delta Kappan,* 80–82.

Batsche, G. M. (1997). Bullying. In G. G. Bear, K. M. Minke, & A. Thomas (Eds.), *Children's needs II: Development, problems and alternatives* (pp. 171–177). Bethesda, MD: National Association of School Psychologists.

Batsche, G., Moore, B. (1992). Bullying fact sheet. In: *Behavioral interventions: Creating a safe environment in our schools.* Bethesda, Maryland: National Mental Health and Education Center for Children and Families; National Association of School Psychologists, 14–16.

Bear, G. G., Telzrow, C. F., & deOliveira, E. A. (1997). Socially responsible behavior. In G. G. Bear, K. M. Minke, & A. Thomas (Eds.), *Children's needs II: Development, problems and alternatives* (pp. 51–63). Bethesda, MD: National Association of School Psychologists.

Behre, W. J., Astor, R. A., & Meyer, H. A. (2001). Elementary and middle school teachers' reasoning about intervening in school violence: An examination of violence-prone school sub-contexts. *Journal of Moral Education, 30*, 131-153.

Benbenishty, R., Astor, R. A., Zeira, A., & Vinokur, A. D. (2002). Perceptions of violence and fear of school attendance among junior high school students in Israel. *Social Work Research, 26*(20), 71–87.

Benenson, J. F., Roy, R., Waite, A., Goldbaum, S., Linders, L., & Simpson, A. (2002). Greater discomfort as a proximate cause of sex differences in competition. *Merrill-Palmer Quarterly, 48*(3), 225–247.

Berkowitz, A. D. (2000, June). *The social norms approach: Theory, research and annotated bibliography*; http://myweb.fltg.net/users/alan/hec.html.

Berkowitz, A. D., & Perkins, H. W. (1986). Problem drinking among college students: A review of recent research. *Journal of American College Health, 35,* 21–28.

Berkowitz, L. (1963). *Aggression: A social psychological analysis.* New York: McGraw-Hill.

Bernstein, J. Y., & Watson, M. W. (1997). Children who are targets of bullying: A victim pattern. *Journal of Interpersonal Violence, 12*(4), 483–498.

Bigelow, B. J., Tesson, G., & Lewko, J. H. (1996). *Learning the rules: The anatomy of children's relationships.* New York: The Guilford Press.

Bjorkqvist, K., & Osterman, K. (1999). Finland. In P. K. Smith, Y. Morita, J. Junger-Tas, D. Olweus, R. Catalano, & P. Slee (Eds.), *The nature of school bullying: A cross-national perspective.* London: Routledge.

Bjorkqvist, K., Osterman, K., & Kaukiainen, (2000). Social intelligence-empathy aggression? *Aggression and Violent Behavior, 5*(2), 191–200.

Boivin, M., Hymel, S., & Hodges, E. (2001). Toward a process view of peer rejection and harassment. In J. Juvonen & S. Graham (Eds.), *Peer harassment in school: The plight of the vulnerable and victimized* (pp. 265–289). New York: The Guilford Press.

Bollorino, F. (Ed.) (Gennaio, 1997). Aggression. *Psychiatry online, Italia, 3*(1). Italia: Priority Lodge Education, Ltd; http:www.priory.com/psych/garelli1.htm.

Bond, L., Carlin, J. B., Thomas, L., Rubin, K., & Patton, G. (2001). Does bullying cause emotional problems? A prospective study of young teenagers. *British Medical Journal, 323,* 480–484.

Bosworth, K., Espelage, D. L., & Simon, T. R. (1999). Factors associated with bullying behavior in middle school students. *Journal of Early Adolescence, 19*(3), 341–362.

Boulton, M. J. (1994). Understanding and preventing bullying in the junior school playground. In P. K. Smith & S. Sharp (Eds.), *School bullying: Insights and perspectives* (pp. 132–159). London: Routledge.

Boulton, M. J. (1997). Teachers' views on bullying definitions, attitudes and ability to cope. *British Journal of Educational Psychology, 67,* 223–233.

Boulton, M. J., Bucci, E., & Hawker, D. D. S. (1999). Swedish and English secondary school pupils' attitudes towards, and conceptions of, bullying: Concurrent links with bully/victim involvement. *Scandinavian Journal of Psychology, 40*(4), 277–284.

Boulton, M. J., & Hawker, D. S. (1997). Non-physical forms of bullying among school pupils: A cause for concern. *Health Education, 97*(2), 61–64.

Boulton, M. J., Trueman, M., Chau, C., Whitehand, C., & Amatya, K. (1999). Concurrent and longitudinal links between friendship and peer victimization: Implications for befriending interventions. *Journal of Adolescence, 22*(4), 461–466.

Bowman, D. (2001a, March 14). Student tips called key to avert violence. *Education Week on the Web.* Editorial Projects in Education, *20*(26), 1, 16; http://www.edweek.org/ew/ewstory.cfm?slug=26shoot.h20.

Boxer, P., & Dubow, E. F. (2002). A social-cognitive information-processing model for school-based aggression reduction and prevention programs: Issues for research and practice. *Applied & Preventive Psychology, 10*(3), 177–192.

Brady, J. (2001). Bullying: An interview with Russell Skiba. *Communiqué, 30*(3), 8.

Brauer, M., Judd, C. M., & Jacquelin, V. (2001). The communication of social stereotypes: The effects of group discussion and information distribution on stereotype appraisals. *Journal of Personality and Social Psychology, 81*(3), 463–475.

British Broadcasting Company News Online (2002, April 15). Youngsters targeted by digital bullies; http://news.bbc.co.uk/1/hi/uk/1929944.stm.

Brody, M. (2000, November). Playing with death. *The Brown University Child and Adolescent Behavior Letter,* 8. Providence, RI: Manisses Communications Group, Inc.

Brooks, R. (2002, June, 4). Stepping outside the box: Some additional thoughts. Part II. *Monthly Articles*; http://www.drrobertbrooks.com.

Brownell, C. A., Zerwas, S., & Balaram, G. (2002). Peers, cooperative play, and the development of empathy in children. *Behavioral and Brain Sciences, 25*(1), 28–29.

Bryant, B. K. (1998). Children's coping at school: The relevance of 'failure' and cooperative learning for enduring peer and academic success. In L. H. Meyer, H. Park, M. Grenot-Scheyer, I. S. Schwartz, & B. Harry. (Eds.), *Making friends: The influences of culture and development* (pp. 353–366). Baltimore, MD: Paul H. Brookes Publishing Company.

Bryce, C. P. (2001). *Insights into the concept of stress.* Washington, DC: World Health Organization.

Butler, S., & Kratz, D. (2000). The Field Guide to Parenting: A Comprehensive Handbook of Great Ideas, Advice, Tips, and Solutions for Parenting Children Ages One to Five. Worcester, MA: Chandler House Press.

Cadwallader, T. W., Farmer, T. W., Cairns, B. D., Leung, M., Clemmer, J. T., Gut, D. M., et al. (2002). The social relations of rural African American early adolescents and proximal impact of the school engagement project. *Journal of School Psychology, 40*(3), 239–258.

Cairns, R. B., & Cairns, B. D. (1991). Social cognition and social networks: A developmental perspective. In D. J. Pepler & K. H. Rubin (Eds.), *The development and treatment of childhood aggression* (pp. 249–278). Mahwah, NJ: Lawrence Erlbaum Associates, Publishers.

Camodeca, M., Goossens, F. A., Terwogt, M. M., & Schuengel, C. (2002). Bullying and victimization among school-age children: Stability and links to proactive and reactive aggression. *Social Development, 11*(3), 332–345.

Carlson, R. V. (1996). *Reframing & reform: Perspectives on organization, leadership, and school change.* New York: Longman Publishers, USA.

Carney, A. G., & Merrell, K. W. (2001). Bullying in schools: Perspectives on understanding and preventing an international problem. *School Psychology International, 22*(3), 364–382.

Cary, P. T., & Swearer, S. M. (2002). Aggression and depression rates across the bully/victim continuum. Poster session presented at the annual spring meeting of the Nebraska Psychological Association, Lincoln, NE.

Cary, P. T., Swearer, S. M., Song, S. Y., & Eagle, J. W. (2001). How bullies, victim and bully-victims differ in their attitudes and perceptions toward bullying. The University of Nebraska (information sheet provided by the authors).

Cary, P. T., Swearer, S. M., Song, S. Y., Haye, K. M., & Sohn, E. (2001). The relationship between depression and aggression across the bully-victim continuum. Poster session presented at the annual meeting of the Association for Advancement of Behavior Therapy, Philadelphia, PA.

Cauce, A. M., Reid, M., Landesman, S., & Gonzales, N. (1990). Social support in young children: Measurement, structure, and behavioral impact. In B. R. Sarason, I. G. Sarason, & G. R. Pierce (Eds.), *Social support: An interactional view* (pp. 64–94). New York: John Wiley & Sons.

Cavendish, R., & Salomone, C. (2001). Bullying and sexual harassment in the school setting. *The Journal of School Nursing, 17*(1), 25–31.

Center for the Study and Prevention of Violence (2001, May 29). Bullying prevention: Recommendations for parents. Fact Sheet Safe Communities ~ Safe Schools; http://www.colorado.edu/cspv/factsheets/SCSS%20Bullying%20-%20Parent%20Recommendations.html.

Charnchoochai, P. (2000, October). Social norm marketing: Applying the goodness of human nature to the problem of binge drinking. Paper published online. University of Colorado at Boulder; http://www.colorado.edu/iec/FALL100AW/BINGE/binge.htm.

Clark, R. D. (1987). Children and teasing. In A. Thomas & J. Grimes (Eds.), *Children's needs: Psychological perspectives* (pp. 610–618). Washington, DC: The National Association of School Psychologists.

Clayton, C., Ballif-Spanvill, B., & Hunsaker, M. (2001). Preventing violence and teaching peace: A review of promising and effective antiviolence, conflict-resolution, and peace programs for elementary school children. *Applied and Preventive Psychology, 10*(11), 1–35.

Cleary, M. (n.d.). Stop bullying! Guidelines for schools. Prepared for the New Zealand Police and Telecom, New Zealand. New Zealand Police Youth Education Service Internet Site; http://www.police.govt.nz.

Coie, J. D., Dodge, K. A., & Coppotelli, H. (1982). Dimensions and types of social status: A cross-age perspective. *Developmental Psychology, 18*, 557–570.

Coie, J. D., & Jacobs, M. R. (2000). The role of social context in the prevention of conduct disorder. In W. Craig (Ed.), *Childhood social development: The essential readings* (pp. 350–371). Oxford, UK: Blackwell Publishers.

Coie, J. D., Underwood, M., & Lockman, D. (1991). Programmatic intervention with aggressive children in the school setting. In D. J. Pepler & K. H. Rubin (Eds.), *The development and treatment of childhood aggression* (pp. 389–410). Mahwah, NJ: Lawrence Erlbaum Associates, Inc.

Conner, M. G. (2001, May). *The risk of violent and homicidal behavior in children*; http://www.oregoncounseling.org/ArticlesPapers/Documents/childviolence.htm.

Connolly, J., Pepler, D., Craig, W., & Taradash, A. (2000). Dating experiences of bullies in early adolescence. *Child Development, 5*(4), 299–310.

Conoley, J. C., Hindmand, R., Jacobs, Y., & Gagnon, W. A. (1998). How schools promote violence. *Family Futures, 1*(1), 8–11.

Corsaro, W. A. (1979). We're friends right? Children's use of access rituals in a nursery school. *Language in Society, 8*, 315–336.

Corsaro, W. A. (1984). Friendship in the nursery school: Social organization in a peer environment. In S. R. Asher & J. M. Gottman (Eds.), *The development of children's friendships* (pp. 207–241). Cambridge, UK: Cambridge University Press.

Corsaro, W. A. (1997). *The sociology of childhood* (pp. 205–252). Thousand Oaks, CA: Pine Forge Press.

Cowie, H. (1998, May 15 and 16) *From bystanding to standing by—The role of peer support against school bullying.* Keynote Address at the European Conference on Initiatives to Combat School Bullying; http://www.gold.ac.uk/euconf/keynotes/cowie.html.

Cowie, H., & Wallace, P. (2000b). What is peer support? In H. Cowie & P. Wallace (Eds.), *Peer support in action: From bystanding to standing by* (pp. 5–22). London: Sage Publications.

Craig, W. M. (1998). The relationship among bullying, victimization, depression, anxiety, and aggression in elementary school children. *Personality and Individual Differences, 24*(1), 123–130.

Craig, W. M., Henderson, K., & Murphy, J. G. (2000, February). Prospective teachers' attitudes toward bullying and victimization. *School Psychology International, 21*(1), 5–21.

Craig, W. M., & Pepler, D. J. (1995). Peer processes in bullying and victimization: An observational study. *Exceptionality Education Canada, 5*(3&4), 81–95.

Craig, W. M., & Pepler, D. J. (1997). Observations of bullying and victimization in the school yard. *Canadian Journal of School Psychology, 13*(2), 41–60.

Craig, W. M., & Pepler, D. J. (2000). Observations of bullying and victimization in the school year. In W. Craig (Ed.), *Childhood social development: The essential readings* (pp. 117–136). Oxford, UK: Blackwell Publishers.

Craig, W. M., Pepler, D., & Atlas, R. (2000). Observations of bullying in the playground and in the classroom. *School Psychology International, 21*(1), 22–36.

Craig, W. M., Pepler, D., Connolly, J., & Henderson, K. (2001). Developmental context of peer harassment in early adolescence: The role of puberty and the peer group. In J. Juvonen & S. Graham (Eds.), *Peer harassment in school: The plight of the vulnerable and victimized* (pp. 243–261). New York: The Guilford Press.

Craig, W. M., Peters, D., & Konarski, R. (1998). *Bullying and victimization among Canadian school children.* Available online from Applied Research Branch, Strategic Policy, Human Resources Development Canada; http://www.hrdc-drhc.gc.ca/publications/research/abw-98-28e.shtml.

Crary, D. (2001a). New attacks may soften tattle taboo. *The Associated Press.* America Online.

Crick, N. (1993, August). Relational aggression: Gender differences in the expression of aggressive behavior. In S. R. Asher (Chair), *Social relationships, social beliefs, and aggression.* Symposium conducted at the annual meeting of the American Psychological Association, Toronto, Canada.

Crick, N. R. (2000). Engagement in gender normative versus nonnormative forms of aggression: Links to social-psychological adjustment. In W. Craig (Ed.), *Childhood social development: The essential readings* (pp. 309–329). Oxford, UK: Blackwell Publishers.

Crick, J. R., & Grotpeter, J. K. (1995). Relational aggression, gender, and social-psychological adjustment. *Child Development, 66,* 710–722.

Crick, N. R., Grotpeter, J. K., & Bigbee, M. A. (2002). Relationally and physically aggressive children's intent attributions and feelings of distress for relational and instrumental peer provocations. *Child Development, 73*(4), 1134–1142.

Crick, N. R., Nelson, D. A., Morales, J. R., Cullerton-Sen, C., Casas, J. F., & Hickman, S. E. (2001). Relational victimization in childhood and adolescence: I hurt you through the grapevine. In J. Juvonen & S. Graham (Eds.), *Peer harassment in school: The plight of the vulnerable and victimized* (pp. 196–214). New York: The Guilford Press.

Crockett, D. P. (2003, February). Future of School Psychology Conference; Keynote. Critical issues facing children in the 2000's. *Communiqué, 31*(5), 7–8.

Crosnoe, R., Erickson, K., & Dornbusch, S. (2002). Protective functions of family relationships and school factors on the deviant behavior of adolescent boys and girls: Reducing the impact of risky friendships. *Youth and Society, 33*(4), 515–544.

Crozier, W. R., & Dimmock, P. S. (1999). Name-calling and nicknames in a sample of primary school children. *British Journal of Educational Psychology, 69*(4), 505–516.

Curwin, R. L., & Mendler, A. N. (1997). *Tough as necessary: Countering violence, aggression, and hostility in our school.* Alexandria, VA: Association for Supervision and Curriculum Development.

Cushman, T., & Johnson, T. (2000, October). Attention: Depression and temperament. *Communiqué, 29*(2), 1, 6–7.

David, C. F., & Kistner, J. A. (2000). Do positive self-perceptions have a "dark-side"? Examination of the link between perceptual bias and aggression. *Journal of Abnormal Child Psychology, 28*(4), 327–337.

Dearing, K. F., Hubbard, J. A., Ramsden, S. R., Parker, E. H., Relyea, N., Smithmyer, C. M., et al. (2002). Children's self reports about anger regulation: Direct and indirect links to social preference and aggression. *Merrill-Palmer Quarterly, 48*(3), 308–336.

DeBruyn, R. L., & Larson, J. L. (1984). *You can handle them all: A discipline model for handling over one hundred different misbehaviors at school and at home.* Manhattan, Kansas: The MASTER Teacher Inc.

Delligatti, N., Akin-Little, A., & Little, S. G. (2003). Conduct disorder in girls: Diagnostic and intervention issues. *Psychology in the Schools, 40*(2), 183–192.

Demko, L. (1996). Bullying at school: The no-blame approach. *Health Education, 96*(1), 26–30.

Dill, V. S. (1998). A peaceable school: Cultivating a culture of nonviolence. Bloomington, Indiana: *Phi Delta Kappa Educational Foundation.*

Dishion, T. J., McCord, J., & Poulin, F. (1999). When interventions harm: Peer groups and problem behavior. *American Psychologist, 54*(9), 755–768.

Dishion, T. J., Patterson, G. R., & Griesler, P. C. (1994). Peer adaptations in the development of antisocial behavior: A confluence model. In L. R. Huesmann (Ed.), *Aggressive behavior: Current perspectives* (pp. 61–95). New York: Plenum Press.

Dodge, K. A. (1991). The structure and function of reactive and proactive aggression. In D. J. Pepler & K. H. Rubin (Eds.), *The development and treatment of childhood aggression* (pp. 201–218). Mahwah, NJ: Lawrence Erlbaum Associates, Publishers.

Duncan, R. D. (1999). Maltreatment by parents and peers: The relationship between child abuse, bully victimization, and psychological distress. *Child Maltreatment, 4*(1), 45–55.

Edens, J. F. (1999). Aggressive children's self-systems and the quality of their relationships with significant others. *Aggression and Violent Behavior, 4*, 151–177.

Edwards, C. H. (2001). Student violence and the moral dimensions of education. *Psychology in the Schools, 38*(30), 249–256.

Eisenberg, M. E., Neumark-Sztainer, D., & Story, M. (2003). Association of weight-based teasing and emotional well-being among adolescents. *Journal of Adolescent Health, 32*(2), 121.

Eisenberg, N., Wentzel, M., & Harris, J. D. (1998). The role of emotionality and regulation in empathy-related responding. *School Psychology Review, 27*(4), 506–521.

Elliot, D. S. (Ed.) (2000). *Blueprints for violence prevention: Bullying prevention program.* Boulder, Colorado: Institute of Behavioral Science, Regents of the University of Colorado.

Elting, J. A., & Demaray, M. K. (2002, February). Coping and social support in middle school children. Poster session presented at the annual convention of the National Association of School Psychologists, Chicago, Illinois.

Embry, D. D. (1997). Does your school have a peaceful environment? Using an audit to create a climate for change and resiliency. *Intervention in School and Clinic, 32*(4), 217–222.

Ericson, N. (2001, June). Addressing the Problem of Juvenile Bullying. Fact Sheet. Washington, DC: The Office of Juvenile Justice and Delinquency.

Eron, L. D., Huesmann, L. R., & Zelli, A. (1991). The role of parental variables in the learning of aggression. In D. J. Pepler & K. H. Rubin (Eds.), *The development and treatment of childhood aggression* (pp. 169–197). Mahwah, NJ: Lawrence Erlbaum Associates, Publishers.

Eslea, M., & Rees, J. (2001). At what age are children most likely to be bullied at school? *Aggressive Behavior, 27*(6), 419–429.

Espelage, D. L. (2002, November). *Bullying in early adolescence: The role of the peer group.* (ERIC Digest, EDO-PS-02-16). Champaign, IL: ERIC Clearinghouse on Elementary and Early Childhood Education; http://ericeece.org/pubs/digests/2002/espelage02.html.

Espelage, D. L., & Asidao, C. S. (2001). Conversations with middle school students about bullying and victimization: Should we be concerned? In R. A. Geffner, M. Loring, & C. Young (Eds.), *Bullying behavior: Current issues, research, and interventions* (pp. 49–62). NY: The Haworth Press, Inc.

Espelage, D. L., & Holt, M. K. (2001). Bullying and victimization during early adolescence: Peer influences and psychosocial correlates. In R. A. Geffner, M. Loring, & C. Young (Eds.), *Bullying behavior: Current issues, research, and interventions* (pp. 123–142). New York: The Haworth Press, Inc.

European Conference on Initiatives to Combat School Bullying (1998). University of London, UK. (Revised August, 1998); http://www.gold.ac.uk/euconf/wrksumms/wrkshp9.html.

Fagan, T. K., Gorin, S., & Tharinger, D. (2000). The National Association of School Psychologists and the Division of School Psychology-APA: Now and beyond. *School Psychology Review, 29*(4), 525–535.

Farmer, A., Jr. & Bierman, K. (2002). Predictors and consequences of aggressive-withdrawn problem profiles in early grade school. *Journal of Clinical Child and Adolescent Psychology, 31*(3), 299–311.

Feinberg, T., & Barbarasch, B. (2002). *Character education: The role for school psychologists;* http://www.nasponline.org/advocacy/span/span_sep02_character.html.

Fine, G. A. (1984). Friends, impression management, and preadolescent behavior. In S. R. Asher & J. M. Gottman (Eds.), *The development of children's friendships* (pp. 29–52). Cambridge, UK: Cambridge University Press.

Fischer, K., Haas, M., Watson, M., & Carr, C. (2002, August). Reserved children more likely to be violent than their outgoing peers. *HGSE News;* http://www.gse.harvard.edu/news/features/fischer08212002.html.

Forehand, R., & Long, N. (1991). Prevention of aggression and other behavior problems in the early adolescent years. In D. J. Pepler & K. H. Rubin (Eds.), *The development and treatment of childhood aggression* (pp. 317–330). Hillsdale, NJ: Lawrence Erlbaum Associates, Publishers.

Foundations of Information Technologies (2002). The University of British Columbia; http://www. slais.ubc.ca/courses/libr500/02-03-wt1/www/L_Serviss/index2.htm.

Franz, D. Z., & Gross, A. M. (2001, January). Child sociometric status and parent behaviors: An observational study. *Behavior Modification, 25*(1), 3–20.

Freedman, J. (1999, July). Easing the teasing: How parents can help their children. Champaign, IL: Clearinghouse on Elementary and Early Childhood Education. (EDO-PS-99-7).

French, D. C., Jansen, E. A., & Pidada, S. (2002). United States and Indonesian children's and adolescent's reports of relational aggression by disliked peers. *Child Development, 73*(4), 1143–1150.

Froschl, M., & Gropper, N. (1999, May). Fostering friendships, curbing bullying. *Educational Leadership, 56*(8), 72–75.

Froschl, M., Sprung, B., & Mullin-Rindler, N. (1998). *Quit it! A teacher's guide on teasing and bullying for use with students in grades K-3.* Washington, DC: NEA Professional Library.

Funke, K., & Hymel, S. (2002, February). The assessment of empathy in children identified as bullies. Poster session presented at the annual meeting of the National Association of School Psychologists, Chicago, Illinois.

Furlong, M., & Smith, D. (1998, April). Angry children: Socialization factors associated with anger and hostility in children. Paper presented at the annual conference of the National Association of School Psychologists. Orlando Florida.

Furniss, C. (2000). Bullying in schools: It's not a crime-is it? *Education and the Law, 12*(1), 9–29.

Gagnon, C. (1991). School-based interventions for aggressive children: Possibilities, limitations and future directions. In D. J. Pepler & K. H. Rubin (Eds.), *The development and treatment of childhood aggression* (pp. 449–455). Mahwah, NJ: Lawrence Erlbaum Associates, Publishers.

Galen, B., & Underwood, M. (1997). A developmental investigation of social aggression among children. *Developmental Psychology, 33*, 589–600.

Garbarino, J. (2001). Viewpoint. *National Dropout Prevention Center/Network Newsletter, 13*(2), 8.

Garrity, C., & Barris, M. A. (1996). Bullies and victims: A guide for pediatricians. *Contemporary Pediatrics, 13*(2), 90–114.

Garrity, C., Jens, K., Porter, W., Sager, N., & Short-Camilli, C. (1994). *Bully-proofing your school: A comprehensive approach for elementary schools.* Longmont, CO: Sopris West.

Gascolgne, J. (2001). The power of positive peer pressure: Using social norm theory to address youth health issues. *The RMC Health Educator, 2*(1), 1–2, 4.

Ge, X., Brody, G. H., Conger, R. D., Simons, R. L., & Murry, V. (2002). Contextual amplification of pubertal transition effects on deviant peer affiliation and externalizing behavior among African American children. *Developmental Psychology, 38*(1), 42–54.

Gersten, R., Chard, D., & Baker, S. (2000). Factors enhancing sustained use of research-based instructional practices. *Journal of Learning Disabilities, 33*(50), 445–457.

Gillham, J., Reivich, K., Jaycox, L., & Seligman, M. E. P. (1995). Prevention of depressive symptoms in school children: Two year follow up. *Psychological Science, 6*(6), 343–351.

Glover, D., Gough, G., Johnson, M., & Cartwright, N. (2000). Bullying in 25 secondary schools: Incidence, impact and intervention. *Educational Research, 42*(2), 141–156.

Goldstein, A. P. (1999). *Low-level aggression: First steps on the ladder to violence.* Champaign, IL: Research Press.

Goldstein, A. P., Glick, B., & Gibbs, J. (1998). *Aggression replacement training: A comprehensive intervention for aggressive youth* (Rev. ed.). Champaign, IL: Research Press.

Goldstein, S. (1995). *Understanding and managing children's classroom behavior* (p. 302). New York: John Wiley & Sons, Inc.

Goodman, R. F. (1999). Bullies: More than Sticks, Stones, and Name Calling. *NY University Child Study Center Letter*, 4–6.

Goosens, F. A., Bokhorst, K., Bruinsma, C., & vanBoxel, H. W. (2002). Judgements of aggressive, withdrawn and prosocial behavior: Perceived control, anger, pity and sympathy in young Dutch children. *Journal of School Psychology, 40*(4), 309–327.

Gorman, A. H., Kim, J., & Schimmelbusch, A. (2002). The attributes adolescents associate with peer popularity and teacher preference. *Journal of School Psychology, 40*(2), 143–165.

Gottheil, N. F., & Dubow, E. F. (2001a). The interrelationships of behavioral indices of bully and victim behavior. In R. A. Geffner, M. Loring, & C. Young (Eds.), *Bullying behavior: Current issues, research, and interventions* (pp. 75–93). New York: The Haworth Press, Inc.

Gottheil, N. F., & Dubrow, E. F. (2001b). Tripartite beliefs models of bully and victim behavior. In R. A. Geffner, M. Loring, & C. Young (Eds.), *Bullying behavior: Current issues, research, and interventions* (pp. 25–47). New York: The Haworth Press, Inc.

Graham. S., & Juvonen, J. (2001). An attributional approach to peer victimization. In J. Juvonen & S. Graham (Eds.), *Peer harassment in school: The plight of the vulnerable and victimized* (pp. 49–72). New York: The Guilford Press.

Graham, S., & Juvonen, J. (2002). Ethnicity, peer harassment, and adjustment in middle school: An exploratory study. *Journal of Early Adolescence, 22*(2), 173–199.

Gray, C. (2001, spring). Gray's guide to bullying Part II: The real world. *The Morning News, 13*(1), p. iii.

Green, S., Nansel, T., Simons-Morton, B., Scheidt, P. & Overpeck, M. D. (2001). Systemic vs. individualistic approaches to bullying. *JAMA, 286*(7), 787–788 (letters); http://jama.ama-assn.org/issues/v286n7/ffull/jlt0815-1.html.

Greenberg, M. T., Domitrovich, C., & Bumbarger, B. (1999). *Preventing mental disorders in school-age children: A review of the effectiveness of prevention programs*. Atlanta, GA: U.S. Department of Health and Human Services, Prevention Research Center for the Promotion of Human Development.

Greener, S. H. (2000). Peer assessment of children's prosocial behavior. *Journal of Moral Education, 29*(1), 47–60.

Griffiths, M. (1999). Violent video games and aggression: A review of the literature. *Aggression & Violent Behavior, 4*, 203–212.

Grills, A. E., & Ollendick, T. (2002). Peer victimization, global self-worth, and anxiety in middle school children. *Journal of Clinical Child and Adolescent Psychology, 31*(11), 59–68.

Gropper, N., & Froschl, M. (2000, April). The role of gender in young children's teasing and bullying behavior. *Equity & Excellence in Education, 33*(1), 48–56.

Gumora, G., & Arsenio, W. F. (2002). Emotionality, emotion regulation, and school performance in middle school children. *Journal of School Psychology, 40*(5), 395–413.

Hamilton Fish Institute (n.d.). *Effective violence prevention programs*, Washington, DC; http://hamfish.org/pub/evpp.html.

Harachi, T. W., Catalano, R. F., & Hawkins, J. D. (1999a). Canada. In P. K. Smith, Y. Morita, J. Junger-Tas, D. Olweus, R. Catalano, & P. Slee (Eds.), *The nature of school bullying: A cross-national perspective* (pp. 296–306). London: Routledge.

Harachi, T. W., Catalano, R. F., & Hawkins, J. D. (1999b). United States. In P. K. Smith, Y. Morita, J. Junger-Tas, D. Olweus, R. Catalano, & P. Slee (Eds.), *The nature of school bullying: A cross-national perspective* (pp 277–295). London: Routledge.

Hardy, C. L., Bukowski, W. M., & Sippola, L. K. (2002). Stability and change in peer relationships during the transition to middle level school. *Journal of Early Adolescence, 22*(2), 117–142.

Harris, J. R. (1995). Where is the child's environment? A group socialization theory of development. *Psychological Review, 102*(3), 458–489.

Harris, S., & Petrie, G. (2002). A study of bullying in the middle school, *NASSP Bulletin, 86*(633), 42–53.

Hartup, W. W. (1999). The company they keep: Friendships and their developmental significance. *Child Development, 67* (pp. 1–13). Reprinted in A. Slater & D. Muir (Eds.), (2000). *The Blackwell reader in developmental psychology* (pp. 452–471). Oxford, UK: Blackwell Publishers.

Hartup, W. W. (1998). The company they keep: Friendships and their developmental significance. In A. Campbell & S. Muncer (Eds.), *The social child* (pp. 143–163). East Sussex, UK: Psychology Press.

Hartup, W. W. (2000). The company they keep: Friendships and their developmental significance. In W. Craig (Ed.), *Childhood social development: The essential readings* (pp. 61–84). East Sussex, UK: Blackwell Publishers.

Haselager, G. J. T., Cillessen, A. H. N., Van Lieshout, C. F. M., Riksen-Walraven, J. M., & Hartup, W. W. (2002). Heterogeneity among peer-rejected boys across middle childhood: Developmental pathways of social behavior. *Developmental Psychology, 38*(3), 446–456.

Hawker, D. S., & Boulton, M. J. (2000). Twenty years' research on peer victimization and psychosocial maladjustment: A meta-analytic review of cross-sectional studies. *Journal of Child Psychology and Psychiatry, 41*(4), 441–455.

Hawkins, J., Herrenkohl, T., Farrington, D., Brewer, D., Catalano, R., Harachi, T., & Cothern, L. (2000). Predictors of youth violence. *Juvenile Justice Bulletin* (pp. 1–11). Washington, DC: U.S. Department of Justice.

Hawkins, L., Pepler, D. J., & Craig, W. M. (2001). Naturalistic observations of peer interventions in bullying. *Social Development, 10*(4), 512–527.

Haynie, D. L., Nansel, T., Eitel, P., Crump, A. D., Saylor, K., Yu, K., & Simons-Morton, B. (2001, February). Bullies, victims, and bully/victims: Distinct groups of at-risk youth. *Journal of Early Adolescence, 21*(1), 29–49.

Hazler, R. J. (1996). Bystanders: An overlooked factor in peer on peer abuse. *The Journal for the Professional Counselor, 11*(2), 11–21.

Hazler, R. J., Miller, D. L., Carney, J. V., & Green, S. (2001, June). Adult recognition of school bullying situations. *Educational Research, 43*(2), 133–146.

Henderson, H. A., & Fox, N. A. (1998). Inhibited and uninhibited children: Challenges in school settings. *School Psychology Review, 27*(4), 492–505.

Henderson, N. R., & Hymel, S. (2002, February). *Peer contributions to bullying in schools: Examining student response strategies.* Poster session presented at the 2002 National Association of School Psychologists Annual Convention, Chicago, IL.

Henington, C., Hughes, J. N., Cavell, T. A., & Thompson, B. (1998). The role of relational aggression in identifying aggressive boys and girls. *Journal of School Psychology, 36*(4), 457–477.

Higgins, C. (1994). Improving the school ground environment as an anti-bullying intervention. In P. K. Smith & S. Sharp (Eds.), *School bullying: Insights and perspectives* (pp. 160–192). London: Routledge.

Hirsch, B. J., Engel-Levy, A., Du Bois, D. L., & Hardesty, P. H. (1990). The role of social environments in social support. In B. R. Sarason, I. G. Sarason, & G. R. Pierce (Eds.), *Social support: An interactional view* (pp. 367–393). New York: John Wiley & Sons.

Hoover, J., & Hazler, R. (1991, February). Bullies and victims. *Elementary School Guidance & Counseling, 25,* 212–219.

Houndoumadi, A., & Pateraki, L. (2001). Bullying and bullies in Greek elementary schools: Pupils' attitudes and teachers'/parents' awareness. *Educational Review, 53*(1), 19–26.

Hubbard, J. A. (2001). Emotion expression processes in children's peer interaction: The role of peer rejection, aggression, and gender. *Child Development, 72*(5), 1426–1438.

Hubbard, J. A., Smithmyer, C. M., Ramsden, S. R., Parker, E. H., Flanagan, K. D., Dearing, K. F., et al. (2002). Observational, physiological, and self-report measures of children's anger: Relations to reactive vs. proactive aggression. *Child Development, 73*(4), 1101–1118.

Huesmann, L. R., & Miller, L. S. (1994). Long-term effects of repeated exposure to media violence in childhood. In L. R. Huesmann (Ed.), *Aggressive behavior: Current perspectives* (pp. 153–186). New York: Plenum Press.

Hughes, J. N., Cavell, T. A., & Prasad-Gaur, A. (2001). A positive view of peer acceptance in aggressive youth: Risk for future peer acceptance. *Journal of School Psychology, 39*(3), 239–252.

Hughes, T., & Giron, K. (2001, April). *Child aggression & treatment.* Paper presented at the annual conference of the National Association of School Psychologists, Washington, D.C.

Hyman, I. A., Dahbany, M., Blum, M., Weiler, E., Brooks-Klein, V., & Pokalo, M. (1997). *School discipline and school violence: The teacher variance approach.* Boston, MA: Allyn and Bacon.

Jahoda, G. (1998). Cultural influences in development. In A. Campbell & S. Muncer (Eds.), *The social child* (pp. 85–109). East Sussex, UK: Psychology Press.

Jeffrey, L. R., Miller, D., & Linn, M. (2001). Middle school bullying as a context for the development of passive observers to the victimization of others. In R. A. Geffner, M. Loring, & C. Young (Eds.), *Bullying behavior: Current issues, research, and interventions* (pp. 143–156). New York: The Haworth Press, Inc.

Johnson, J. (1996). The no-fault school: Understanding groups-understanding schools. In R. Constable, J. P. Flynn, & S. McDonald (Eds.), *School social work: Practice and research perspectives* (3rd ed., pp. 307–327). Chicago, IL: Lyceum Books, Inc.

Juvonen, J., Nishina, A., & Graham, S. (2001). Self-views versus peer perceptions of victim status among early adolescents. In J. Juvonen & S. Graham (Eds.), *Peer harassment in school: The plight of the vulnerable and victimized* (pp. 105–124). New York: The Guilford Press.

Kaltiala-Heino, R., Rimpela, M., Rantanen, P., & Rimpela, A. (2000). Bullying at school—an indicator of adolescents at risk for mental disorders. *Journal of Adolescence, 23*(6), 661–674.

Kaukiainen, A., Salmivalli, C., Lagerspetz, K., Tamminen, M., Vauras, M., & Poskiparta, E. (2002). Learning difficulties, social intelligence, and self-concept: Connections to bully-victim problems. *Scandinavian Journal of Psychology, 43*(3), 269–278.

Kayton, R. (n.d.). *Helping your child cope with teasing: Help your child avoid becoming a victim*; http://family,go.com/PrinterFriendly/

Kelley, B., Loeber, R., Keenan, K., & DeLamatre, M. (1997). Developmental pathways in boys' disruptive and delinquent behavior. *Juvenile Justice Bulletin*, 1–19. Washington, DC: U.S. Department of Justice.

Keltikangas-Jarvinen, L. (2002). Aggressive problem-solving strategies, aggressive behavior, and social acceptance in early and late adolescence. *Journal of Youth and Adolescence, 31*(4), 279–287.

Keogh, B. K. (2003). *Temperament in the classroom: Understanding individual differences.* Baltimore, MD: Paul H. Brookes Publishing Company.

Khatri, P., Kupersmidt, J. B., & Patterson, C. (2000). Aggression and peer victimization as predictors of self-reported behavioral and emotional adjustment. *Aggressive Behavior, 26*(5), 345–358.

Khosropour, S. C., & Walsh, J. (2001). That's not teasing-That's bullying: A study of fifth graders' conceptualization of bullying and teasing. Paper presented at the annual conference of the American Educational Research Association, Seattle, Washington.

Kiesner, J., Cadinu, M., Poulin, F., & Bucci, M. (2002). Group identification in early adolescence: Its relation with peer adjustment and its moderator effect on peer influence. *Child Development, 73*(1), 196–208.

Killen, M. (2002). Early deliberations: A developmental psychologist investigates how children think about fairness and exclusion. *Teaching Tolerance, 22*, 44–49.

Killen, M., & Stangor, C. (2001). Children's social reasoning about inclusion and exclusion in gender and race peer group contexts. *Child Development, 72*(1), 174–186.

Kochenderfer, B., & Ladd, G. (1996). Peer victimization: Manifestations and relations to school adjustment in kindergarten. *Journal of School Psychology, 34*(3), 267–283.

Kochenderfer-Ladd, B., & Skinner, K. (2002). Children's coping strategies: Moderators of the effects of peer victimization? *Developmental Psychology, 38*(2), 267–278.

Kowalski, R. M. (2000). "I was only kidding!": Victims and perpetrators of teasing. *Personality and Social Psychology Bulletin, 26*(2), 231–241.

Kratochwill, T. R., & Stoiber, K. C. (2000). Uncovering critical research agendas for school psychology: Conceptual dimensions and future directions. *School Psychology Review, 29*(4), 591–603.

Kruger, L. (2002, November 8). *Bullying discussion. Message posted to the Global School Psychology Network*, news:// www.dac.neu.edu/cp/consult/.

Kutnick, P., & Manson, I. (1998). Social life in the primary school: Towards a relational concept of social skills for use in the classroom. In A. Campbell & S. Muncer (Eds.), *The social child* (pp. 165–187). East Sussex, UK: Psychology Press.

Ladd, G. W. (1999). Peer relationships and social competence during early and middle childhood. *Annual Review of Psychology, 50*, 333–359.

Ladd, G. W., Kochenderfer, B. J., & Coleman, C. C. (2000). Friendship quality as a predictor of young children's early school adjustment. In W. Craig (Ed.), *Childhood social development: The essential readings* (pp. 139–166). Oxford, UK: Blackwell Publishers.

Ladd, B. K., & Ladd, G. W. (2001). Variations in peer victimization: Relations to children's maladjustment. In J. Juvonen & S. Graham (Eds.), *Peer harassment in school: The plight of the vulnerable and victimized* (pp. 25–48). New York: The Guilford Press.

LaFontana, K. M., & Cillessen, A. (2002). Children's perceptions of popular and unpopular peers: A multimethod assessment. *Developmental Psychology, 38*(5), 635–647.

Lagerspetz, K. M., & Bjorkqvist, K. (2000). Indirect aggression in boys and girls. In L. R. Huesmann (Ed.), *Aggressive behavior: Current perspectives* (pp. 131–150). New York: Plenum Press.

Lampert, J. B. (1998, February). Voices and visions: Adolescent girls' experiences as bullies, targets, and bystanders. Dissertation. Dissertation Abstracts International. (5808-A0:2986).

Landau, S., Milich, R., Harris, M. K., & Larson, S. E. (2001). "You really don't know how much it hurts:" Children's and preservice teachers' reactions to childhood teasing. *School Psychology Review, 30*(3), 329–343.

Laner, M. R., Benin, M. H., & Ventrone, N. A. (2001). Bystander attitudes toward victims of violence: Who's worth helping? *Deviant Behavior, 22*(1), 23–42.

Lazar, Z. (2002, February). Bullying: A serious business. *Child*, 78–84.

Lazarus, P. J. (2001, May) Breaking the code of silence: What schools can do about it. *Communiqué, 29*(7), 28–29.

LeBlanc, J. C. (2001, September). Bullying: It's not just a school problem. *Pediatrics & Child Health, 6*(7). http://www.pulsus.com/Paeds/06_07/lebl_ed.htm.

Ledingham, J. E. (1991). Social cognition and aggression. In D. J. Pepler & K. H. Rubin (Eds.), *The development and treatment of childhood aggression* (pp. 279–285). Mahwah, NJ: Lawrence Erlbaum Associates, Publishers.

Leff, S., Kupersmidt, J., Patterson, C., & Power, T. (1999). Factors influencing teacher identification of peer bullies and victims. *School Psychology Review, 28*(2), 505–517.

Leff, S. S., Power, T. J., Manz, P. H., Costigan, T. E., & Nabors, L. A. (2001). School-based aggression prevention programs for young children: Current status and implications for violence prevention. *School Psychology Review, 30*(3), 344–362.

Lewis, T. J., Powers, L. J., Kelk, M. J., & Newcomer, L. L. (2002). Reducing problem behaviors on the playground: An investigation of the application of schoolwide positive behavior supports. *Psychology in the Schools, 39*(2), 181–190.

Liberman, R. (2001, June). Bullying: A slow fuse to childhood rage. *Communiqué, 29*(8), p. 38.

Limber, S. P. (1996, Fall). Bullying among school children. *School Safety*, 8–9, 30.

Limber, S. P., & Nation, M. M. (1998, April). Bullying among children and youth. *Juvenile Justice Bulletin*. Rockville, MD: Juvenile Justice Clearinghouse.

Lindgren, H. G. (1996, October). "Bullying"—How to stop it!" Lincoln, Nebraska (January, 1997); *University of Nebraska Cooperative Extension* (NF 309), Lincoln, Nebraska: http://www.ianr.unl.edu/pubs/family/nf309.htm.

Lines, C., Plog, A., & Porter, W. (2002, February). *The ABC's of school psychological safety: Assets (and assessment), bully-proofing, and the caring community*. Poster session presented at the annual convention of the National Association of School Psychologists, Chicago, Illinois.

Lumsden, L. (2002). *Preventing bullying* (ERIC Digest 155). Eugene, Oregon: ERIC Clearinghouse on Educational Management; http://ericcass.uncg.edu/virtuallib/bullying/1068.html.

Maccoby, E. E. (2000). Gender and relationships: A developmental account. In W. Craig (Ed.), *Childhood social development: The essential readings* (pp.201–219). Oxford, UK: Blackwell Publishers.

Macklem, G. L. & Kalinsky, R. (2002, February). *Teasing and bullying behaviors: Focus on prevention and interventions for bullies, targeted children and passive participants.* Mini-skills workshop presented at the annual convention of the National Association of School Psychologists, Chicago, Illinois.

Mahady-Wilton, M. M., Craig, W. M., & Pepler, D. J. (2000). Emotional regulation and display in classroom victims of bullying: Characteristic expression of affect, coping styles and relevant contextual factors. *Social Development, 9*(2), 226–244.

Maharaj, A. S., Ryba, K., & Tie, W. (2000a). Bullying as school violence: Prevention and elimination. *The Bulletin of the New Zealand Psychological Society, Inc., 98*, 42–48.

Maharaj, A. S., Ryba, K., & Tie, W. (2000b). Deconstructing bullying in Aotearoa/New Zealand: Disclosing its liberal and colonial connections. *New Zealand Journal of Educational Studies, 35*(1), 9–23.

Mains, B., & Robinson, G. (1992). *Stamp out bullying: Never mind the awareness, what can we do?* Bristol, UK: Lame Duck Publishers.

Malecki, C. K., & Demaray, M. K. (2002). Measuring perceived social support: Development of the child and adolescent social support scale (CASSS). *Psychology in the Schools, 39*(1), 1–18.

Marlowe, D. H. (2000). *Psychological and psychosocial consequences of combat and deployment with special emphasis on the Gulf War* (chapt. 6). Santa Monica, CA: RAND.

Martin, C. L., & Fabes, R. A. (2001, May). The stability and consequences of young children's same-sex peer interactions. *Developmental Psychology, 37*(3), 431–446.

Massey, O. T., Armstrong, K., Boroughs, M., Santoro, G., & Perry, A. (2002, March). *Evaluating the safe schools/healthy students initiative: Bullying, violence and the experience of safety in schools.* Symposium presented at the annual convention of the National Association of School Psychologists, Chicago, Illinois.

Matson, G., Ju, J., Knierim, A. M., Hansen, M., & Knierim-Fatras, M. (Eds.) (2002). "Bullying": Principals' pervasive problem. *School Principal's Legal Alert.* NJ: Alexander Hamilton Institute.

McClowry, S. G. (1995). The development of the School-Age Temperament Inventory (SATI). *Merrill-Palmer Quarterly, 41*, 271–285.

McCoy, E. (1997). *What to do . . . when kids are mean to your child.* Pleasantville, NY: The Reader's Digest Association, Inc.

McDonald, S. & Moriarty, A. (1996). Conflict resolution. In R. Constable, J. P. Flynn, & S. McDonald (Eds.), *School social work: Practice and research perspectives* (3rd ed., pp. 290–298). Chicago, IL: Lyceum Books, Inc.

McGurk, H., & Soriano, G. (1998). Families and social development: The 21st century. In A. Campbell and S. Muncer (Eds.), *The social child* (pp. 113–142). East Sussex, UK: Psychology Press.

McMaster, L. E., Connolly, J., Pepler, D., & Craig, W. (2000). Peer to peer sexual harassment in early adolescence: A developmental perspective. *Development and Psychopathology, 14*, 91–105.

McWhirter, J. J., McWhirter, B. T., McWhirter, A. M., & McWhirter, E. H. (1998). *At-risk youth: A comprehensive response* (2nd ed., pp. 238–256). Pacific Grove, CA: Brooks/Cole Publishing Company.

Mellor, A. (1999). Scotland. In P. K. Smith, Y. Morita, J. Junger-Tas, D. Olweus, R. Catalano, & P. Slee (Eds.), *The nature of school bullying: A cross-national perspective* (pp. 91–111). London: Routledge.

Menesini, E., Eslea, M., Smith, P.K., Genta, M.L., Giannetti, E., Fonzi, A., & Costabile, A. (1998). Cross-national comparison of children's attitudes towards bully/victim problems in school. *Aggressive Behavior, 23*(4), 245–257.

Menesini, E., Fonzi, A., Ciucci, E., Almeida, A., Ortega, R., Lera, M. J., et al. (1999, December). Bullying and emotions: Report of the working party. *Nature and prevention of bullying*, TMR Initiative of the European Commission; http://www.gold.ac.uk/tmr/reports/aim2_firenze2.html.

Miller, A. L., & Olson, S. L. (2000). Emotional expressiveness during peer conflicts: A predictor of social maladjustment among high-risk preschoolers. *Journal of Abnormal Child Psychology, 28*(4), 339–352.

Miller, G., & Rubin, K. (1998). Victimization of school-age children: Safe schools strategies for parents and educators. In A. S. Canter & S. A. Carroll (Eds.), Helping children at home and school: Handouts from your school psychologist (Rev. ed., by S. Carroll, pp. 527–530). Bethesda, MD: The National Association of School Psychologists.

Mostow, A. J., Izard, C. E., Fine, S., & Trentacosta, C. J. (2002). Modeling emotional, cognitive, and behavioral predictors of peer acceptance. *Child Development, 73*(6), 1775–1787.

Mounts, N. S. (1997, Summer). What about girls? Are they really not aggressive? *Human Development and Practice, 3*(2); http://www.hec.ohio-state.edu/famlife/bulletin/volume.3/bull26b.htm.

Mullin-Rindler, N. (1998). *Helping children deal with bullying*. Unpublished paper. MA: Wellesley College Center for Research on Women.

Mullin-Rindler, N. (2001a, Spring). Bullying and gender: Is there a connection? *National Dropout Prevention Center/Network Newsletter. 13*(2), 3.

Mullin-Rindler, N. (2001b, June). Confronting Teasing and Bullying in School. *Project on Teasing and Bullying*. Unpublished paper. MA: Wellesley College Center for Research on Women.

Mullin-Rindler, N. (2001). *Dealing with Provocative Victims*. Project on Teasing and Bullying. Unpublished paper. MA: Wellesley College Center for Research on Women.

Mullin-Rindler, N. (2001). Project on Teasing and Bullying: *Research, Education & Action*. Wellesley Centers for Women; http://www.wcwonline.org/bulling/staffdev.html.

Murray, J. P. (1997). Media violence and youth. In J. D. Osofsky (Ed.), *Children in a violent society* (pp. 77–78). New York: The Guilford Press.

Muscari, M. (2002). Media violence: Advice for parents. *Pediatric Nursing. 28*(6), 585–591.

Nansel, T. R., Overpeck, M. D., Haynie, D. L., Ruan, W. J., & Scheidt, P. C. (2003). Relationships between bullying and violence among US youth. *Archives of Pediatrics & Adolescent Medicine, 157*(4), 348–353.

Nansel, T. R., Overpeck, K., Pilla, R. S., Ruan, J., Simons-Morton, B., & Scheidt, P., (2001). Bullying behaviors among US youth: Prevalence and association with psychosocial adjustment. *JAMA, 285*(16), 2094–2100.

National Education Association (n.d.). National Bullying Awareness Campaign (NBAC). Washington, DC; http://www.nea.org/schoolsafety/bullying.html.

National Norms Resource Center (2003). Social norms; An introduction. Frequently asked Questions about the social norms approach. DeKalb, IL; http://www.socialnorm.org/faqs.html.

Neimark, N. F. (1998, October). The fight or flight response. *Mind/Body Education Center*; http://www.mindbodymed.com/EducationCenter/fight.html.

Newman, D. A., Horne, A. M., & Bartolomucci, C. L. (2000a). *Bully busters: A teacher's manual for helping bullies, victims, and bystanders*. Champaign, IL: Research Press.

Newman, D. A., Horne, A. M., & Bartolomucci, C. L. (2000b). *Bullybusting: A psychoeducational program for helping bullies and their victims*. Champaign, IL: Research Press.

Newmark-Sztainer, D., Falkner, N., Story, M., Perry, C., Hannan, P. J., & Mulert, S. (2002). Weight-teasing among adolescents: Correlations with weight status and disordered eating behaviors. *International Journal of Obesity, 26*(1), 123–131.

Oakden, R. (1997). Playground passes. *Teachers plus: Free teaching resources*; http://www.prairie.ca/~roakden/playpass.htm.

O'Connell, P., Pepler, D., & Craig, W. (1999). Peer involvement in bullying: Insights and challenges for intervention. *Journal of Adolescence, 22*(4), 437–452.

Office of Civil Rights, (2001, January). Washington, DC: US Department of Education http://www.ed.gov/offices/OCR/ocmews.html.

Olweus, D. (1991). Bully/victim problems among schoolchildren: Basic facts and effects of a school based intervention program. In D. J. Pepler & E. H. Rubin (Eds.), *The development and treatment of childhood aggression* (pp. 411–449). Mahwah, NJ: Lawrence Erlbaum Associates, Publishers.

Olweus, D. (1993). *Bullying at school: What we know and what we can do.* Oxford, UK: Blackwell Publishers.

Olweus, D. (1994). Bullying at school: Long-term outcomes for the victims and an effective school-based intervention program. In L. R. Huesmann (Ed.), *Aggressive behavior: Current perspectives* (pp. 97–130). New York: Plenum Press.

Olweus, D. (1999a). Norway. In P. K. Smith, Y. Morita, J. Junger-Tas, D. Olweus, R. Catalano, & P. Slee (Eds.), *The nature of school bullying: A cross-national perspective* (pp. 28–48). London: Routledge.

Olweus, D. (1999b). Sweden. In P. K. Smith, Y. Morita, J. Junger-Tas, D. Olweus, R. Catalano, & P. Slee (Eds.), *The nature of school bullying: A cross-national perspective* (pp. 7–27). London: Routledge.

Olweus, D. (2001a). *Olweus' core program against bullying and antisocial behavior: A teacher handbook* (Version III). Bergen, Norway: University of Bergen.

Olweus, D. (2001b). Peer harassment: A critical analysis and some important issues. In J. Juvonen & S. Graham (Eds.), *Peer harassment in school: The plight of the vulnerable and victimized* (pp. 3–20). New York: The Guilford Press.

O'Moore, M. (1997). Critical issues for teacher training to counter bullying and victimization. *European Conference on Initiatives to Combat School Bullying: Keynote Addresses*; http://ericcass.uncg.edu/virtuallib/bulling/1016.html.

O'Moore, M., & Kirkham, C. (2001, July). Self-esteem and its relationship to bullying behavior. *Aggressive Behavior, 27*(4), 269–283.

Orobio deCastro, B., Veerman, J. W., Koops, W., Bosch, J. D., & Monshouwer, H. J. (2002). Hostile attribution of intent and aggressive behavior: A meta-analysis. *Child Development, 73*(3), 916–934.

Osofsky, H. J., & Osofsky, J. D. (2001). Violent and aggressive behaviors in youth: A mental health and prevention perspective. *Psychiatry, 64*(4), 285–295.

Owens, L., Shute, R., & Slee, P. (2000). "Guess what I just heard!": Indirect aggression among teenage girls in Australia. *Aggressive Behavior, 26*(1), 67–83.

Owens, L., Slee, P. T., & Shute, R. H. (2000). 'It hurts a hell of a lot . . .' The effects of indirect aggression on teenage girls. *School Psychology International, 21*(4), 359–376.

Owens, L., Slee, P., & Shute, R. (2001). Victimization among teenage girls: What can be done about indirect harassment? In J. Juvonen & S. Graham (Eds.), *Peer harassment in school: The plight of the vulnerable and victimized* (pp. 215–241). New York: The Guilford Press.

Pakaslahti, L., & Keltikangas-Jarvinen, L. (2000). Comparison of peer, teacher, and self-assessments on adolescent direct and indirect aggression. *Educational Psychology, 20*(2), 177–190.

Pakaslahti, L., Karjalainen, A., & Keltikangas-Jarvinen, L. (2002). Relationships between adolescent prosocial problem-solving strategies, prosocial behavior, and social acceptance. *International Journal of Behavioral Development, 26*(2), 137–144.

Parks, C. D., & Sanna, L. J. (1999). *Group performance and interaction.* Boulder, CO: Westview Press.

Patterson, G. R. (1986). The contribution of siblings to training for fighting: A microsocial analysis. In D. Olweus, J. Block, & M. Radke-Yarrow (Eds.), *Development of antisocial and prosocial behavior: Research, theories, and issues.* New York: Academic Press. Reported in D. J. Pepler, J. Connolly, & W. M. Craig (1997). Bullying and victimization: The problems and solutions for school-aged children. Canada: National Crime Prevention Council.

Patterson, G. R., DeBaryshe, B. D., & Ramsey, E. (2000). A developmental perspective on antisocial behavior. In W. Craig (Ed.), *Childhood social development: The essential readings* (pp. 333–348). Oxford, UK: Blackwell Publishers.

Paulk, D., Swearer, S., Song, S., & Carey, P. (1999, August). *Teacher-, peer-, and self-nominations of bullies and victims of bullying.* Paper presented at the annual convention of the American Psychological Association, Boston, MA.

Pellegrini, A. D. (2001a). Sampling instances of victimization in middle school: A methodological comparison. In J. Juvonen & S. Graham. (Eds.), *Peer harassment in school: The plight of the vulnerable and victimized* (pp. 125–146). New York: The Guilford Press.

Pellegrini, A. D. (2001b). The roles of dominance and bullying in the development of early heterosexual relationships. In R. A. Geffner, M. Loring, & C. Young (Eds.), *Bullying behavior: Current issues, research, and interventions* (pp. 63–73). New York: The Haworth Press, Inc.

Pellegrini, A., & Bartini, M. (1999, August). Bullying and victimization in early adolescence: Description and prevention. *Paper presented at the annual convention of the American Psychological Association,* Boston, MA.

Pellegrini, A. D., & Long, J. D. (2002). A longitudinal study of bullying, dominance, and victimization during the transition from primary school through secondary school. *British Journal of Developmental Psychology, 20*(2), 259–280.

Pepler, D., Connolly, J., & Craig, W.(1997, June). Bullying and victimization: The problems and solutions for school-aged children. (MP32-28/98-28E). *National Crime Prevention Council,* Canada (Modified 2000, December); http://www.crime-prevention.org/english/publications/children/violence.

Pepler, D. J., & Craig, W. (2000, April). Making a Difference in Bullying: Understanding and Strategies for Practitioners. (ISSN 084-99749); http://pavlov.psyc.queensu.ca/~craigw/makediff.pdf.

Pepler, D. J., Craig, W. M., Connolly, J., & Henderson, K. (2001). Bullying, sexual harassment, dating violence, and substance abuse among adolescents. In C. Wekerle & A. Wall, (Eds.), *The violence and addiction equation: Theoretical and clinical issues in substance abuse and relationship violence* (pp. 153–169). Philadelphia, PA: Brunner-Routledge.

Pepler D., Craig, W. M., & O'Connell, P. (1999). Understanding bullying from a dynamic systems perspective. In A. Slater & D. Muir (Eds.), *Developmental psychology* (pp. 32–43). Oxford, UK: Blackwell Publishers.

Pepler, D. J., Craig, W. M., Ziegler, S., & Charach, A. (1994). An evaluation of an anti-bullying intervention in Toronto schools. *Canadian Journal of Community Mental Health, 13*(2), 95–110.

Pepler, D. J., King, G., & Byrd, W. (1991). A social-cognitively based social skills training program for aggressive children. In D. J. Pepler & K. H. Rubin (Eds.), *The development and treatment of childhood aggression* (pp. 361–386). Mahwah, NJ: Lawrence Erlbaum Associates, Publishers.

Pepler, D. J., & Sedighdeilami, F. (1998). *Aggressive girls in Canada: Should we worry about them?* Presented at Investing in children: A National Research Conference, 1998; http://www.hrdc-drhc.gc.ca/sp-ps/arb-dgra/publications/research/investing.shtml.

Perry, D. G., Hodges, E. E., & Egan, S. K. (2001). Determinants of chronic victimization by peers: A review and a new model of family influence. In J. Juvonen & S. Graham (Eds.), *Peer harassment in school: The plight of the vulnerable and victimized* (pp. 73–104). New York: The Guilford Press.

Peterson, K. D. (2002, Summer). Positive or negative? *Journal of Staff Development, 23*(3); http://wwwnsdc.org/library/jsd/peterson233.html.

Pettegrini, A. D., & Long, J. D. (2002). A longitudinal study of bullying, dominance, and victimization during the transition from primary school through secondary school. *British Journal of Developmental Psychology, 20,* 259–280.

Pettijohn, T. F. (1998). *PSYCHOLOGY :A ConnecText* (4th ed.). Columbus, OH: McGraw-Hill.

Phillips, L. (2000, December). *Youth and violence: Medicine, nursing, and public health: Connecting the dots to prevent violence.* From the Commission for the Prevention of Youth Violence.

Phillipsen, L. C., Bridges, S. K., McLemore, T. G., & Saponaro, L. A. (1999). Perceptions of social behavior and peer acceptance in kindergarten. *Journal of Research in Childhood Education, 14*(1), 68–77.

Pikas, A. (2002). New developments of the shared concern method. *School Psychology International, 23*(3), 307–326.

Poland, S. (2002). Safe schools and springtime stress, post 9-11: Prevention issues. National Association of School Psychologists. *Communiqué, 30*(7), Insert, 1–3.

Potier, B. (2002, September). Inhibition in children predicts aggression GSE research shows surprising findings. *Harvard Gazette;* http://www.news.harvard.edu/gazette/2002/09.19/16-violence.html.

Ray, G. E., Norman, M., Sadowski, C. J., & Cohen, R. (1999). The role of evaluator-victim relationships in children's evaluations of peer provocation. *Social Development, 8*(3), 380–394.

Reinke, W. M., & Herman, K. C. (2002). Creating school environments that deter antisocial behaviors in youth. *Psychology in the Schools, 39*(5), 549–559.

Rigby, K. (2000). Effects of peer victimization in schools and perceived social support on adolescent well-being. *Journal of Adolescence, 23*(1), 57–68.

Rigby, K. (2001). *What is bullying? Defining bullying: A new look at an old concept;* http://www. education.unisa.edu/bulling.

Rigby, K. (2002). *A meta-evaluation of methods and approaches to reducing bullying in pre-schools and in early primary school in Australia.* Commonwealth Attorney-General's Department, Canberra, Australia.

Rigby, K., & Barnes, A. (2002). The victimized students dilemma to tell or not to tell. *Youth Studies Australia, 21*(3), 33–36.

Rigby, K., & Slee, P. T. (1999). Australia. In P. K. Smith, Y. Morita, J. Junger-Tas, D. Olweus, R. Catalano and P. Slee (Eds.), *The nature of school bullying: A cross-national perspective* (pp. 324–339). London: Routledge.

Ritzel, D. O. (2002). Social norms and social marketing in driver education and traffic safety. *The Chronicle;* http://www.adtsea.iup.edu/adtsea/TheChronicle/fall_02/social_norms.htm.

Robinson, T. (2001). Intervention to reduce media viewing improves aggressive children's behavior. *Archives of Pediatrics and Adolescent Medicine, 155,* 17–23.

Rodkin, P., Farmer, T., Pearl, R., & Van Acker, R. (2000, January). Heterogeneity of popular boys: Antisocial and prosocial configurations. *Developmental Psychology, 36*(1), 14–24.

Roland, E. (2002). Bullying, depressive symptoms and suicidal thoughts. *Educational Research, 44*(1), 55–67.

Roland, E., & Idsoe, T. (2001, November). Aggression and bullying. *Aggressive Behavior, 27*(6), 446–462.

Rosen, K. (1998). The family roots of aggression and violence: A life span perspective. In L. L'Abate (Ed.), *Family psychopathology: The relational roots of dysfunctional behavior* (pp. 333–357). New York: The Guilford Press.

Ross, D. (1996). *Childhood bully and teasing: What school personnel, other professionals and parents can do.* Alexandria, Virginia: American Counseling Association.

Rothbart, M. K., & Jones, L. B. (1998). Temperament, self-regulation, and education. *School Psychology Review, 27*(4), 479–491.

Rothschild, B. (1997). *Post-Traumatic Stress Disorder identification and diagnosis;* http://www.healing-arts.org/tir/n-r-rothschild.htm.

Rubin, K. H., Bream, L. A., & Rose-Krasnor, L. (1991). Social problem solving and aggression in childhood. In D. J. Pepler & K. H. Rubin (Eds.), *The development and treatment of childhood aggression* (pp. 219–248). Mahwah, NJ: Lawrence Erlbaum Associates, Publishers.

Rudolph, K. D., & Clark, A. G. (2001). Conceptions of relationships in children with depressive and aggressive symptoms: Social-cognitive distortion or reality? *Journal of Abnormal Child Psychology, 29*(1), 41–56.

Rummel, R. J. (19975). *Understanding conflict and war: Vol. 1: The dynamic psychological field.* Beverly Hills, California: Sage Publications; http://www.mega.nu:8080/ampp/rummel/dpf.chap22.htm.

Salmivalli, C. (1999). Participant role approach to school bullying: Implications for interventions. *Journal of Adolescence, 22*(4), 453–459.

Salmivalli, C., Huttunen, A., and Lagerspetz, K. M. J. (1997). Peer networks and bullying in schools. *Scandinavian Journal of Psychology, 38*, 305–312.

Salmivalli, C., Kaukiainen, A., Kaistaniemi, L., & Lagerspetz, K. M. (1999). Self-evaluated self-esteem, peer-evaluated self-esteem, and defensive egotism as predictors of adolescents' participation in bullying situations. *Personality and Social Psychology Bulletin, 25*(10), 1268–1278.

Salmivalli, C., Kaukiainen, A., & Lagerspetz, K. (2000). Aggression and sociometric status among peers: Do gender and type of aggression matter? *Scandinavian Journal of Psychology, 41*(1), 17–24.

Salmivalli, C., & Nieminen, E. (2001). Proactive and reactive aggression among school bullies, victims, and bully-victims. *Aggressive Behavior, 28*(1), 30–44.

Sanchez, E., Robertson, T. R., Lewis, C. M., Rosenbluth, B., Bohman, T., & Casey, D. M. (2001). Preventing bullying and sexual harassment in elementary schools: The Expect Respect model. In R. A. Geffner, M. Loring, & C. Young (Eds.), *Bullying behavior: Current issues, research, and interventions* (pp. 157–180). New York: The Haworth Press, Inc.

Sandstrom, M. J., & Coie, J. D. (1999). A developmental perspective on peer rejection: Mechanisms of stability and change. *Child Development, 70*(4), 955–966.

Sarason, S. B. (1996). *Revisiting "The culture of the school and the problem of change"* (pp. 283–298, 309–344). New York: Teachers College Press.

Sarason, B. R., Pierce, G. R., & Sarason, I. G. (1990). Social support: The sense of acceptance and the role of relationships. In B. R. Sarason, I. G. Sarason, & G. R. Pierce. (Eds.), *Social support: An interactional view* (pp. 97–128). New York: John Wiley & Sons.

Saufler, C. (1998, April). A survey of bullying behavior among Maine third graders. Maine Project Against Bullying; http://lincoln.midcoast.com/~wps/against/bullying.html.

Scambler, D. J., Harris, M. J., & Milich, R. (1998). Sticks and stones: Evaluation of responses to childhood teasing. *Social Development, 7*(2), 234–249.

Schofiled, J. W. (1984). Complementary and conflicting identities: Images and interaction in an interracial school. In S. R. Asher & J. M. Gottman (Eds.), *The development of children's friendships* (pp. 53–90). Cambridge, UK: Cambridge University Press.

Schuster, B. (1999). Outsiders at school: The prevalence of bullying and its relation with social status. *Group Processes & Intergroup Relations, 2*(2), 175–190.

Schwartz, D. (2000). Subtypes of victims and aggressors in children's peer groups. *Journal of Abnormal Child Psychology, 28*(2), 181–192.

Schwartz, D., Dodge, K. A., Coie, J. D., Hubbard, J. A., Cillessen, A. H., Lemerise, E. A., et al. (1998). Social-cognitive and behavioral correlates of aggression and victimization in boys' play groups. *Journal of Abnormal Child Psychology, 26*(6), 431–440.

Schwartz, D., Farver, J. M., Chang, L., & Lee-Shin, Y. (2002). Victimization in South Korean children's peer groups. *Journal of Abnormal Child Psychology, 30*(2), 113–125.

Schwartz, D., McFadyen-Ketchum, S., Dodge, K. A., Pettit, G. S., & Bates, J. E. (1999). Early behavior problems as a predictor of later peer group victimization: Moderators and mediators in the pathways of social risk. *Journal of Abnormal Child Psychology 27*(3), 191–201.

Schwartz, W. (1999). Developing social competence in children. *Choices in preventing youth violence.* (Briefs #3). New York, NY: Institute for Urban and Minority Education. Teachers College, Columbia University.

Scott, A. M. (2000, March). *The relationship between temperament and conflict resolution abilities.* Paper presented at the annual convention of the National Association of School Psychologists, New Orleans, Louisiana.

Serbin, L. A., Moskowitz, D. S., Schwartzman, A. E., & Ledingham, J. E. (1991). Aggressive, withdrawn, and aggressive/withdrawn children in adolescence: Into the next generation. In D. J. Pepler & K. H. Rubin (Eds.), *The development and treatment of childhood aggression* (pp. 55–78). Mahwah, NJ: Lawrence Erlbaum Associates, Publishers.

Seward, L. M. (n.d.) Bullying, teasing, and victimization and the social cognition of adolescence; http://www.personal.psu.edu/faculty/n/x/nxd10/bullying/group9/laura2.html.

Shapiro, J. P., Baumeister, R. F., & Kessler, J. W. (1991). A three component model of children's teasing: Aggression, humor, and ambiguity. *Journal of Social and Clinical Psychology, 10*, 459–472.

Shapiro, J. P., Burgoon, J. D., Welker, C. J., & Clough, J. B. (2002). Evaluation of the Peacemakers Program: School-based violence prevention for students in grades 4 through 8. *Psychology in the Schools, 39*(1), 87–100.

Sharp, S., & Cowie, H. (1994). Empowering pupils to take positive action against bullying. In P. K. Smith & S. Sharp (Eds.), *School bullying: Insights and perspective* (pp. 108–131). London: Routledge.

Sharp, S., & Thompson, D. (1994). The role of whole-school policies in tackling bullying behavior in schools. In P. K. Smith & S. Sharp (Eds.), *School bullying: Insights and perspective* (pp. 57–83). London: Routledge.

Sharp, S., Thompson, D., & Arora, T. (2000). How long before it hurts?: An investigation into long-term bullying. *School Psychology International, 21*(1), 37–46.

Sheridan, S. M., & Gutkin, T. B. (2000). The ecology of school psychology: Examining and changing our paradigm for the 21st century. *School Psychology Review, 29*(4), 485–502.

Shields, A., & Cicchetti, D. (2001). Parental maltreatment and emotion dysregulation as risk factors for bullying and victimization in middle childhood. *Journal of Clinical Child Psychology, 30*(3), 349–363.

Shields, A., & Cicchetti, D. (2001). Parental maltreatment and emotion dysregulation as risk factors for bullying and victimization in middle childhood. *Journal of Developmental & Behavioral Pediatrics, 23*(1), 61–65.

Shortly, C. L. (1991, October). The development of aggression and prosocial behavior in early childhood. (*Coordinators' Notebook N. 10*). Washington D.C.: World Bank, The Consultative Group on Early Childhood Care and Development.

Silver, R. C., Wortman, C. B., & Crofton, C. (1990). The role of coping in support provision: The self-presentational dilemma of victims of like crises. In B. R. Sarason, I. G. Sarason, & G. R. Pierce (Eds.), *Social support: An interactional view* (pp. 397–426). New York: John Wiley & Sons.

Skernen, (n.d.). Teasing Intervention; http://www.skernen.netfirms.com/teasing_intervention.htm.

Skiba, R., & Fontanini, A. (2000). Bullying prevention: Early identification & intervention. *Communiqué, 29*(7), Insert, 1–3.

Skiba, R., & Peterson, R (2000). *Violence prevention and conflict resolution curricula: Creating a positive climate.* Bloomington, In: Safe and Responsive Schools Project.

Smith, P. K. (1999). England and Wales. In P. K. Smith, Y. Morita, J. Junger-Tas, D. Olweus, R. Catalano, & P. Slee. (Eds.), *The nature of school bullying: A cross-national perspective* (pp. 68–90). London: Routledge.

Smith, P. K., Cowie, H., Olafsson, R. F., & Liefooghe, A. P. D. (2001, November). Definitions of bully-related terms from children in different cultures. Nature and prevention of bullying: The causes and nature of bullying and social exclusion in schools and ways of preventing them. *TMR Network Project;* http://www.gold.ac.uk/tmr/reports/aim1_gold1.html.

Smith, P. K., Cowie, H., Olafsson, R. F., & Liefooghe, A. P. (2002). Definitions of bullying: A comparison of terms used, and age and gender differences, in a 14 country international comparison. *Child Development, 73*(4), 1119–1133.

Smith, P. K., Cowie, H., & Sharp, S. (1994). Working directly with pupils involved in bullying situations. In P. K. Smith & S. Sharp (Eds.), *School bullying: Insights and perspectives* (pp.193–212). London: Routledge.

Smith, P. K., & Morita, Y. (1999). Introduction. In P. K Smith, Y. Morita, J. Junger-Tas, D. Olweus, R. Catalano, & P. Slee (Eds.), *The nature of school bullying: A cross-national perspective* (pp. 1–4). London: Routledge.

Smith, P. K., & Shu, S. (2000). What good schools can do about bullying: Findings from a survey in English schools after a decade of research and action. *Childhood, 7*(2), 193–212.

Smith, S. (2002). Female bullying gets more attention, sparks new debate. Sentinel and Enterprise.com (Last updated 6/11/02); http://www.sentinelandenterprise.com/Stories/0,1413,106% 7E50000%7E666362,00.html.

Social Norms Marketing Research Project; http://www.edc.org/hec/snmrp/.

Song, S. Y., & Swearer, S. M. (2002, February). *An ecological analysis of bullying in middle school: Understanding school climate across the bully-victim continuum.* Paper presented at the annual convention of the National Association of School Psychologists, Chicago, IL.

Song, S., Swearer, S., Eagle, J., & Cary, P. (2000, April). *Bullying and school achievement: Understanding a complex relationship.* Poster presented at the annual convention of the National Association of School Psychologists, New Orleans, LA.

Soutter, A., & McKenzie, A. (2000). The use and effects of anti-bullying and anti-harassment policies in Australian schools. *School Psychology International, 21*(1), 96–105.

Stacey, H. (2000). Mediation and peer mediation. In H. Cowie & P. Wallace (Eds.), *Peer support in action: From bystanding to standing by* (pp.23–35). London: Sage Publications.

Stein, N. (2001). Introduction-What a difference a discipline makes: Bullying research and future directions. In R. A. Geffner, M. Loring, & C. Young (Eds.), *Bullying behavior: Current issues, research, and interventions* (pp. 1–5). New York: The Haworth Press, Inc.

Stetson, E., Hurley, A., & Miller, G. (2001). *Promoting empathy in elementary school children.* Mini-Skills presentation at the annual conference of the National Association of School Psychologists, Washington, D.C.

Stevens, V., DeBourdeaudhuij, I., & Van Oost, P. (2001). Anti-bullying interventions at school: Aspects of programme adaptations and critical issues for further programme development. *Health Promotion International, 16*(2), 155–167.

Stevens, V., Van Oost, P., & De Bourdeaudhuij, I. (2001). Implementation process of the Flemish antibullying intervention and relation with program effectiveness. *Journal of School Psychology, 39*(4), 303–317.

Strawn, D., & Paradiso, D. (2001, April). *Bullying: Research and interventions.* Paper presented at the annual convention of the National Association of School Psychologists, Washington, D.C.

Sudermann, M., Jaffe, P., & Schiek, E. (1996). *Bullying: Information for parents and teachers*; London Family Court Clinic; http://www.lfcc.on.ca/bully.htm.

Sullivan, K. (1999). Aotearoa/New Zealand. In P. K. Smith, Y. Morita, J. Junger-Tas, D. Olweus, R. Catalano, & P. Slee (Eds.), *The nature of school bullying: A cross-national perspective* (pp. 340–355). London: Routledge.

Sutton, J., & Keogh, E. (2000). Social competition in school: Relationships with bullying, Machiavellianism and personality. *British Journal of Educational Psychology, 70*(3), 443–456.

Sutton, J., Smith, P. K., & Swettenham, J. (1999). Bullying and 'theory of mind': A critique of the 'social skills deficit' view of anti-social behavior. *Social Development, 8*(1), 117–127.

Schwartz, D. (2000). Subtypes of victims and aggressors in children's peer groups. *Journal of Abnormal Child Psychology, 28*(2), 181–192.

Schwartz, W. (1999). Developing social competence in children. (Choices Briefs #3). Institute for Urban and Minority Education, Teachers College. *Choices in Preventing Youth Violence.* NY: Columbia University.

Swearer, S. M., Cary, P. T., Song, S. Y., & Eagle, J. W. (2000, August). *Self-monitoring as a means of assessing bullying and victimization.* Poster presented at the American Psychological Association National Conference, Washington, DC.

Swearer, S. M., Cary, P. T., Song, S. Y., & Eagle, J. W. (2000). *Depression rates among middle school bullies, bully-victims, and victims.* Poster session presented at the annual meeting of the Association for the Advancement of Behavior Therapy, New Orleans, LA.

Swearer, S. M., Cary, P. T., Song, S. Y., & Eagle, J. W. (2001). *A longitudinal analysis of depression rates among middle school bullies, bully-victims, and victims.* Poster presented at the 2001 World Congress of Behavioral and Cognitive Therapies Convention, Vancouver, BC.

Swearer, S. M., & Doll, B. (2001). Bullying in schools: An ecological framework. *Journal of Emotional Abuse, 2*(2/3), 7–23.

Swearer, S. M., Eagle, J. W., Song, S. Y., & Cary, P. T. (2001). *A longitudinal analysis of the relationship between anxiety and the bully-victim continuum in preadolescents.* Poster presented at the 2001 World Congress of Behavioral and Cognitive Therapies Convention, Vancouver, B.C.

Swearer, S. M., Song, S. Y., Cary, P. T., Eagle, J. W., & Mickelson, W. T. (2001). Psychosocial correlates in bullying and victimization: The relationship between depression, anxiety, and bully/victim status. In R. A. Geffner, M. Loring, & C. Young (Eds.), *Bullying behavior: Current issues, research, and interventions* (pp. 95–121). New York: The Haworth Press, Inc.

Sweeting, H., & West, P. (2001). Being different: Correlates of the experience of teasing and bullying at age 11. *Research Papers in Education, 16*(3), 225–246.

Tanner, L. (2002, June). AMA adopts anti-bully measure; http://www.ama-assn.org.

Tattum, D., & Tattum, E. (1992). *Social education and personal development.* London: David Fulton Publishers.

Teglasi, H. (1998a). Introduction to the mini-series: Implications of temperament for the practice of school psychology. *School Psychology Review, 27*(4), 475–478.

Teglasi, H. (1998b). Temperament constructs and measures. *School Psychology Review, 27*(4), 564–585.

Teglasi, H., & Epstein, S. (1998). Temperament and personality theory: The perspective of cognitive-experiential self-theory. *School Psychology Review, 27*(4), 534–550.

Teglasi, H., & Rothman, L. (2001). STORIES: A classroom-based program to reduce aggressive behavior. *Journal of School Psychology, 39*(1), 71–94.

Terwogt, M., & Stegge, H. (1977). Children's perspective on the emotional process. In A. Thomas & S. Chess (Eds.), *Temperament and development* (pp. 249–269). New York: Brunner/Mazel.

Thompson, M., O'Neill, G. C., & Cohen, L. J. (2001). *Best friends, worst enemies: Understanding the social lives of children.* New York: Ballantine Books.

Thornton, T. N., Craft, C. A., Dahlberg, L. L., Lynch, B. S., & Baer, K. (with Potter, L., Mercy, J. A., and Flowers, E. A.) (2000). *Best practices of youth violence prevention: A sourcebook for community action.* Atlanta, GA: Centers for Disease Control and Prevention.

Tur-Kaspa, H. (2002). Social cognition in learning disabilities. In B. Y. L. Wong & M. L. Donahue (Eds.), *The social dimensions of learning disabilities: Essays in honor of Tanis Bryan* (pp. 11–31). Mahwah, NJ: Lawrence Erlbaum Associates, Publishers.

Twemlow, S. W., Fonagy, P., & Sacco, F. C. (2001, March). An innovative psychodynamically influenced approach to reduce school violence. *Journal of the American Academy of Child and Adolescent Psychiatry, 40*(3), 377–379.

U.S. Department of Education, (1998a, November 3). Bullying: Peer abuse in schools. *Preventing bullying—A manual for schools and communities*; http://www.ldonline.org/ld_indepth/social_skills/preventing_bullying.html.

U.S. Department of Education, National Center for Education Statistics (1998b, November). *Student victimization at school.* Washington, DC.

Verkuyten, M., & Thijs, J. (2000). Peer victimization and self-esteem of ethnic minority group children. *Journal of Community & Applied Social Psychology, 11*(3), 227–234.

Verschueren, K., & Marcoen, A. (2002). Perceptions of self and relationship with parents in aggressive and nonaggressive rejected children. *Journal of School Psychology, 40*(6), 501–522.

Voss, L. D., & Mulligan, J. (2000). Bullying in school: Are short pupils at risk? Questionnaire study in a cohort. *British Medical Journal, 320,* 612–613.

Walker, H. M., Colvin, G., & Ramsey, E. (1995). Instructing and managing the antisocial student on the playground. *Antisocial behavior in school: Strategies and best practices* (pp. 189–214). Pacific Grove: Brooks/Cole Publishing Company.

Warman, D. M., & Cohen, R. (2000). Stability of aggressive behaviors and children's peer relationships. *Aggressive Behavior, 26*, 277–290.

Weiner, J., & Schneider, B. H. (2002). A multisource exploration of the friendship patterns of children with and without learning disabilities. *Journal of Abnormal Child Psychology, 30*, 127–141.

White, K. J., Sherman, M. D., & Jones, K. (1996). Children's perceptions of behavior problem peers: Effects of teacher feedback and peer-reputed status. *Journal of School Psychology, 34*(1), 53–72.

Whitney, I., Rivers, I., Smith, P. K., & Sharp, S. (1994). The Sheffield project: Methodology and findings. In P. K. Smith & S. Sharp (Eds.), *School bullying: Insights and perspectives* (pp. 21–56). London: Routledge.

Whitney, I., & Smith, P. K. (1993). A survey of the nature and extent of bully/victim problems in junior/middle and secondary school. *Educational Research, 35*, 3–25. Reported in Skiba, R., and Fontainini (2001, May). Bullying prevention: Early identification and intervention. Safe & Responsive Schools. *Communiqué, 29*(1), 1–3.

Whitney, I., Smith, P. K., & Thompson, D. (1994). Bullying and children with special educational needs. In P. K. Smith & S. Sharp (Eds.), *School bullying: Insights and perspectives* (pp. 213–240). London: Routledge.

Wiler, R. (1993). Strategies for changing bullying behaviors. *Kansas Bullying Prevention Program.* Can be obtained from Project DARE. Kansas.

Willenz, P. (1999). Middleschool bullying especially tough-Not limited to loners. *American Psychological Association;* http://www.eurekalert.org/releases/apa-bin081199.html.

Wolke, D., Woods, S., Bloomfield, L., & Karstadt, L. (2000). The association between direct and relational bullying and behavior problems among primary school children. *Journal of Child Psychology and Psychiatry, 41*(8), 989–1002.

Wright, J. C., Lindgren, K. P., & Zakriski, A. L. (2001). Syndromal versus contextualized personality assessment: Differentiating environmental and dispositional determinants of boy's aggression. *Journal of Personality and Social Psychology, 81*(6), 1176–1186.

Yoon, J. S., Hughes, J. N., Cavell, T. A., & Thompson, B. (2000). Social cognitive differences between aggressive-rejected and aggressive-neglected children. *Journal of School Psychology, 38*(6), 551–570.

Zaff, J. F., Calkins, J., Bridges, L. J., & Margie, N. G. (2002, September). Promoting positive mental and emotional health in teens: Some lessons from research. *Child Trends Research Brief.* Washington DC: Child Trends. Information can be found at www.childtrends.org.

Zhou, Q., Eisenberg, N., Losoya, S. H., Fabes, R. A., Reiser, M., Guthrie, I. K., et al. (2002). The relations of parental warmth and positive expressiveness to children's empathy-related responding and social functioning: A longitudinal study. *Child Development, 73*(3), 893–915.

Index